# An Integrative Theory of Leadership

# An Integrative Theory of Leadership

## Martin M. Chemers

*University of California, Santa Cruz*

Ψ Psychology Press
Taylor & Francis Group

New York   London

First Published by
Lawrence Erlbaum Associates, Inc., Publishers
10 Industrial Avenue
Mahwah, NJ 07430

Transferred to Digital Printing 2009 by Psychology Press
270 Madison Ave, New York NY 10016
27 Church Road, Hove, East Sussex, BN3 2FA

**Library of Congress Cataloging in Publication Data**

Chemers, Martin M.
    An integrative theory of leadership / Martin M.
    Chemers
          p.   cm.
    Includes bibliographical references and index.
    ISBN 0-8058-2678-5 (c : alk. paper). —ISBN 0-8058-
    2679-3 (p : alk. paper)
        1. Leadership.  2. Organization.  I. Title.
        HD57.7.C484   1997
        658.4'092—dc21                              97-893
                                                        CIP

**Publisher's Note**
The publisher has gone to great lengths to ensure the quality of this reprint
but points out that some imperfections in the original may be apparent.

*For Joel—he's not heavy...*

# Contents

# *Preface*

Contemporary leadership theory has been described as complex, fragmented, and contradictory, making its study frustrating for the scholar and its application difficult for the practitioner. It is the thesis of this volume that leadership theory can be integrated and the empirical findings reconciled. In the chapters that follow, a comprehensive review of the leadership literature is attempted. Theories and approaches are compared and contrasted, searching for common elements and coherent perspectives. Finally, an integrative model is presented with implications for theory and practice.

The book provides basic overviews of the full range of contemporary leadership theory giving the neophyte scholar a broad introduction to the topic. In-depth analyses of the theoretical coherence and empirical support for specific theories provide the advanced researcher with alternative views and hopefully stimulating perspectives. The book is intended to serve as a supplement to advanced courses in social or organizational psychology and management studies.

Special emphasis is placed on cultural and subcultural issues. The book examines the cross-cultural generalizability of leadership theories developed in the United States and abroad. Potential differences in leadership style and performance between men and women and between Euro-American and minority group leaders are carefully scrutinized. Positivist and constructionist perspectives are compared with an eye to integrating the strongest points of each approach. Each chapter ends with a conclusions section designed to help the reader move toward an eventual integration.

Writing this book has been an fascinating and exhilarating enterprise. I have come away with an even greater appreciation for the ingenuity of my fellow scholars in the field of leadership. My adviser, Fred Fiedler, to whom I owe a great deal, once responded to a criticism of his theoretical approach as being too complicated. He replied, "One needs a pretzel-shaped theory to describe a pretzel-shaped universe." During the writing of this book, I sometimes felt that my desire to integrate complex and seemingly contradictory theories was giving me a pretzel-shaped psyche.

I received a variety of different kinds of support from many different quarters. The most important of this came, as always, from my wife, colleague, and friend

Barbara. The value of her moral support and encouragement was exceeded only by the excellent editorial advice she gave me on innumerable drafts. Extremely useful editorial commentary also came from Fred Fiedler who critiqued an early version of the manuscript, capping 30 years of mentorship, as well as from John Harvey and Art Jago. Most of the work on this book was done when I was a faculty member at Claremont McKenna College, and I am indebted to the financial support provided by Henry Kravis through the Kravis Leadership Institute. And finally, I would like to thank my students whose desire to learn makes teaching and writing worthwhile.

*—Martin M. Chemers*
*Santa Cruz, California*

# Chapter 1

## The Functions of Leadership in Organization

### THE NATURE OF THE BOOK

A definition of leadership that would be widely accepted by the majority of theorists and researchers might say that "leadership is a process of social influence in which one person is able to enlist the aid and support of others in the accomplishment of a common task." The major points of this definition are that leadership is a group activity, is based on social influence, and revolves around a common task. Although this specification seems relatively simple, the reality of leadership is very complex. Intrapersonal factors (i.e., thoughts and emotions) interact with interpersonal processes (i.e., attraction, communication, influence) to have effects on a dynamic external environment. Each of these aspects brings complexity to the leadership process. It is the purpose of this book to try to make that complexity a bit more manageable, thus increasing our ability to understand what effective leadership is.

The contemporary empirical literature on leadership often seems fragmented and contradictory. It is the thesis of this book that a solid structure can be built to organize and integrate what we know about leadership. The key building blocks of that structure will be an understanding of the basic functions of leadership, that is, what leaders must do to be effective, and the critical processes of leadership, that is, how the functions fit together in the accomplishment of the task.

The chapters that follow provide a comprehensive review of the major approaches to leadership. Each is discussed with an eye toward explaining the basic principles, the research evidence, and where appropriate, the relationship of the theory or research program to other theories. The ultimate goal of this review of the literature is to provide a basis for the presentation of an integrative model of leadership that brings together function and process, and provides an armature for integrating what we know.

1

## A Beginning

In this opening chapter, I try to place the leadership role in perspective, illustrating how leadership contributes to the realization of organizational goals. The mechanisms by which organizations create and structure the leadership role is related to the environments in which the organizations function. The discussion concludes with an explanation of how environmental characteristics influence the evolution of organizational types and leadership roles with attendant conceptions of ideal leadership.

## ORGANIZATIONAL FUNCTIONS

Groups and organizations are by nature inefficient. If one person could accomplish a job, the creation or assignment of a group would not be warranted. Groups require coordination of the efforts of their members. The time and energy spent in that coordination are diverted from productive activity. Organizations, which are groups of groups, demand even greater resources applied to coordination. Nonetheless, most of the productive activities in modern society cannot be accomplished by one person working alone. Organizations are essential to the realization of the goals of productive endeavor, and leaders are essential to organizational coordination. Let us examine the major functions of organizations and see how leadership is central to the fufillment of those functions.

## Internal Maintenance

The primary function that an organization must achieve is the regularization of activities to provide a stable base for productive operation. The organization must maintain an internal integrity that allows it to respond to routine events in reliable and predictable ways.

Every organization is faced with a large number of demands that repeatedly require the same response. Universities must enroll students in classes, assign them to dormitories, collect tuition and housing fees, monitor academic progress, clean facilities, and so on. Many of these activities are uniform or routine in their form and occurrence and are dealt with in the same way each time they happen.

The activities become regularized to save time and energy. If the responses to routine events weren't standardized, every day would be like the first day of organizational life. The names of the buildings, the distribution of classes, the method of computing grade point averages would all have to be invented daily. The organization would never be able to accomplish anything but these "setting up" activities.

That these activities are properly carried out is essential to the organization's integrity in the same way that maintaining a state of stable equilibrium is essential to the survival of any living organism. The human body, by analogy, must maintain body temperatures, nervous system activity, blood saline levels, and other systems within narrowly prescribed limits. In order to do this, the organism has sensors to monitor vital systems. When the systemic parameters are outside the prescribed limits, the organism responds with preprogrammed adjustments to restore equilibrium within the limits.

If the sensors detect that blood temperature is above the appropriate level, the body begins to perspire, setting in motion evaporative cooling processes that will restore equilibrium. Blood temperature below normal results in shivering and the burning of stored energy to generate heat.

An organization must maintain similar monitoring and adjustment systems. Rules, regulations, and standard operating procedures must govern everyday activities. The organization is striving for stability so that it may function from one day to the next. The key aspects of this internal maintenance function are *reliability*, *predictability*, and *accountability*.

Reliability means that recurrent events are responded to in the same way every time they occur. The reliability of response enhances predictability. Members of the organization know what is likely to occur and when. The fact that responses are supposed to be reliable and predictable makes accountability possible. If a key activity does not occur, knowing when, how, where, and by whom it was supposed to be accomplished makes it possible to identify the cause of the error and correct it.

The achievement of internal maintenance makes it possible for the organization to make productive movement. Without internal maintenance, an organization cannot exist for long. A human being who couldn't maintain a stable physiological equilibrium would soon perish. However, the importance of the internal maintenance function can sometimes make organizations overly focused on the attainment of order and stability and consequently, they may lose sight of the other essential organizational function, external adaptability.

## External Adaptability

A person with a normal temperature, excellent nutrition, and a clean set of clothes who steps into traffic in front of a fast-moving truck is not going to be a stable organism for long. When an organization maintains a fixed course in the face of a changing environment, it resembles the old Western movie's driverless stagecoach flying off the cliff when the road takes a sudden turn.

Organizations must know what is going on around them and adapt to changes in the evironment. The ability to change is the critical element of innovation in organizations and is necessary for adaptability. The key aspects of external adaptability are *sensitivity*, *flexibility*, and *responsiveness*.

An organization or system that exists in an environment that is not perfectly static must be sensitive to the changes around it. The organization that does not attend to its environment calls to mind the joke about the airliner that has lost its navigational bearings, but is making "very good time."

Making good time in the wrong direction is not the hallmark of outstanding organizations. Successful organizations in unstable environments must be sensitive to change and flexible enough to respond. Such organizations have mechanisms for restructuring traditional approaches in light of new conditions.

The McDonald's hamburger restaurant chain, for example, while a highly structured and internally integrated organization, must be sensitive and responsive to competitor's products (e.g., chicken sandwiches), or changes in customer tastes (e.g., an emphasis on food items with lower fat content). Such responsiveness results in adaptability to changes in the external environment.

## Balancing Contradictory Demands

Although it is easy to say that organizations must ensure both internal stability and responsiveness to change, the fact that these two functions are basically contradictory is the bedevilment of both practicing managers and organizational theorists. Unfortunately, procedures that organizations might adopt to ensure reliability and predictability will usually reduce flexibility and responsiveness. Standard operating procedures are, after all, "standard," not flexible or adaptive. Conversely, the strategies an organization might use to enhance its ability to change will make it harder to guarantee that routine events will be handled in exactly the same way each time they occur.

Organizational survival is a question of balance. The appropriate balance between stability and adaptiveness depends on the nature of the organization's environment. Organizations that live in very stable and predictable environments benefit from the efficiencies of highly regularized procedures. A manufacturing company with predictable markets and suppliers (e.g., a company that makes kitchen matches) can develop highly routinized ways of purchasing materials and producing and marketing their products. Regularity enhances efficiency and reliability.

On the other hand, an organization that must function in a highly competitive and unstable set of conditions (e.g., a computer design company) needs to sacrifice the benefits of reliability to enhance responsiveness. In order to know what the competition is up to and how emerging technologies can be exploited, the company must design its internal structure and devote a substantial portion of its resources to facilitating external adaptability functions. For example, the company's applied research and development department might play the focal role in short-term planning. It might also build a close linkage with customers into the organization's information systems.

How does an organization identify and maintain the proper placement on the stability–change continuum? How are these organizational functions realized? The answer to those questions is that leaders play a central role in helping organizations to develop appropriate systems for meeting internal and external demands.

## THE ORGANIZATIONAL FUNCTIONS OF LEADERSHIP

The active ingredient in organizations is people. The vital functions of organizational life are accomplished by women and men working together. Thus, when we speak about coordinating organizational activities, we really mean coordinating the efforts of people. Social groups have developed the role of "leader" to accomplish this coordination function.

Leadership is a process of social influence through which one person is able to enlist the aid of others in reaching a goal. A number of activities are included in the leadership role, and it is illuminating to look at these activities in relation to the organizational functions of internal maintenance and external adaptability identified earlier.

When the group or team is functioning in an orderly, structured, and well-understood environment, the leader's primary responsibilities include guidance and motivation. The leader's job is to assign people to tasks or responsibilities, to outline what is expected, and to facilitate and encourage goal attainment.

In later chapters, I discuss the behavioral options available to leaders for carrying out the guidance and motivation functions. These activities can be accomplished in a number of ways, but they must be done.

When groups or organizations are operating in less predictable environments that call for an emphasis on external adaptability, the leader's crucial functions entail problem solving and innovation. The leader must help to create the kind of atmosphere that encourages the sensitivity, flexibility, and creativity that allows the group to deal with the uncertainty of new or complex demands. The leader as change agent must possess a legitimate authority for influencing followers. That legitimacy flows from the leader's special status.

## Status Differentiation

The concept of leadership implies a differentiation of authority and responsibilities between group members. Social psychologists and sociologists refer to this differentiation in power and responsibility as *status*. Sherif and Sherif (1969) described status as

> a member's position (rank) in a hierarchy of power relations in a social unit (group or system) as measured by the relative effectiveness of initiative (a) to control interaction, decision-making, and activities, and (b) to apply sanctions in the cases of non-participation and non-compliance. (p. 140)

Every human society that has been studied has some sort of status system. In some groups or societies, the relative distinctions between individuals are quite minor, and the system is very simple. For example, among some hunting and gathering societies, such as the Pygmies of the Ituri forest in Zambia or the !Kung bushmen of Kalahari Desert in southern Africa, the only status distinction is the recognition of a "headman," usually the oldest male member of the band, who is accorded somewhat more influence in group decision making and a more desirable location for his family's dwelling. The headman is essentially "first among equals."

In other societies, such as the imperial bureaucracies of Asia or the hereditary chieftainships of Polynesia, complex and highly differentiated systems of power and privilege are sustained. Some individuals have a great deal more power than others, and one person's income could be thousands of times that of another. Later in this chapter, I discuss the conditions that give rise to one type of status system or another, but first we must examine the reasons for the pervasiveness of status systems. What is the purpose of differentiating members of a social unit?

## The Functions of Status Bestowal

The differentiation of members of a group by status entails both the intended functions that make such differentiation a positive aspect of group life and the negative or unintended functions that can make status differentiation a threat to the viability of the group.

   *Positive Functions.*    As noted in the earlier discussion of internal maintenance and external adaptability, many organizational processes are "double-edged swords." The intended, positive functions of a particular organizational practice are often connected with less desirable, unintended functions. This is very much the case with status differentiation.

   The positive functions of status are vital to the sustenance of any organization. If the tasks that faced a social unit were equally important to the unit's survival, there would be no need to differentiate its members. Any member could do any job, if all jobs were equal in their impact. However, because individuals differ in their abilities, and because the tasks that a social unit faces differ in terms of their importance, it becomes very significant for an organization to assign its most capable members to its most important tasks. We can leave aside, for the moment, the definition of "capable," and focus on the question of importance.

   If members of the unit are grouped to accomplish a task that is too large, too difficult or, too dangerous for individual effort, a leader is chosen to coordinate the labors of the members. The leader's actions generally are more important to the success of the endeavor than are the actions of any other individual in the group. It is important then that the person chosen for this responsibility is the one most likely to carry it out successfully. The first purpose of status, then, is the *elevation of competence.*

   If the organization of the unit's activities are complex enough to necessitate higher level groupings, that is, multiple levels of authority, it will usually be the case that activities of each higher level will be more important to the success of the unit, simply by virtue of the more pervasive impact of those activities. Military organizations provide a straightforward example of this principle. The squad leader commands a group of 8 to 10 soldiers. A platoon leader directs the activities of three or four squads. A company commander is responsible for several platoons, and so on. At each higher level, the leader is responsible for more people, more materials, and for increasingly important tasks.

   The second objective of status differentiation is based on this need for a leader to organize and direct the work of others. As the Sherifs pointed out in their definition of status, positions in a hierarchy vary in their authority. Because authority should be commensurate with responsibility, another purpose of status is the *assignment of authority*. The person who is accountable for the responsibility is differentiated so that others in the unit recognize that authority.

Increased responsibility and authority are generally acknowledged as making a position more demanding and often more onerous. Some incentive is typically offered to make the assignment equitable. The third function of status is the *distribution of rewards*. It is important to note that rewards need not be material or tangible. For example, the Plains Indian who made a contribution to the welfare of the tribe, such as bravery in battle or successful hunting, received the honor of wearing a commemorative eagle feather and had the satisfaction of public recognition, but did not receive any material benefit.

Nonetheless, the designation of special status, the assignment of increased authority, and the purveyance of visible rewards help to enhance the prominence of the high-status individual. Enhanced visibility and prominence make possible the fourth function of status differentiation, the *modeling of normative expectancies*. The person with special status becomes a role model whose behavior helps to define the norms for others in the group. Those who would like to hold positions of status are encouraged to behave in accordance with the social expectations demonstrated by the high-status individual.

The specific behaviors encouraged in a group and the performance of these behaviors which results in status bestowal depend on the goals of the group. What a society is trying to achieve depends on the demands that the environment places on the group. In some societies, the optimal utilization of environmental resources calls for creativity, whereas in another society success is achieved through consistent application of time-honored methods. These environmentally determined goals will vary dramatically from one society or organization to another. Within each society, however, the goals and the behaviors needed to accomplish the key tasks must be clear, distinctive, and well understood. For example, if a society depends on the resourcefulness and creativity of each individual, the society must encourage independence and resourcefulness by rewarding those behaviors when they occur and the individuals who display them.

If we reflect on the first four aspects of status differentiation, we can see that they have the effect of reinforcing and perpetuating organizational approaches that have worked in the past. The group members that are elevated to positions of higher status are chosen because of their accomplishments in the recent or distant past, not for a future that has yet to occur. The characteristics of the role models are likewise those of people who succeeded in the past. In other words, status bestowal encourages stability and enhances internal maintenance functions.

As already noted, however, stability can mean stagnation when the social unit is confronted by a dynamic environment. If status differentiation processes are not to exert a strangling effect on a society's ability to adapt to change, status must *facilitate innovation*, the fifth positive function of status.

Edwin Hollander's (1958) work on leadership, status, and influence makes the clearest explication of the innovative function of status. Hollander developed the "idiosyncrasy credit" construct to explain how individuals in groups accumulate credits which allow them to act in nonnormative or idiosyncratic ways.

Usually, when individuals do not act in accordance with group norms, they are sanctioned in some way. When such incidents of deviant behavior reach a high enough level, the person is ostracized from the group. However, if an individual has built up a backlog of idiosyncrasy credits, he or she can spend them, essentially to buy some leeway to act in idiosyncratic ways.

Idiosyncrasy credit reflects the extent to which an individual is valued by the group and therefore tolerated despite nonconformity. Credit is earned in two ways; (a) by making contributions to the group's efforts to achieve its goals, that is, by showing competence, and (b) by acting in conformity with group norms, that is, by showing solidarity with the group's values. In other words, the group members who are allowed to break with tradition and introduce new ideas into a group are those with the strongest records of competence and loyalty. Status, which is very similar in concept to idiosyncrasy credit, becomes the vehicle by which innovation and change are safely programmed into group life.

Functioning at its best, status differentiation identifies and elevates into positions of responsibility the most competent and loyal group members, provides them with the authority to handle enhanced responsibilities, and compensates them with rewards for doing so. Leaders then become role models reinforcing the norms for desirable behavior, and introducing new ideas into the group.

*Negative Functions.*    Unfortunately, status differentiation has its darker side. Because status is so strongly associated with prominence and reward, it becomes very desirable. Ambitious individuals feel anxious about their attempts to gain status, and once status is attained, about their ability to hang on to it. This status anxiety is responsible for a number of aberrations of the intended functions of status.

One such unintended function is what might be called a *"means–end reversal."* The intended function of status is to allow and encourage the group members to make contributions to the group. Status is the means for the group to achieve its goals. However, when the accrual of status becomes the end in itself, it ceases to be the means for group success. Individuals may engage in behaviors designed to gain or protect status rather than to contribute to group life. Energies are diverted from goal attainment to status striving. For example, the junior manager who spends time and energy buttering up his supervisor in order to obtain a promotion is wasting personal and organizational resources.

One manifestation of the means–end reversal is the distortion of communications in the social unit. Research has shown that in a variety of group settings (e.g., industrial organizations, professional seminars, juries, and laboratory groups), status determines the content and the targets of communication.

For example, Bales and Strodtbeck (1951) found that jury deliberations tended to be dominated by the members of the highest social status. Hurwitz, Zander, and Hymovitch (1953) found that status controlled the direction of communication in professional discussions with high-status people doing the most talking, and everyone in the group directing their communications towards the high-status members. In a study of managerial communication, Read (1962) found that the truthfulness of upward communication depends on the relative power of the superior to affect the status of the subordinate. Managers with powerful supervisors were more likely to misrepresent their true progress in order to maintain a positive impression with their boss.

In other words, when status becomes the paramount consideration in a group, the content and direction of communications are no longer relevant to the goals of the task, but are subordinated to status pursuit. Overcentralization of communication by and toward high-status group members can cause information overload on those individuals and can keep important information away from those who may need it. Distortions in the content of communication fill the decision-making channels of the group with noise, that is, bad information. A group whose members' attentions are focused on enhancing status rather than on doing a good job is a severely handicapped unit.

All of the problems associated with status reach their zenith in the phenomenon of rigidification. In order to achieve the positive effects of status, a social system must be very fluid with the most competent group members rising easily to positions of greatest responsibility. However, one of the most prevalent ways that those in power try to maintain power is by solidifying the status structure. By reducing fluidity and movement, those at the top of the status structure protect their positions.

At the level of the larger society, status rigidification can occur when accidents of birth, such as royal heritage, social class, caste, or ethnicity are used to determine who is eligible for positions of status. The members of the group in power maintain their positions of privilege, but the society as a whole suffers when the talent pool from which potential leaders may be drawn is severely restricted. Individuals who are not members of the dominant group are not allowed to rise in status and responsibility regardless of their merit. Over time, the level of leadership competence deteriorates in rigidified societies and the society's effectiveness is outdistanced by societies with more open status bestowal systems.

Within work organizations, rigidification can result when powerful individuals try to monopolize decision-making prerogatives and other forms of control. Territoriality, cronyism, and petty competition impair the ability of competent people to rise in the organization or to work together productively once in authority. Functioning at its worst, status differentiation results in a system of unfair privilege and stultifying control that kills motivation and makes broad teamwork impossible. The enormous challenge for successful leadership is to harness the positive functions of status, while avoiding or diminishing the negative aspects. Given the daunting nature of this challenge, it is small wonder that effective leadership is often in woefully short supply.

Up to this point, I have begged the question of how a social unit determines the capabilities that a person should have to be elevated to a position of responsibility. In essence, what constitutes competence? What is effective leadership? The lessons of history provide a partial answer to these questions.

# THE CULTURAL EVOLUTION
# OF EFFECTIVE LEADERSHIP

Leadership is a process involving social interaction, and like all such processes, the question of what behaviors are desirable must be understood within the social context. The appropriateness and desirability of leadership and other social behavior is determined by the values of the culture in which the behavior occurs. In some cultures, the specifications of acceptable behavior for a particular role are quite precise and little leeway is allowed in expression. Pelto (1968) called such cultures "tight." Other cultures are normatively somewhat looser, giving a role occupant a greater range of appropriateness in which to function. What is true, however, is that every culture (whether religious, national, or organizational culture) does prescribe which behaviors are normative in a social context.

Culture is the way in which a social unit adapts to its environment over time. Triandis (1993) made the analogy that, "Culture is to society what memory is to individuals. It is the depository of what has worked and not worked in the past" (p. 171). Culture is the interface that connects the group with the environmental context in which it must function. The nature of the environment sets limits on the form that the culture must take to successfully exploit that interface. Once the form of the social unit's interaction with the environment is determined, the rest of the culture is molded to fit around that "cutting edge" form. In words that we have used earlier, the culture is first determined by "external adaptability," and then the "internal maintenance" processes are brought into coherence.

Perhaps an example will help to illustrate the relationship of adaptation and maintenance. If an environment, perhaps due to climate or lack of arable land, makes hunting and gathering more feasible than agriculture, the people living in that environment are more likely to prosper if they adopt that method of subsistence. However, successful hunting and gathering cultures usually depend on cooperative sharing of the food resoucefully gathered, frequently by individuals working independently. This implies that hunting and gathering cultures must encourage cooperation while developing independent and resourceful members. Democratic political structures (e.g., tribal councils) and egalitarian religious systems help to encourage the growth of self-sufficient and cooperative group members.

This is not to say, by any means, that the environment absolutely and completely determines the form that external adaptability takes, nor that external adaptability has a tight, one-to-one relationship to the form of the internal culture. In each case, demarcation of limits or of a range of possibilities is made. Certain arid climates make agriculture an unlikely form of economic adaptation, and make hunting and gathering economies more likely. Yet, not all hunting and gathering societies are exactly alike. Nonetheless, we can predict a lot about the way a group will organize itself if we acknowledge the strategies it has adopted to maximize its survival.

We can also learn a great deal about how effective leadership is defined by observing the nature of the leadership role in different types of societies. Different forms of economic strategy (e.g., hunting vs. farming) result in different organizational structures placing specific demands on the leadership role and the kinds of persons who fill that role. We can observe how leadership is evaluated in relation to the types of subsistence technologies that have evolved across the course of human history. Such an examination tells us not only about the historical record, but also helps us to place in perspective the role of leadership in contemporary organizational culture.

The evolution of food-getting technology (subsistence) can be divided up in a number of ways, but one set of categories has fairly widespread agreement. Subsistence technologies proceeded from *hunting and gathering* through *horticulture* (gardening or small-scale agriculture) to *agriculture* (extensive field-crop production). Technology helps determine two critical features of the society; (a) the most productive way to organize collective effort to implement the technology, and (b) the amount of surplus wealth created by the technology. These two factors help determine the kinds of personalities that are most beneficial for members of a society to possess and the kinds of organizational structures that are most efficient.

Hunting and gathering techniques vary. In some societies, people hunt or gather individually or in small groups, whereas in other groups or at other times, bigger groups may organize a large-scale hunt. However, what all of these cultures share is a relatively unpredictable supply of food, putting a premium on the resourcefulness of individuals to utilize the resources of their environment creatively, and a high level of cooperation and sharing among group members to forestall and reduce the impact of temporary shortages. The lack of the technology's capacity to generate or maintain large surpluses reduces the advantage of competition or status striving. There is little benefit to the society to have people competing, because their competition does not enhance the accumulation of food, and it weakens the cooperative ties necessary for survival.

The kind of adult personality that is valued in such groups is that which makes a person independent and resourceful enough to exploit an unpredictable environment, yet modest and unassuming enough to maintain cordial interpersonal relations with others. Such societies tend to be very egalitarian, as might be expected in groups of independent individuals. Influence tends to be done through persuasion rather than coercion, and decision making is relatively democratic, that is, through councils. Thus, the nature of leadership is an important aspect of a society's adaptation.

Anthropologist Stanley Diamond (1969) distiguished the way in which leadership roles are distributed in a society. *Situational* leadership roles are temporary roles designated for some particular task, and the emergence of the role is based on the special ability of an individual with respect to the task at hand. Thus, if the group is undertaking a hunt of some particular animal, one or more members of the group might be given leadership roles because of their experience and expertise at hunting that particular animal. Those leadership responsibilities and authority would last only as long as the group was focused on the particular activity.

*Generalized* roles are those that individuals fill because of some general progress through the life cycle. A man might be elected to membership in a warrior society or a woman designated as a "clan mother" with responsibilities in clan governance when each reaches a certain age.

*Restricted* roles exist where a relatively small number of positions are available, such as might be the case in autocratic societies where there is only one king or emperor or perhaps a ruling junta. Societies with restricted role allocation are sometimes called "closed" systems.

Hunting and gathering societies were likely to follow either the situational or generalized modes of allocation of leadership roles. The kind of leadership compatible with this social system was therefore quite democratic and sensitive to the interpersonal dynamics necessary for cooperative life and persuasive influence. Aggressiveness or arrogance was not acceptable for such leaders.

Hunting and gathering people were, of course, familiar with the potential for cultivation of the available plant foods which they gathered. In fact, rudimentary cultivation activities, such as diverting water to a desirable food source or protecting it from encroachment by other plants was common. The declining availability of game or other food sources or simply the increased sense of security provided by regularly cultivated food sources may have spurred the transition to some form of small-scale cultivation or gardening.

The transition to horticulture increased the opportunities for the society to exploit its environment to generate surpluses. Social arrangements that have the effect of intesnifying the economic base became adaptive for the group. Adult personality characteristics (e.g., ambition) which encourage hard work were desirable. However, the social groups were still quite fluid and formal structures of rank and status are not typical. A type of semiegalitarian leadership, sometimes labeled *managerial leadership* (Rosen, 1983), was common in such situations.

For example, Sahlins (1958, 1972) described the phenomenon of the Melanesian "Big Men," who were redistributor leaders. These individuals enhanced the productivity of the agricultural system by encouraging and directing large feasts in which great quantities of pork and yams accumulated by the Big Man and his associates were exchanged with another Big Man's entourage. The Big Man who gave the feast gained prestige and status in proportion to the amount of food provided. The receiver of the food must have arranged, in a reasonable time period, a reciprocal exchange in which the amount of food given exceeded the first feast. If he failed to do so, he lost status whereas the first Big Man gained it. The society as a whole benefited from the increased food supply generated by these competitions.

In order to amass the large amounts of food necessary for the feast, the Big Man had to gather, maintain, and exhort a group of associates who cultivated increased amounts of food which they shared with the Big Man for the feast. The associates benefited from their ties to the Big Man by sharing in the food made available in the reciprocal exchanges and the prestige provided by the Big Man's reflected glory. However, the amount of work the associates had to do to meet the Big Man's ever-increasing demands for pigs and yams was a decidedly negative aspect of their relationship.

The Big Men had no real hierarchical authority to require the support of their associates. The tools at their disposal included inspiration, negotiation, and manipulation. Through a combination of role modeling and cajolery, they tried to persuade their followers that the increased effort was worthwhile. In addition, through subtle negotiation involving the loans of pigs to associates at one point in time to be collected with interest at a later point, the Big Men managed the resources available to them.

Potential candidates for Big Man status were recognized in early adolescence and encouraged by friends and relatives to engage in feasts. They gradually developed the skills of persuasion and negotiation needed to fill the role and contribute to the society. Although the emphasis on persuasion resembles the leadership style of hunters and gatherers, the addition of material exchanges of value and the greater use of negotiation and directiveness shifts the leadership style toward a more "leader focused," less egalitarian mode.

Under some circumstances, the redistributor models evolved into true rank structures with decidedly autocratic overtones. This shift was made possible by some critical features of the social/economic system. First, food surpluses had to reach sufficient accumulations to allow the leader to hire a retinue of followers who were paid by and loyal to that person. This represented the beginnings of an army or police force. A second necessary feature was some barrier to the leader's followers shifting their allegiances when the leader's demands became too onerous. Islands, like those of Polynesia, or deserts or other inhospitable ecotones like the deserts surrounding the Mesoamerican centers, made it hard for disgruntled followers to move. Hostile, warlike relations with neighboring groups also discouraged movement.

Many of these features were present in the large-scale agrarian societies, along with some other characteristics that encourage the development of hierarchical power structures and restrict access to leadership roles. Large agricultural economies, especially in arid climates where massive irrigation systems were necessary, required the coordination of many workers. The increased food supplies allowed for the growth of larger populations. Public works, such as irrigation systems or the construction of religious structures (e.g., pyramids, ziggarauts, etc.) employed large numbers of people who were directed by multilevel management systems.

Many of these agrarian societies were expansionist, maintaining large armies. Like the public works bureaucracies of Asia (e.g., China, Persia, India) or feudal rank structures of Europe, armies devolved into hierarchical systems. Large groups needing tight control developed strict command structures fostering particular leadership practices.

In addition to the influences of mere size on the structure of agrarian societies, the farming technology had strong influences on the most appropriate system of governance and the kind of people who occupied leadership roles. Whereas it was adaptive for hunters and gatherers to be independent and resourceful, such was not the case for farmers. The greatest virtue of the farmer was reliability. The raising of field crops required that certain crucial activities be done in the correct manner and on time. Crops had to be planted at specific times, cared for in specific ways, and harvested at appropriate times.

The decision on when and how these activities should take place was not made by a group of equals debating possibilities. The planting times were determined by the inexorable progression of the seasons. The enormous interest that many early agrarian civilizations had in astronomy reflects the importance of marking time so that appropriate planting dates are not missed. Methods of cultivation, water distribution, and other facets of agriculture were specified by collective authorities, not by independent individual decisions. The allocation of leadership roles was, in Diamond's terms, restricted. Very few members of the society occupied leadership positions, whereas the vast majority formed the undifferentiated labor pool. The extreme differentiation of high-status individuals from all others gave the ruler tremendous power to organize collective functions.

The most valued personality trait for the masses was obedience. People were expected to do what they were told, and they expected to be told what to do. An autocratic leadership style, high on direction and low on participation, was the dominant pattern. However, this pattern of strict control of decision making was often combined with great expressed concern for the welfare of the less powerful. The good, fatherly king or emperor followed a pattern of "benevolent paternalism."

From our modern perspective, we might find some of these leadership styles more attractive than others. The important thing to recognize is that each of these styles was adaptive for a certain set of conditions. The style fits the environmental demands placed on the society and the leadership system. What is also interesting to contemplate is that the features of the environment that influenced each of these subsistence technologies, for example, the predictability of information and the rate of change in important conditions of the environment, are still relevant aspects of the environments of modern organizations.

We have contemporary organizations that face conditions similar to the hunting and gathering societies of the dim past. They deal with complex and unpredictable environments calling for resourcefulness and independence in employees, and for management styles that encourage and facilitate those characteristics. The boutique advertising agency, the investment banking firm specializing in mergers and acquisitions, and the computer software design firm, for example, operate in market environments similar to the hunting and gathering society. What they hunt is information, and it can be as elusive as any deer or peccary.

At the other end of the continuum are organizations whose environment is more predictable and stable, and who produce extremely large batches of a product before changing the design or manufacturing process. In other words, they are more like agrarian societies. At this particular moment in history, those predictable types of organizational environments seem to be disappearing. The globalization of business, the accelerating pace of technological change, and the intense competitiveness of international markets appear to have wiped out the stable environment for all organizations. The classic example of the large production bureaucracies, such as the automobile manufacturers, no longer have stable and predictable markets of the type that once led Henry Ford to say that his customers could have any color car they wanted as long as it was black.

However, history cautions us not to assume that the trends of today will continue indefinitely. Periods of intense competition are often followed by more stable periods in which the winners consolidate their hold on what they have garnered.

The current trend, for example, for the large automobile companies in the United States to enter production and marketing partnerships with their Japanese competitors is an attempt to reduce the disruptiveness and uncertainty of intense competition. Some economists predict that the number of giant, multinational automobile companies may well be reduced to three or four in the next few decades. These few companies may operate in a period of reduced competition and greater predictability, and it may be too early to predict the ultimate demise of the large, bureaucratic organization.

## SUMMARY

This chapter has addressed the need for organizations to develop stable and orderly internal structures which also have the capacity to sense change in the environment and to adapt to it. Status bestowal is a way of accomplishing the necessary organizational functions by elevating competent people to positions of responsibility and by giving them the wherewithal to organize, direct, and inspire the efforts of other people. The discussion of the evolution of subsistence technology and the relationship of technology to culture and leadership style illustrates how organizational goals and leadership are intricately intertwined.

## Organization of the Book

Having laid out the broad parameters of leadership in groups, organizations, and societies, I devote the subsequent chapters to a more in-depth analysis of what actually makes particular leaders effective. The next chapter takes a "first slice" look at leadership from the perspective of the early empirical research literature and contemporary popular writings on managerial leadership. These two approaches are grouped together because they begin from a "one best way" premise that good leadership must be the same in every situation. As will be shown, such a premise is untenable in light of the empirical findings. Nonetheless, popular writings illuminate what our culture believes about leadership and provide a good starting point for my in-depth analyses.

Chapters 3 through 9 take us deeply into the complexity of contemporary leadership theory and research. Chapters 3 and 4 present the contingency perspective that holds that the style of leadership that will have the most positive effects on group process and productivity depends (is contingent) on the nature of the leadership situation. Different situations (in terms of clarity, follower support, leader's authority, etc.) require different kinds of leadership.

Chapters 5 and 6 focus on the relationship between leaders and followers, revealing the range of such relationships from cold transactional bargains to emotionally transcendant and transformational experiences.

Chapters 7 through 9 bring some caveats and qualifications to our what was presented in earlier chapters. In chapter 7, we learn about the role of perception in leadership and with it, the effects of bias and misperception. Chapters 8 and 9 address the possibility of differences in leadership styles and relationships among peoples of different nationalities and cultures and possibly between men and women in our own culture.

Chapters 1 to 9 set the stage for the development of an integrative framework. The key functions of leadership and the processes by which the functions are accomplished become the basis for a broader understanding of the phenomenon and help to point toward some potentially productive directions for research and application. At the end of each chapter, summaries help to point out the important features that form the basis for the eventual integration.

# *Chapter 2*

## Early Research on Leadership

I have, thus far, drawn leadership in broad brush strokes, and it would be useful to move to a level of greater specificity. To ask the question, "Exactly what should leaders *do* to be effective?" Over the course of history and across the sweep of cultures, a good deal has been written about effective leadership. In our own era, writings about leadership have become quite popular. We turn now to see what insights can be gleaned from those sources.

## *POPULAR CONCEPTIONS OF IDEAL LEADERSHIP*

Throughout human history, social and political observers have recognized the importance of leadership and have contemplated the most appropriate form for it to take. For the most part, these conceptions were not scientific findings communicated to other scholars. Rather, they were the beliefs of social philosophers, practitioners of leadership, or the followers who observed leadership.

The views expressed in these writings sometimes flow from an overarching philosophical position, as was the case with Plato or Hobbes, or they may embody principles inductively derived through the observation of exemplary leaders of the past, as was the case in the writings of Macchiavelli or Confucius. They usually reflect the influence of strong cultural assumptions about the bases of human nature, for example, an emphasis on individualism in the European writings contrasted with the collectivism of the Asians. They are almost always influenced by the contemporary political struggles of the time, or more recently, by global economic trends.

These writings often reflect a greater concern with what should be than with what really is. Their greatest value may, in fact, lie in the insight they give us into how the values of a society are reflected in the leadership pattern considered ideal. The focus of this book is on leadership in modern organizations, so I forego a detailed discussion of ancient conceptions and confine my focus to some contemporary exemplars of the popular approach.

Combining armchair theorizing with informal observation, business professors Warren Bennis and Burt Nanus (1985) studied 60 private sector and 30 public sector leaders of outstanding reputation. The methods of selection were a bit haphazard, relying on people identified in business magazines or news reports, and the sample was decidedly biased in the direction of the middle-aged, White, male managers found at the helm of most large American organizations. However, the authors were most interested in selecting leaders of organizations characterized as innovative and responsive to the turbulent and challenging world of modern organizations, that is, leaders who had "achieved fortunate mastery over present confusion" (Bennis & Nanus, 1985, p. 21).

The method of data collection involved unstructured interviews ranging from a few hours to a few days. The leaders under study were asked a few questions about their strengths and weaknesses, their management philosophies, and important career decisions, and the interviews flowed in whatever directions seemed fruitful to interviewer and interviewee. Analysis of the data was accomplished by the authors' reading and rereading their interview notes until some common themes began to emerge. Bennis and Nanus ackowledged at the outset of their monograph that their approach was quite far from a scientific methodology. The vagaries and imprecision of these methods would be troubling if one's goal in reading this work were to find the causes of effective leadership. But, if the reader regards the conclusions as reflecting what successful leaders and those who study and read about them *think* are the causes of effective leadership, the conclusions drawn stand on firmer ground.

Bennis and Nanus identified four "strategies" of effective leaders. The first of these is the articulation of a compelling vision. Effective leaders must have a clear picture of what they are trying to accomplish. Second, they must be able to communicate this vision to others, especially followers, with a clarity and vibrancy that creates a "shared meaning." Third, leaders must be seen as trustworthy by adopting on unwavering commitment to a vision that allows followers to see that the leader is in for the long haul. Finally, and perhaps most importantly, successful leaders are able to make the fullest use of their personal resources of intelligence, energy, and commitment because they are confident about their capabilities and optimistic about the eventual success of their efforts.

In recent years, a number of other books, articles, and training programs have trod similar paths. Sometimes, these writings were based on interviews or questionnaires given to leaders or followers, and sometimes they were based on the wisdom and experience of a single observer, practitioner, or theorist. By and large, they come back to a few common points. People who are perceived as successful and effective leaders usually have an inspiring goal or an inspiring way of describing the goal; they are trustworthy, honest, and fair; and they are confident, optimistic, and energetic. This is contemporary America's view of the ideal leader.

As essential feature of popular views of leadership is that they tend to be uniform across situations. There is a "one-best-way" to lead that is the same in every leadership situation. This sort of simplified view of a very complex process was the starting point for early empirical research on the topic as well. A brief review of that work will help to illustrate why popular theories, although appealing, do not provide sufficient understanding.

## EARLY RESEARCH IN LEADERSHIP

Research literatures that deal with very complex objects of study are often characterized by a series of false starts and dead ends. This is especially true of leadership research. Given the infinite complexity of human behavior, the analysis of the interpersonal and group dynamics that surround leadership involves infinity taken to the $n^{th}$ power. A trip down leadership research's memory lane can help to delineate some of the good and reasonable hypotheses that lay strewn along the path.

## The Search for the Leadership Trait

A common view of leadership, historically, has been that there was something about the leader as a person that provided the unique qualifications for that person's ascendancy. The 19th century philosopher, Thomas Carlyle (1841/1907), offered a "Great Man Theory" of leadership that held that great leaders possessed some special trait or characteristic that allowed them to rise to positions of prominence regardless of setting or situation. To a degree, this argument represents an apology for social privilege in that it implies that anyone in a leadership position must deserve to be there by virtue of a special capability. Nonetheless, we are drawn to explanations of human behavior that lay the focus on causality in the individual.

The beginnings of the scientific study of leadership date from the early years of the 20th century. Around that time, psychologists were making progress in the development of measures of individual differences, such as Binet and Simon's seminal work on the development of the first test of intelligence in 1905 (Binet & Simon, 1908). The success of early intelligence measures led psychologists toward the measurement of other aspects of an individual that were consistent and reliable predictors of behavior or performance, that is, traits.

From the early 1900s up to the Second World War, trait investigations were the dominant research strategy in leadership. In his classic review of this literature, Stogdill analyzed the evidence in favor of the trait approach (Stogdill, 1948). In most of the studies that Stogdill surveyed, the focus was on identifying reliable differences in personal characteristics between leaders and followers in a variety of organizational settings.

Leadership status was operationalized in a number of ways; by observations of the behavior of people in groups; by rankings, votes, or sociometric choices of peers and other associates; by the holding of formally assigned positions, such as fraternity president, industrial manager, or public administrator; and by biographical and case history analyses. The subjects of study included preschoolers, elementary, high school, and college students, and adults. The traits measured ran the gamut from indices of height, weight, physique, appearance, energy, and health to intelligence, speech fluency, knowledge, judgment, introversion–extroversion, adaptability, originality, dominance, persisistence, social skills, and on and on. In all, the results from 124 separate investigations were compiled.

Stogdill's conclusions were not sanguine. He found that almost all of the traits studied were related to leadership to a degree, but none was sufficiently and universally associated with leadership enough to provide an explanation of leadership emergence or to predict who might become a leader. Weak support was found for general classes of traits that reflected capacity or ability, achievement, responsibility, and participation. These findings were not deemed surprising, because it is by participating in group activities in a responsible and capable manner that leaders are recognized and chosen. However, Stogdill's (1948) final conclusion was so prescient and important in the context of later research that it bears quoting:

> A person does not become a leader by virtue of the possession of some combination of traits, but the pattern of personal characteristics of the leader must bear some relevant relationship to the characteristics, activities, and goals of the followers. Thus, leadership must be conceived in terms of the interaction of variables which are in constant flux and change.... The persistence of individual patterns of human behavior in the face of constant situational change appears to be the primary obstacle encountered not only in the practice of leadership, but in the selection and placement of leaders. (pp. 63–64)

Although Stogdill did not dismiss the study of traits, noting that reliable differences in ability, activity, and character were associated with leadership, his analysis foreshadowed the more complex contingency theories of a later era in which personal characteristics were related to important situational variables. In any case, Stogdill's dour conclusions, followed by similar reviews, such as, Mann (1959), led discouraged researchers to look for leadership explanations in other directions. They were not, however, ready for the interactional perspective that Stogdill suggested and continued to look for a simple answer to a very complex problem.

Although I am extolling Stogdill's foresight, as well as setting up my own arguments to appear later in the book, it is worthwhile to note that he also recognized the role of cultural and historical aspects of leadership characteristics. He sights two interesting historical–literary studies, one by Frankfort, Frankfort, Wilson, and Jacobsen (1949) and another by Sarachek (1968). The former reported the three qualities of divinity that the ancient Egyptians attributed to their kings, "Authoritative utterance is in they mouth, perception is in thy heart, and thy tongue is the shrine of justice" (p. X). Stogdill distilled the traits of authority, discrimination, and just behavior from this quote. Sarachek deduced the leadership traits valued by the ancient Greeks through an analysis of the descriptions of the leaders in Homer's *Iliad*: (a) justice and judgement—Agamemnon; (b) wisdom and counsel—Nestor;

(c) shrewdness and cunning—Odysseus; and (d) valor and action—Achilles. Stogdill (1974) concluded that the changes from the Egyptians to the Greeks to modern times (e.g., our less positive view of shrewdness and cunning) reveal that conceptions of ideal leadership change from one time and culture to another.

## The Search for Effective Leader Behaviors

*Leadership Styles.*    Somewhere between the broad personality trait and the specific behavior sits the "leadership style." Styles reflect relatively stable patterns of response to social situations. For a brief period, leadership research focused on the possibility that these styles might be better explanatory constructs than personality traits had proven to be.

Kurt Lewin, who became one of the most influential figures in American social psychology, was an Austrian Jew driven from his homeland by the Nazi *Anschluss*. Lewin was greatly troubled by the rise and spread of fascism in the world, and he undertook a research program to determine the relative benefits of the democratic leadership style.

Lewin trained graduate students to lead small groups of boys employing a democratic, autocratic, or laissez-faire leadership style (Lewin, Lippitt, & White, 1939). Democratic leaders involved the boys in participative decisions about group activities, whereas in the autocratically led groups, all decisions were made by the leader. In the laissez-faire condition, actual leadership activity was kept to a minimum, with the leader allowing the boys to work and play essentially without supervision.

The democratically led groups had the highest levels of individual satisfaction and functioned in the most positive and orderly fashion. The autocratically led groups had the highest level of aggressive activity, especially when the leader was not present. A follow-up study by Lippitt and White (1943) found that autocratically led groups engaged in the highest levels of productive task activity, but only when the leader was present. When the supervisor left the room, goal-directed behavior dropped drastically.

An experimental study with adult subjects compared a hierarchical supervision program (i.e., directive and structuring) with an autonomy program (i.e., democratic and participative). The differences in productivity between the two approaches was minimal, but the hierarchical program was more efficient due to lower labor costs.

As with most areas of leadership research, subsequent research indicated that the problem was more complex than originally conceived. Vroom (1959) found that employee characteristics affect the relative utility of leadership styles. Employees high in authoritarianism and low in the need for independence performed best under autocratic supervision, whereas employees low in authoritarianism and high in the need for independence performed best with democratic supervisors. Similarly, Haythorn, Couch, Haefner, Langham, and Carter (1956) showed that subordinates who were themselves somewhat authoritarian were more satified with authoritarian leadership than those who were not. Leadership style research appeared to be, if not a dead end, at least a convoluted labyrinth.

*Identifying Leader Behavior Patterns.*    Following World War II, researchers disillusioned by the relative failure of the trait approach turned their attention toward leader behaviors. They hoped that an emphasis on the observable aspects of leadership might prove productive both in terms of delineating the specific nature of leadership activity and in identifying the patterns of behavior that are related to effective leadership. The first goal was better achieved than the second.

The most comprehensive program of research on leadership behavior was intigated in 1945 at Ohio State University by Carroll Shartle (1950). The goal of this program was to develop an instrument for the accurate measurement of leader behavior. Hemphill (1950) developed a list of some 1,800 potential behavioral descriptors. The list was eventually culled down to a set of 150 items that became the basis for the Leader Behavior Description Questionnaire (LBDQ), one of the longest lasting and most widely used measures in leadership research.

Subsequent factor analyses of the questionnaire (Halpin & Winer, 1957) revealed that most of the variance in the leader behavior descriptions was contributed to by two factors or behavioral clusters. The first of these, *consideration*, included behaviors indicating open communication between leader and followers, mutual trust and respect, follower participation in decision making, and interpersonal warmth. The second factor, *initiation of structure*, referred to behaviors designed to organize and structure group activities, define relationships, and direct followers toward task accomplishment.

Around the same time that the LBDQ was in development, researchers at the University of Michigan (Kahn, 1953; Katz & Kahn, 1951) were studying leader behavior from another perspective. Using interviews with the subordinates of industrial supervisors, the Michigan group identified two general styles of leadership, labelled *production-oriented* and *employee-oriented*. Production-oriented supervisors emphasized planning, direction, and productivity, whereas the employee-oriented supervisor was typified by good rapport with subordinates, an open and accepting style, and a concern for the problems and feelings of subordinates.

In yet another series of studies conducted at Harvard University, Bales and his associates (Bales & Slater, 1955) developed a method for recording the behavior of group members as the group's activities unfolded. *Interaction Process Analysis,* used to log the behavior of college students interacting in leaderless discussion groups, revealed two distinct types of emergent leaders. Some of the most active individuals engaged in organizing, summarizing, and directive behaviors and were called *task-specialists*. The second type, the *socio-emotional specialists*, acted to reduce interpersonal tensions, raise morale, and instigate group participation.

In another program of research using observations of leader behavior (Carter, 1953; Couch & Carter, 1952), three major categories of behavior were identified. These were *group goal facilitation*, signifying leader attempts to move the group toward task achievement; *group sociability*, reflecting the extent to which the leader interacted socially with group members and tried to gain acceptance; and *individual prominence*, meaning behaviors by the leader that would make him or her stand out. Interestingly, Carter (1953) found that behaviors that characterized leaders in one task did not necessarily characterize them in another.

These four research programs, utilizing distinct methodologies, seemed to reach a consensus. Two distinct styles or patterns of leadership behavior were recurrent. One pattern focused on accomplishing the assigned task, by organizing and directing the work of others. The other pattern attempted to maintain a positive emotional interpersonal atmosphere among the group members.

The rare but welcome confirmation of at least one leadership finding was comforting. Leadership researchers now felt that they were able to relate the behavioral factors to important organizational outcomes, such as productivity, satisfaction, and turnover, and to determine which style of leadership was most effective.

### *Relating Leader Behavior to Organizational Outcomes.* T h e
most extensive program of research on the relative effectiveness of leadership behavior patterns was carried out by the very productive group of researchers at Ohio State. Studies were done with military samples, primarily Air Force crews; in educational organizations, such as colleges and secondary schools; and in industrial organizations. The LBDQ factors were related to superior and subordinate evaluations of leaders and to a variety of dependent measures including team performance, follower satisfaction, group harmony and cohesiveness, grievance and turnover rates, and more. (See Stogdill, 1974, or Korman, 1966 for extensive reviews of specific findings.)

Although many individual studies found significant effects relating consideration or initiation of structure to particular outcome measures, the overall pattern of findings was not heartening. In one study, ratings of the leader's consideration behavior was positively related to follower satisfaction and group harmony, whereas initiation of structure was related to goal attainment or productivity as rated by a superior. However, in another study, both factors were related to the same outcome, for example, productivity or satisfaction.

From one set of studies to another, the relationships between the behavior factors and outcome measures shifted, being positively related in one study to negatively related or unrelated in another. Sometimes different raters (i.e., superiors, peers, or subordinates) disagreed on the leader's behavior. This lack of consistency in the relationship of the behaviors to important organizational outcomes defeated the hope that leader behavior measures were the simple answer to the leadership conundrum.

Perhaps the most reasonable summary of the studies on leadership behavior says that higher ratings on the leader behavior factors are most often associated with positive individual and organizational outcomes. It is important to stress, however, that ratings of behavior are not the same thing as actual behavior. Ratings of behavior reflect the perceptions of the rater, and perceptions are influenced by many factors in addition to actual behavior.

In later chapters, I describe extensive research programs on leadership perception and cognition that quite clearly showed that leader behavior ratings are influenced by the knowledge of how well the leader's group has performed. For example, identical videotapes of a leader interacting with a group resulted in very different ratings of the leader's behavior when the raters were told that the group performed poorly or successfully (e.g., Phillips & Lord, 1981).

To a considerable degree, the consideration and initiation of structure factors represent idealized descriptions of the two major functions of leadership, goal attainment and group morale. It is not surprising that high scores on these measures are associated with good group outcomes. Unfortunately, the direction of causality in these relationships is not clear. We don't know if the behavior causes the outcome, or if the positive outcome leads to the retrospective perception of the behavior. Followers or superiors who hold positive perceptions of a leader may describe that leader in positive ways, that is, as being high on the behavior factors. The particular pattern of ratings may reflect the follower's beliefs about what a good leader does as much as they reflect what the leader actually did.

Another problem with the literature on leader behavior is the same issue that was discussed with respect to personality traits. There is no reason to believe that one style of behavior will be appropriate in every situation. Should we expect that an educational leader will be effective with the same behaviors that serve a military commander well, or even that the military commander's behavior will have the same effect during a combat situation that it has during a training exercise or recreational activity?

It seems sensible to propose that effective leaders should be high on both types of behavior. The goal attainment functions of leadership can be accomplished with structuring leadership, whereas group harmony, morale, and satisfaction can be attained through more interpersonally sensitive actions. Does it make sense, however, to think that a leader can do all of these behaviors at the same time? Leaders may have to focus on one activity or another, and it may be that some of the behaviors included in one factor are contradictory or inimicable to those of another factor.

In chapter 1, I argued that certain organizational functions are contradictory to others. For example, systems that enhance reliability tend to reduce creativity. A similar case can be made with respect to leader behavior. For example, being highly directive is clearly incompatible with fostering high levels of follower participation. The question of whether and under what circumstances a leader can display both considerate and structuring behavior is a complex and unresolved issue in leadership research even today. In the 1950s, the results relating leader behavior to performance represented another disappointing episode in the search for meaningful effects.

## Situational Factors in Leadership

Although situational influences on leadership were not focal topics for early researchers, they were not altogether ignored either. A number of studies revealed that aspects of the context in which the leader functioned could have important effects on leadership emergence and subsequent behavior.

At the most basic level, Hemphill (1949) argued that the motivation to attempt to assert influence in groups, that is, to lead, depended on three perceptions held by the potential leader. First, the person must believe that the influence attempts will be accepted by other group members. Second, the potential leader must perceive a sufficiently high probability that they will be able to accomplish the task or achieve the goal. Third, the leader must feel that the rewards of goal attainment will be attractive and worthwhile. A question that arises from this analysis is what conditions in the leadership situation make a prospective leader feel that they are likely to be successful in the role.

A number of studies show that being in the right place at the right time has a lot to do with becoming a leader. For example, studies of communication networks indicate that individuals who are in central positions in such networks and have greater opportunities to interact with others are more likely to be chosen as leaders. In a study of B-29 bomber crews, Dorothy McBride Kipnis (1957) found that members of the 11-man crew whose position in the intercom system gave them greater prominence were more likely to be chosen as influential by other crew members.

Leavitt (1951) experimentally created different types of communication networks by varying the channels available for the members of 5-person groups to converse with one another. Some of these networks had one central node, and the person in that position could communicate with every other group member, all of whom could communicate only with the central person. In other networks, people could communicate with one or two other people, but no one could communicate with more than two, and in still other arrangements, every group member could communicate with every other member. In the highly centralized network, the person occupying the central position was chosen to be the group leader in 100% of the groups. In the less centralized groups, no particular position enjoyed an advantage in leadership emergence.

Similar results were found in studies of spatial and seating arrangements (Bass, Klubeck, & Wurster, 1953; Howells & Becker, 1962; Sommer, 1961; Steinzor, 1950). People who sit at the head of the table or in positions that give them the opportunity for face-to-face contact with other people are more likely to be chosen as leaders. Clearly, the opportunity for interaction plays a role in emergence.

Influence attempts that receive support from other group members may also provide an impetus for increased attempts at leadership. For example, in an ingenious experiment, Bavelas, Hastorf, Gross, and Kite (1965) manipulated feedback to members of a leaderless discussion group. In front of each group member, a shielded set of light bulbs (one red and one green) provided feedback confidentially to each person about the quality of their contributions to group activity. An ostensibly good verbal contribution resulted in a green light being lit, whereas a red light indicated a detrimental input. The experimenters then randomly determined which group members would receive the positive and negative feedback. Individuals who were given the green light spoke more and longer, and as a result, were much more likely to be chosen as group leaders. This outcome was obviously quite independent of any personal characteristics of the individuals involved.

Using specially trained confederates rather than red and green lights, Gruenfeld, Rance, and Weissenberg (1969) found the same effect. When followers agreed with a potential leader's initial suggestions or comments, that person was more likely to increase the number of influence attempts compared to a person who received less supportive feedback. Thus, the likelihood that one will become a leader and the subsequent vigor with which the leader will act may depend on factors like physical location or follower receptiveness that are external to the leader.

In a study of naval officers, Shartle (1951) showed that an organizational role can have profound effects on the manner in which a leader behaves. Shartle studied executive officers, the seconds-in-command on ships of the line, and found that the best predictor of how an officer would behave in the executive officer position was how the last occupant of that position had behaved. The previous occupant's behavior predicted the new officer's behavior better than did the new officer's personality or the way he had behaved in his last position.

Other analyses (McGrath & Altman, 1966; Morris, 1966; Morris & Hackman, 1969) show that a group's task had a strong effect on the behavior of the leader and other group members. Certain tasks are more likely to elicit directive behavior from a leader, whereas other tasks seem to promote participation by followers.

## SOME CONCLUSIONS

The first 50 or so years of leadership were a story of frustration and futility, but current students of the field can glean some important points from these pioneering efforts. First, it is clear that simple answers emphasizing universal approaches of traits, behaviors, or styles are unlikely to be sufficient to explain the dynamics of the leadership process. What then might be the candidates for a set of variables to include in a more complex and integrative approach to understanding the phenomenon?

The research on personality traits, both in the early part of the century and since that time, suggests that stable, personal dispositions cannot be ignored. In a 16-year study of achievement motivation among managers, McClelland and Boyatzis (1980) showed that enduring motivational patterns measured early in a manager's career could predict success more than 10 years later. Other careful studies show that stable aspects of the leader can indeed have predictive validity (House, 1981; Kenny & Zaccaro, 1983).

These recent studies do not really contradict Stogdill's (1948, 1974) conclusions. Rather, they place those conclusions in perspective. Stogdill did not say that personal differences had no explanatory utility for understanding leadership. He only said that they were not sufficient for a complete understanding which must integrate important aspect of the situation.

Some good candidates for important aspects of the situation would certainly include the leader's position in the organization; the policies, procedures, and climate of the organization; and the culture of the society in which the organization is embedded. These factors might be broadly identified as the leader's role.

Situations can vary, however, even for occupants of the same role. For example, a first-line foreman's situation in a large industrial organization could be very different from one foreman to another. The followers' acceptance and suppport for the leader is an important determinant of how the individual approaches the role. Similarly, the nature of the group's task and the authority relations within and between the group and the surrounding organization are all part of the leadership equation.

## A PREVIEW OF THE INTEGRATIVE MODEL

The futile search for simple answers that characterized the early research on leadership makes apparent the complexity and elusiveness of the phenomenon. Some 40 to 50 years of research reinforced that conclusion. In the chapters that follow, the various approaches, disparate and sometimes contradictory, are presented. Before embarking on a such a journey, however, it might be wise to seek a map, even a relatively crude one, that shows our eventual destination. These will be the general principles to keep in mind as you progress through this book.

It is the thesis of this volume that an integration of contemporary leadership theory and research is possible, but it requires a new way of looking at leadership. This integrative approach stresses common functions and processes of leadership, that cut across particular theories. Effective leadership is thought to emcompass three major functions; *image management*, which refers to a leader's ability to project an image that is consistent with observers' expectations; *relationship development*, which reflects the leader's success in creating and sustaining motivated and competent followers; and *resource utilization*, which alludes to the leader's capability for deploying the assets of self and others to mission accomplishment.

The processes by which these functions are combined to create effective groups and organizations are governed by the "match" principle. Leaders are able to project a compelling image when their actions match commonly held templates of how effective leaders should appear. They are able to build meaningful relationships when their behaviors match followers' needs and expectations. They are able to effectively deploy available resources when their strategies match the demands of the organizational environment. These are the functions and processes of effective leadership. As we proceed through the chapters, key features of contemporary theory will be highlighted to support the bases for the integration that is presented in Chapter 10.

# Chapter 3

## The Contingency Model
## and Its Sequelae

### A NEW APPROACH TO THE
### STUDY OF LEADERSHIP

In the early 1960s, discouraged by the sparse yield of the trait and behavioral approaches followed in the early studies, the field of leadership research was ready for a new paradigm. What arose to fill that need was the contingency model of leadership effectiveness (Fiedler 1964, 1967), and the field turned in a dramatic new direction.

In some ways, Fred Fiedler was an unlikely prospect to bring to leadership research a shift in approach so profound that Harry Triandis (1993) later said that all of leadership research could be conceptually divided into the period that preceded and that which followed the introduction of Fiedler's contingency model (Fiedler, 1964, 1967). Trained as a clinical psychologist at the University of Chicago, Fiedler began doing research on leadership when he joined the faculty at the University of Illinois. To the study of group dynamics and performance, Fiedler brought both a clinician's feel for the interpersonal aspects of the phenomenon and a willingness to stick with a complex and confusing research problem.

During his early research on the effectiveness of clinical theraptists, Fiedler (1951) asked therapists to describe their patients and themselves. He found that therapists whose ratings revealed a psychologically distant attitude toward patients were less effective than those who were more accepting. In a series of modifications, Fiedler eventually developed a measure in which leaders were asked to rate the "worst coworker with whom they had ever worked; the one individual who most interfered with successful task accomplishment." This measure was called the least preferred coworker (abbreviated as LPC) scale.[1]

In a series of studies, Fiedler correlated the leader's score with group outcomes. From the first, Fiedler viewed the appropriate outcome criterion in group studies to be how well the group performed on its assigned task. He argued that symphony conductors, professional football coaches, and steel shop foreman, are rewarded by how well their groups play music, win ballgames, or make steel, not by how happy the group members are. Thus, his studies, most of which were conducted in work organizations, measured group performance by organizational criteria of productivity whenever possible.

In correlating his measure of psychological distance to group performance, Fiedler like many researches of that time was still trying to identify the leadership trait. Perhaps, leaders who were cool and aloof from subordinates would be more effective than those who felt closer to their followers, or vice versa. Some early studies indicated that the distant leader was more effective.

For example, in a study of open-hearth steel shop foreman (Cleven & Fiedler, 1956), the groups of leaders who had given lower ratings to their least preferred coworker (called low LPC leaders) outperformed the high LPC led groups on measures of the tonnage of steel produced per shift. Similar results turned up in studies of the facility of tank crews in destroying targets during training exercises (Fiedler, 1958), of B-29 bomber crew performance on training runs (Fiedler, 1955), and of the accuracy of surveying teams (Fiedler, 1954). In each case, the teams led by low LPC, "psychologically distant" leaders performed better than teams led by high LPC, "psychologically close" individuals.

Like so many leadership researchers before him, Fiedler was soon blithely sliding down that mountain of broken dreams, that is, the belief that he had identified the elusive leadership effectiveness trait. No sooner had he published a book extolling the virtues of the psychologically distant leadership style (Fiedler, 1958) than studies began to yield results in which the high LPC leaders were more effective than low LPC leaders. Studies of the financial success of Illinois farming cooperatives (Godfrey, Fiedler, & Hall, 1959), of laboratory groups working on ambiguous or creative tasks (Fiedler, Meuwese, & Oonk, 1960) and of groups performing under stressful conditions (Meuwese & Fiedler, 1964) yielded the results favoring psychologically close leadership.

What was even more important to Fiedler's eventual breakthrough was the fact that in some of these studies, the relationship between LPC and performance varied dramatically from one condition to another. One example was the study of laboratory groups working on creative tasks (Fiedler et al., 1960) which was conducted

---

[1]The full scale contains 18 bipolar adjective scales on which the leader rated the least-preferred coworker, including pleasant–unpleasant; friendly–unfriendly; accepting–rejecting; relaxed–tense; close–distant; supportive–hostile; harmonious–quarrelsome; cheerful–gloomy; open–guarded; loyal–backbiting; trustworthy–untrustworthy; considerate–inconsiderate; agreeable-disagreeable; sincere-insincere; kind-unkind (Fiedler & Chemers, 1984).

in Holland. In that study, leaders who were either formally appointed or who emerged informally led groups that were either culturally homogeneous (i.e., all Catholic or all Calvinist, an important aspect of social life in that country) or culturally heterogeneous. The observed relationships varied dramatically with the low LPC leaders being decidedly more effective in one set of groups whereas the high LPC led groups were far superior in another condition.

The variability in which leader type was most effective from one study to another and even from one condition to another within a single study brought Fiedler to the realization that a major moderator must be missing from the leadership equation; an insight that had eluded a great many other leadership researchers of the time. He theorized that the nature of the relationship between LPC and group performance was dependent or "contingent" on some other aspect of the leadership situation, and in 1964, he published the first formal exposition of a "contingency theory" of leadership.

# THE CONTINGENCY MODEL
# OF LEADERSHIP EFFECTIVENESS

Stogdill's (1948) suggestion that a complete theory of leadership would involve the interaction of the leader's personality with important aspects of the leadership situation waited 16 years to find its presentation in the contingency model of leadership effectiveness. In a chapter in Berkowitz (1964) *Advances in Experimental Social Psychology* and then in his own 1967 book, *A Theory of Leadership Effectiveness*, Fiedler reorganized his work of the previous 15 years, and in the process, dramatically changed the way people studied leadership, as well as many other social psychological phenomena.

Fiedler (1967) argued that because leadership is primarily the exercise of social influence, the ease with which a leader is able to influence his or her followers should make a big difference in how "favorable" the leadership situation is for the leader. In analyzing the factors in a group task situation that could make it easier or harder for a leader to influence followers, Fiedler felt that the quality of the interpersonal relations between the parties was the paramount consideration. When the leader was liked and respected by followers, attempts at influence would be much more likely to be successful. A second consideration was the nature of the task assigned to the group, particularly the degree of clarity and structure in the task. Tasks with clear goals and procedures not only gave the leader the sense of knowing what to do, but also provided a framework within which to exercise authority and influence. The third variable that Fiedler included in the situational specification was the amount of authority that the leader held by virtue of a formal position or designation of leadership.

In many of the studies that Fiedler had done up to that time, measures of these three variables were already available or could be inferred from the circumstances or conditions. For example, the interpersonal ambience (later dubbed "leader–member relations") was sometimes measured with a "group atmosphere" scale consisting of semantic differential scales (e.g., friendly–unfriendly, cooperative–uncooperative, enthusiastic–unenthusiastic). When such data was not available, conditions like cultural homogeneity or heterogeneity could be used to infer the quality of the relations.

The second factor in the specification of the situation, task structure, could be determined by having knowledgeable raters judge the objective parameters of the task. Dimensions of task structure developed by Marvin Shaw (1963), reflecting the degree to which the task's goals, procedures, and means of evaluation were clear and specific, were applied to the tasks on which Fiedler's groups had worked using an expanded rating scale developed by Hunt (1967).

Hunt (1967) developed a similar scale for assessing the degree of formal power in a leadership position. The leader's authority to reward and punish followers and the leader's expertise to judge subordinate performance were central to the position power measure.

These three variables were ordered in terms of importance with leader–member relations being the most important and position power the least. By dividing each of the three variables into a high and a low level and then combining them, 8 possible classifications or octants were created. When the variables were ordered by importance, the octants yielded a dimension of "Situational Favorableness." The 700 groups that had performed in the earlier studies were sorted into the 8 octants of the model. The relationship between the leader's LPC score and the group's performance within each set of groups was noted, and the resultant relationship comprised the curve shown in Fig. 3.1.

The dimension of Situational Favorableness is arranged along the bottom of the graph, ranging from high favorableness, where relations with followers, task structure, and position power provide the leader great ease of influence, through moderate

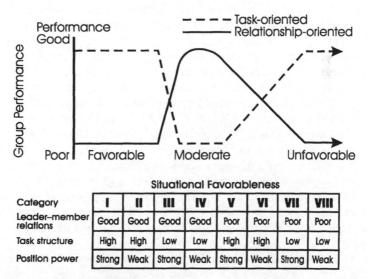

| Category | I | II | III | IV | V | VI | VII | VIII |
|---|---|---|---|---|---|---|---|---|
| Leader–member relations | Good | Good | Good | Good | Poor | Poor | Poor | Poor |
| Task structure | High | High | Low | Low | High | High | Low | Low |
| Position power | Strong | Weak | Strong | Weak | Strong | Weak | Strong | Weak |

FIG. 3.1. Relationship between LPC score and group performance for 8 levels of situational favorableness (from Fiedler, 1978).

situations to very unfavorable situations. The other axis of the graph presents the relative effectiveness of high and low LPC led groups across the situational dimension. The curve indicates that in very favorable or very unfavorable situations, the low LPC leaders were more effective in achieving high group productivity, whereas in moderate situations, the high LPC leaders were more successful. How are we to understand these findings, and what are their implications?

# The Validity, Meaning, and Implications of the Contingency Model

The implications of the contingency model were dramatic and profound. The findings meant that the idea of one universally effective leadership trait or style was a myth. Effective leadership was an "if–then" proposition with some leaders being effective in some situations, but not others. It was also quite clear that leadership, like other social psychological phenomena, was dependent on a subtle set of interpersonal relationships rooted in a particular context of task and authority.

## The Validity of the Model

The contingency model had a pervasive impact on the field of leadership and social psychology almost immediately. However, the work was not without its detractors. The manner in which the model was developed contributed to doubts about its validity. The psychological construct reflected in the LPC score was not clear. The measure and its interpretation had been modified from its original purposes and interpretation, and no one was quite sure what the measure signified. The model itself, with the Situational Favorableness dimension based on three variables, interacting in a curvilinear function with the LPC scale seemed overly complex. In defense of the model's complexity, Fiedler, (1964, personal communication) often said that "a pretzel shaped theory was needed to explain a pretzel shaped universe)." Finally, the fact that the model was developed inductively from data already collected invited speculation that the retrospective curve fitting was overly dependent on chance and would not hold up to subsequent testing.

Shortly after the publication of Fiedler's (1967) book, Graen and his associates published a scathing criticism of the contingency model in the prestigious journal, *Psychological Bulletin* (Graen, Alvarez, Orris, & Martella, 1970). The Graen criticism was followed by a number of other examinations of the model, some of which were thoughtful and germane and some less so (Ashour, 1973; McMahon, 1972; Schriesheim & Kerr, 1977). The thrust of the criticisms centered on a set of issues related to (a) the nature and specification of the constructs, (b) the methods for testing the predictions of the model, and (c) the explanatory rationale underlying the model.

The first and third issues (1) and (3) relate to the theoretical elegance of the model more than they do to the validity of its predictions. The question of primary importance concerns whether the predictions of the model based on the early studies hold up in subsequent tests of the model, that is, the technical validity of the theory. Graen et al. (1970) argued that fitting a curve to data already collected encourages the development of a theory that accommodates the limited data on hand and may capitalize on chance. The criticism further noted that in many tests of the model, the predicted relationships did not reach traditionally acceptable levels of significance, and inferences were based on nonsignificant trends. Graen et al. (1970) buttressed their argument by reporting the results of their own experimental test of the contingency model that failed to yield supportive results.

Fiedler (1971) answered the critique by pointing out that Graen et al.'s (1970) experiment suffered from serious methodological flaws of its own. Fiedler presented the results of a large number of laboratory and field studies conducted after the development of the model and in support of the model's predictions. Unfortunately, most of the studies cited by Fiedler were again only marginally significant.

Later, carefully controlled experimental studies that strongly supported the model (e.g., Chemers & Skryzypek, 1972) were contrasted by disconfirmations in other research (Vecchio, 1977). The problems inherent in comparing and interpreting single studies or even groups of studies may have allowed the contingency model validity question to linger on for a long time. However, meta-analysis strategies that became popular in the 1980s were particularly well suited to breaking the deadlock surrounding the validity question.

In meta-analysis, the results of individual studies are converted to standard scores that can be aggregated and tested for overall significance. Strube and Garcia (1981) reported the results of a meta-analysis of 145 tests of the Contingency Model that indicated extremely strong support for the model. They also noted that the results of studies completed after the exposition of the model, what Graen et al. (1970) called "evidential" studies, were stronger in support of the model than were the original studies on which the model was based. In another meta-analysis employing a more stringent methodology, Peters, Hartke, and Pohlmann (1983) also found support for the validity of the model.

Although these meta-analyses provide strong support for the basic predictive validity of the model, they do not answer criticisms questioning the meaning of the LPC construct or the underlying explanatory rationale for the model.

## The Meaning of the Least Preferred Coworker (LPC) Construct

The most pointed, if somewhat vernacular, criticism of the LPC construct is embodied in the question, "What the hell is LPC, anyway?" During the course of research with the LPC measure, it has alternatively been interpreted as a measure of (a) psychological distance, (b) motivational orientation, (c) cognitive complexity, and (d) a hierarchy of primary and secondary motivations.

*Psychological Distance.* In its original inception as an offshoot of the measure of psychotherapists, the scale was seen as a measure of psychological distance. However, the later measure of a poor coworker seems better understood in terms of the degree of uniform negativity in the rating. In other words, why are some individuals so much more negative than others in their descriptions of a poor coworker?

*Motivational Orientation.*   The context in which to interpret that negativity may be provided by recalling the instructions for the stimulus to be rated as the least preferred coworker, that is, "the one coworker in your entire work history with whom you had the most difficulty getting a job done." The context to which the rater's attention is drawn involves the failure to perform an assigned task. The resultant rating may then reflect the intensity of negative feelings toward a person who impedes task accomplishment and by inference, may reflect the degree of importance that the rater attaches to task accomplishment. The negative emotionality may be related to the extent of frustration felt when goal attainment is blocked, and again by inference, may reflect the importance of the blocked goal (Fishbein, Landy, & Hatch, 1969). This train of reasoning leads to regarding the low LPC person (i.e., the person who gives a low rating to their least preferred coworker) as one who is very motivated to attain task accomplishment. The person who rates a poor coworker relatively positively is seen as more concerned with the interpersonal or relational aspects of the group experience (Fiedler, 1964, 1967).

Regarding the LPC scale as reflecting motivation toward and preoccupation with task or relationship concerns brings the construct into conceptual alignment with the kinds of variables identified by the behavioral researchers of the 1950s, that is, initiation of structure and consideration, production-orientation and employee-orientation, task specialist and socioemotional specialist, and others. This commonality across approaches helps to tie LPC into the broader leadership literature. It is important to recognize, however, that the LPC construct was not regarded as a measure of behavior, but rather one of motivation or orientation (Fiedler, 1967; Fiedler & Chemers, 1974).

*Motivational Hierarchy.*   The basic view of low LPC persons as task-oriented and high LPC persons as relationship oriented was eventually found to be not entirely satisfactory. Although the two leader types usually behaved in ways consistent with the task and relationship designation, there were studies in which, at least in some conditions, the low LPC leaders showed more considerate behavior whereas the high LPC leaders were more structuring.

To account for these discrepancies, Fiedler (1972) proposed a motivational hierarchy interpretation of LPC. Consistent with Maslow's (1954) need hierarchy, Fiedler suggested that leaders might have a primary motivation and a secondary motivation. Under demanding conditions where it is not clear that all needs will be satisfied, people are motivated to focus on their primary goals, that is, task goals for the low LPC leaders and relationship goals for the high LPCs. However, in very favorable situations when the satisfaction of primary needs seems assured, people have the psychological luxury to pursue secondary goals, and low LPC persons become more relationship oriented, whereas high LPC leaders seek task accomplishment.

*Cognitive Complexity.*    A study by Mitchell (1970) indicated that high LPC, "relationship-motivated" persons scored higher on a measure of cognitive complexity than did low LPC persons. Foa, Mitchell, and Fiedler (1971) proposed that cognitive complexity may underlie the LPC scale because high LPC persons, by the very nature of their high rating of a poor coworker, differentiated between task and interpersonal issues. One could also argue that the moderate control situations in which high LPC leaders were more effective called for a more complex approach, because such situations have a mix of favorable and unfavorable aspects.

This evolution in the interpretation of the LPC score followed much the same path as the general development of the contingency model, generating some of the same problems that we observed in the discussion of the model's validity. As new data were gathered, interpretations were modified in an inductive fashion to fit the latest results. Although the large number of studies using the LPC variable attests to the vibrancy of the model, and the willingness of researchers to modify their theories with the accretion of data is a sign of flexibility, the resultant multiple and changing explanations led to a confusion that weakened both the clarity and the confidence with which the measure was regarded. Thankfully, an excellent review and analysis by Rice (1978) helped to clarify the nature and meaning of the LPC measure.

*Value–Attitude Interpretation.*    Robert Rice was one researcher who was frustrated with the confusion surrounding the meaning of the LPC variable. Rice argued that rather than a series of ad hoc interpretations, a comprehensive review with data aggregated in a meaningful fashion was necessary to elucidate the meaning of LPC.

Rice (1978) randomly selected 66 studies from a pool of 114 studies that included the LPC variable. These 66 studies yielded 1,445 relationships between LPC and other variables. Rice compiled and categorized these relationships in an extremely thorough and careful analysis that stands as the "gold standard" of LPC reviews. He found that the LPC score, itself a judgment of a coworker, was most strongly related to other kinds of judgments made by the leader. These judgments yielded a general pattern that was consistent with the view that low LPC leaders were task oriented and high LPC leaders were relationship oriented.

For example, whereas high LPC persons were generally more positive in their judgments of other people, low LPCs were more positive in their judgments of people who contributed to task success, such as good coworkers and loyal subordinates. When asked to describe the kind of persons who were their least preferred coworkers, high LPCs depicted persons who might be disruptive of interpersonal relations whereas low LPCs described a poor worker, that is, one who is stupid, careless, or slow.

When comparing the two types of leader on judgments of their groups and task environments, low LPCs were found to be more complex, more accurate, and more optimistic when discussing aspects of group life related to task accomplishment, whereas high LPCs were more complex, more accurate, and more optimistic about the interpersonal environment.

Low LPCs responded with more favorable attitudes about themselves and their groups when the group had been successful in task accomplishment. This effect was not found for high LPCs, but they were more positive about themselves and others when their groups were interpersonally successful.

When the examination turned to the behavior of the two leader types, Rice reported that the vast majority of significant findings supported the view of lows as task oriented and highs as relationship oriented. Low LPCs did more task focused activity, such as clarifying the task, controlling the discussion, keeping the group on task, and generally dominating the group process. High LPC leaders, on the other hand, were characterized as encouraging the participation of subordinates, being supportive of group members, and trying to boost morale in the group. However, there were indeed occasions when the behaviors of these leaders shifted, but in ways that were not incompatible with the general view. For example, low LPC leaders engaged in more considerate behavior toward their subordinates when their group had been successful on the task.

Rice (1978) concluded that the LPC score could be most usefully regarded as reflecting a difference in values. Low LPC persons value task accomplishment, and high LPC persons value interpersonal accomplishment. These two values became contructs (Kelly, 1955) through which various aspects of the environment were evaluated. Thus, each type of leader forms attitudes toward other people, groups, and behavioral intentions on the basis of the relationship to the leader's basic values and goal attainment.

The value–attitude interpretation is not inconsistent with earlier views, but it is much more elegant. Thus, low LPC leaders are not more psychologically distant from other people in general, only from the type of people (i.e., poor coworkers) who thwart the attainment of valued goals. High LPC leaders are more psychologically distant from those who interfere with good relationships and group harmony. Rather than one type of leader being more cognitively complex than another, they are each complex (and accurate, favorable, and optimistic) in the valued domain. We can expect that each type of leader will engage in behaviors that they feel are likely to help them attain valued goals. Most of the time, this will mean that low LPCs are task oriented, structuring, and orderly, and high LPC leaders are considerate, participative, and sensitive. However, in some situations, each leader type might act in ways that are different from the typical pattern, but not inconsistent with their ultimate goals. The value–attitude approach provides a reasonable synthesis of the the findings concerning the LPC construct.

## Causal Explanations of Contingency Effects

What can we conclude, then, about the causal processes underlying the observed relationships? A broad reading of the contingency model literature brings the following conclusions. First, the LPC construct reflects the relative degree to which a person in a leadership position values and strives for task or interpersonal success, and the extent to which they employ relatively task-focused, structuring, and directive behavior or relatively morale-focused, considerate, and participative behavior to achieve those goals. Second, each of these types of leaders has variable success in attaining high levels of group productivity and organizational performance dependent on the degree to which the leadership situation provides the leader with a sense of predictability, certainty, and control. Task-motivated leaders perform significantly and consistently better in situations in which the leader has either very high or very low levels of control, whereas the relationship-motivated leader performs best in situations of moderate control. Why should this be so?

*High Control Situations.*    In situations of high control, the leader has a supportive group of followers, understands how to accomplish the task, and has moderate to high levels of authority. Under these conditions, the group must simply be kept on track and highly motivated in order to achieve high productivity. A leadership style that creates high expectations for performance in a structured and goal-directed atmosphere, without undue pressure, is likely to be quite successful. The task-oriented leader feels relaxed and at ease in this situation because primary goals are likely to be met. The task-motivated leader can keep the group moving forward with an emphasis on performance that results in continued attention to goal attainment.

The relationship-motivated leader in high control may become bored or distracted. The things that he or she is interested in, such as being liked by others, are already attained, and the skills that are well developed, such as participative problem solving, are not really necessary. The relationship-oriented leader finds nothing to energize or maintain attention. However, even the most clear-cut task and the most supportive group can be messed up. If a bored or distracted relationship-motivated leader ignores details and wastes time in unnecessary morale boosting or problem-solving exercises, the group will not perform as well as possible, and certainly not as well as the businesslike groups run by the task-oriented leaders.

*Moderate Control Situations.*    A much more complex and ambiguous environment is present in situations of moderate control. The intermediate level of the dimension involves a mix of variables that both enhance and diminish predictability and control. The leader might have a supportive group but a very unclear and unstructured task. Conversely, the task might be quite well organized, but interpersonal relations are problematic. Ambiguous situations might benefit from different leadership processes than would the more homogeneous high or low control situations.

If a leader faces a situation with strong follower support but an unclear task, participative leadership in which followers add their knowledge and creativity to task definition and problem solution would be very effective. In a situation where the task is clear but difficulty is created by an uncooperative or unmotivated group, an emphasis on consideration and morale building can move the group toward a more productive orientation. The relationship-oriented leader is likely to react to task or interpersonal ambiguity in these characteristic ways.

The task-motivated leader is likely to respond in a less effective manner. When the task is unclear, the goal-directed leader might rush toward structure, choosing the first solution that seems feasible. Frequently, task-motivated leaders avoid group discussions that create an even greater sense of uncontrollability in favor of solitary problem solving and planning. By reducing the input of others, the overly structuring leader limits creativity and diminishes the opportunity for a truly constructive outcome.

When the task-oriented leader is confronted by a well-structured and clear task with an unethusiastic group of followers, the leader is inclined to push ahead, ignoring the interpersonal relations, or attempt to control followers with directions or threat of punishment. Whereas difficult tasks can sometimes be engineered into submission, difficult subordinates rarely can. By attempting to enforce order, the task-motivated leader increases the likelihood of greater problems.

*Low Control Situations.*   A soft voice may turn away wrath, but it can also be drowned out by the din of chaos. The low control situation presents the leader with a task that is not well understood, to be solved with a hostile and uncooperative group in conditions of limited authority. The old military adage comes to mind; "when a group is under heavy attack, any order is better than no order."

The single-minded, no-nonsense style of the task-motivated leader can provide at least a minimal amount of organization to the situation to get the group moving forward. The relationship-motivated leader, in an attempt to consider all angles and everyone's concerns, may end up wheel spinning without progress. The task-motivated, "kick 'em in the pants" style will not result in high levels of performance, but it will, nonetheless, have better effects than the alternative.

In each of the situations, the task- or relationship-motivated leader is likely to behave in particular patterns based on deeply held and long-practiced inclinations. Whether one style or another will be effective depends on the demands of the specific situation. This explanation of contingency model effects is based on a somewhat "mechanical" view. In other words, the leadership situation presents specific problems that have a higher probability of solution with some procedures than with others. In this reasoning, for example, the more contributors there are to the solution of an unstructured problem, the greater the likelihood of a superior solution. In such explanations, it is assumed that the parameters of the leadership situation determine the most useful leadership orientation. Leader behaviors interact with situational demands to produce high or low group performance.

However, other potential explanations of contingency model place less emphasis on the objective effects of the situation and more emphasis on the leader's "phenomenological" experience of the situation. Two recent lines of research with their roots in the contingency model suggest that some more subtle and subjective processes may also contribute to the observed effects of the person–situation interaction.

## COGNITIVE RESOURCE THEORY

In keeping with his history of inductively derived theory, Fiedler's scientific curiosity was again aroused by some empirical findings that agreed with neither common sense nor with accepted scientific wisdom. His interest eventually led Fiedler to the development of cognitive resource theory (Fiedler & Garcia, 1987). The seeds of the theory were sown in two experiments that compared the leadership performance of experienced military officers with untrained, inexperienced recruits and found no differences between the groups led by the recruits and those led by the officers (Fiedler, 1966; Fiedler & Chemers, 1968). These results were obtained despite the facts that the groups worked on military analog tasks and that the officers were graduates of military academies, averaging 10 years of military service experience, and having higher scores on an intelligence test than did the recruits. The finding that neither training nor experience in a highly "leadership-intensive" occupation predicted leadership performance demanded further investigation.

Fiedler reanalyzed data from earlier studies in which experience or training information was available, including studies of leadership in post offices (Fiedler, Nealey, & Wood, 1968), research laboratories, craft shops, and grocery stores (Hunt, 1967). The consistent results of these analyses prompted Fiedler (1970) to write an article entitled "Leadership Experience and Leader Performance—Another Hypothesis Shot to Hell."

Fiedler reasoned that if experience and training were irrelevant to performance, perhaps another knowledge-related resource, intelligence, might be a better predictor. However, findings indicated that leader intelligence bore a weak and generally nonsignificant relationship to leadership performance (Bons & Fiedler, 1976; Fiedler & Garcia, 1987).

The development of the contingency model taught Fiedler that when a reasonable, logical, straightfoward hypothesis fails to yield a simple, straightforward set of results, it is time to dig a little deeper and look for the situational variables that might moderate the not-so-simple relationship. Fiedler and his associates undertook an extensive research program to examine possible moderators of the relationships between cognitive resources (i.e., experience and intelligence), and leader performance (Blades & Fiedler, 1973; Bons & Fiedler, 1976; Fiedler & Leister, 1977; Fiedler, Potter, Zais, & Knowlton, 1979: For a more complete discussion of the individual studies than is possible in the space available here, see Fiedler, 1993, or Fiedler & Garcia, 1987).

This research revealed a powerful moderating role for stress. In these studies, stress was measured through leader self-report measures or by analyzing the nature of the leader's job and working conditions. Performance was almost always operationalized by organizational criteria of success, either through objective measures or through superior ratings. The findings indicated that when leaders were under high levels of stress, the relationship between leader intelligence and unit performance was nil, and in some cases even negative. Under low levels of stress, intelligence was positively correlated with performance criteria. Leadership experience, on the other hand, was strongly positively correlated with performance under high levels of stress, but uncorrelated with performance when stress was low.

Fiedler and Garcia (1987) explained that stressful conditions and the anxiety they generate interfere with careful and thoughtful analysis. Intelligent leaders, who are used to using their considerable creative and analytic capacities to solve problems, get immersed in frantic and nonproductive efforts to think their way out of trouble. Leaders with high levels of experience, however, can fall back on both known techniques and previously tested solutions to the problem at hand. Experience leads to well-learned response patterns that are much less susceptible to stress-generated interference (Zajonc, 1965).

In addition to these pervasive effects of stress, Fiedler and his associates also noted some other factors that further moderate the link between cognitive resources and performance. One such variable is the extent to which the leader is directive (Blades & Fiedler, 1973). The leader's knowledge or creativity can only affect the group's output if the leader actively uses those resources to make decisions and solve problems. Correlations between intelligence and performance under low stress conditions or between experience and performance under high stress conditions are much stronger when the leader is rated as engaging in higher levels of directive behavior.

In summary, Fiedler and Garcia (1987) presented a causal chain in which a leader's cognitive resources (intelligence under low stress conditions and experience under high stress conditions) have their most positive impact on group performance when the leader actively directs follower activity.

What conditions might determine when a leader acts directively? In chapter 2, an argument was made that leaders are likely to attempt to exert influence when they think that followers are willing to accept their leadership and when they think that they are capable of achieving group goals (Gruenfeld, Rance, & Weissenberg, 1969; Hemphill, 1949). Fiedler and Garcia (1987) reported some data suggesting that contingency model variables, such as follower support and task structure, may indeed affect leader directiveness.

## MATCH, STRESS, AND CONFIDENCE

Recently, an exciting possibility for the integration of the contingency model and cognitive resource theory arose from a series of studies directed at understanding the psychological concomitants of being "in-match." In the literature on work stress, a number of theorists argued that person–situation interactions, such as those postulated by contingency theories, should be the best predictors of stress on the job (McGrath, 1976). Schuler (1980) also favored this view, but felt that the complexity of organizational dynamics makes it difficult to identify the appropriate variables to include in such a contingency formulation.

The potential application of leadership theories to the study of stress etiology led to a collaboration between leadership researcher, Martin Chemers, and Fred Rhodewalt, a social psychologist with interests in health and personality psychology. Chemers and Rhodewalt and their associates began a series of studies to examine person–situation models of job stress. The application of Fiedler's contingency model seemed apt for a number of reasons. First, it was a well-developed theory with specific variables, available measurement devices (Fiedler & Chemers, 1984), and well-articulated predictions. Some suggestive data already pointed in the direction of match effects on psychological states. In dissertations conducted in Chemers' laboratory at the University of Utah, Garcia (1983) found that in-match persons made stronger attributions to their personal responsibility for performance outcomes than did out-of-match persons. Nahavandi (1983) reported that in-match leaders of small laboratory groups expressed higher levels of interest and personal involvement in the group experience than did out-of-match leaders.

In a pilot study (Chemers, Hays, Rhodewalt, & Wysocki, 1985), 62 department chairs at a large university were asked to respond to the contingency model measures (i.e., LPC, leader–member relations, task structure, and position power; Fiedler & Chemers, 1984), as well as to measures of job stress (Fiedler et al., 1979) and stress-related illness. Findings strongly indicated that in-match chairs reported significantly lower levels of stress and stress-related illness than did out-of-match administrators.

In a follow-up study involving 385 secondary school administrators (Chemers, Hill, & Sorod, 1986), similar results were obtained. In-match administrators, as specified by the contingency model predictions, reported less stress and stress-re-lated illness, as well as significantly more positive scores on measures of job satisfaction (Smith, Kendall, & Hulin, 1969).

In a somewhat related approach, Ayman and Chemers (1991) examined the effects of leadership match on reactions of subordinates. They asked 100 middle managers in several Mexican corporations to complete the Leader Match scales (Fiedler & Chemers, 1984), and their subordinates completed measures of satisfac-tion with supervision and other job aspects. The subordinates of in-match leaders reported significantly higher levels of supervisor satisfaction than did the subordi-nates of out-of-match managers.

In an attempt to gain a clearer picture of the effects of match on the responses of leaders and followers, Chemers, Ayman Sorod, and Akimoto (1991) conducted an extensive laboratory experiment. Leaders, followers, and observers completed a series of questionnaires on their perceptions and reactions to the group experience. Those reactions fell into three general categories; (a) mood, or how pleasant and interesting the group experience was; (b) control, reflecting the degree to which the leader was actively organizing and directing group activity; and (c) cooperation, indicating the degree to which the group worked together harmoniously.

Analyses revealed that the in-match leaders reported significantly more positive moods, significantly higher ratings of their own control, and marginally higher ratings of cooperation than did out-of-match leaders. Followers of in-match leaders reported significantly higher ratings of both leader control and group cooperation than did followers of out-of-match leaders. Observer's ratings yielded effects favoring the in-match leaders on all three factors.

Taken together, these studies provide fairly strong support for the idea that the phenomenological experience of leadership match is a mood of excitement and involvement, a feeling of confidence and control, and a sense of harmonious leader–follower relationships, that is, an enthusiastic and confident leader who directs and guides group processes, and who also makes followers feel that they are involved and contributing.

A few important parallels between these results and other leadership research are worth pointing out. The sense of confidence and control experienced by the in-match leader is conceptually very similar to the sense of confidence and optimism that the popular theories (e.g., Bennis & Nanus, 1985) regard as a central component of successful leadership.

Second, the perception of the leader as directive, structuring, and in control may be congruent with the leader directiveness variable that is part of cognitive resource theory (Blades & Fiedler, 1973; Fiedler & Garcia, 1987). In cognitive resource theory, directiveness is essential for the application of the leader's intellectual and experiential resources to achieve task success. It may be that "match" provides the sense of confidence and control that encourages the leader to be more active and directive.

The coherence of these findings provide us with three possible explanations for the observed effects of match on group and organizational performance. Leaders who are in-match are likely to be more enthusiastic and active, to make more effective use of their own and their followers' resources, and to elicit perceptions of competence and control that inspire greater commitment and enthusiasm among followers.

It is important to note, however, that these paths to group performance are at least partially independent of one another. Leaders and followers can be quite confident and satisfied and still perform poorly. Leaders can be active and directive, and stress might still interfere with the successful employment of their cognitive resources. In other words, being confident and active does not assure success. Nonetheless, a psychological state characterized by excitement, confidence, and personal responsibility probably goes a long way toward providing a positive environment for productivity and effective leadership.

## SUMMARY AND CONCLUSIONS

In this chapter, the complexity of our explanations of leadership processes took a quantum leap. The one-best-way approaches of the early empirical research on leadership traits and behaviors and the popular view of the capable and dynamic leader who can succeed in any situation must be tempered by what we have learned from the contingency model.

The research by Fiedler and those who followed after reveals that effective leadership is strongly affected by the match or fit between the leader's orientation, inclinations, and skills and the demands of the leadership situation. The leader's relative emphasis on task versus relationship concerns appears to be an important characteristic. Likewise, the degree to which the leadership situation is clear and structured as opposed to being ambiguous and unpredictable is certainly part of the leadership equation. Contingency effects manifest themselves in both group productivity and perfomance and in the thoughts and emotions of group members. In-match leaders seem to result in highly performing groups that are calm, confident, and cooperative.

In the next chapter, other contingency formulations are presented. We see how the effects of a leader's supervisory behavior may depend on both the subordinate's task and personality. We also see that the strategy chosen by a leader to make decisions must be understood in the context of situational contingencies. Ultimately, an integrative theory of leadership must accommodate the role of leader–situation match.

# Chapter 4

---

# More Contingency Theories

The presentation of Fiedler's Contingency model in the 1960s created considerable controversy, but it also provided leadership researchers with a new, more productive approach to the problem. A second generation of contingency theories followed the contingency model and reflected a variety of perspectives. The two most prominent of the second generation contingency theories were House's (1971) path–goal theory of supervision and Vroom and Yetton's (1973) normative decision theory. This chapter deals extensively with these two models, as well as with some related theories that did not have as great an impact on the research literature, but nonetheless offer valuable insights.

## THE PATH–GOAL THEORY OF LEADERSHIP

One of the weaknesses of Fiedler's contingency model that was discussed in the last chapter was its failure to describe or directly analyze the processes by which the leader's motivational orientation affects group processes and outcomes. One obvious path for leadership effects to follow is through the psychological states of the followers, the people who must aid the leader in accomplishing the mission. Following this logic, leadership can be construed in terms of its effects on the motivation and satisfaction of followers.

Many motivational theories of the time were influenced by instrumentality notions (Vroom, 1964) that conceptualized motivation in terms of an actor's perception of the likelihood that certain behaviors would result in (i.e., be instrumental for) gaining desired outcomes. Georgopoulos, Mahoney, and Jones (1957) offered a "path–goal" instrumentality model that argued that motivation to engage in a behavior was a function of the product of the person's perception of the

44

probability that the behavior would lead to a goal and the perceived importance of the goal. A natural question concerns what sorts of factors influence an actor's perceptions of the path–goal probabilities. In particular, how might a leader's actions influence the path–goal perceptions held by subordinates?

The path–goal approach has the virtue of identifying the specific variables that must be addressed in defining follower motivation. Evans (1970) hypothesized that these path–goal perceptions were the moderators of the effects of leader behaviors such as initiation of structure and consideration (Fleishman & Harris, 1962). He reasoned that the behaviors did not always have the same effects on group outcomes such as productivity or satisfaction, because they did not always have the same effects on path–goal perceptions.

Evans argued that considerate and participative supervision enhanced the subordinates' perceptions of the availability of goals associated with higher order needs (i.e., self-esteem, feelings of accomplishment), but did nothing to make the subordinate feel more certain about how to go about attaining those goals. Initation of structure, on the other hand, provided clarification of the appropriate path (e.g., high productivity, high quality, obedience), although not necessarily assuring the availability of rewards. Thus, in conjunction, the two behaviors should have the most positive effect. Structuring leader behavior should have a very positive effect on motivation when consideration levels are high, but no effect when consideration behavior is absent.

Evans (1970) collected data from samples of workers in a public utility company and from nurses in a general hospital. Respondents rated the considerate and structuring behaviors of their supervisors, and their own perceptions of availability and importance of goals (e.g., promotion, pay), the instrumentality of various paths to those goals (e.g., helping others, producing high quantity of output), the frequencies with which they followed those paths, and their job satisfaction.

The results provided moderate support for the hypotheses. Both leader behaviors, consideration and structuring, were found to be significantly related to perceptions of path–goal instrumentality, but the predicted interaction of the behaviors was not found. The product of path–goal instrumentality and goal importance (i.e., how likely it was that the path would lead to a goal and how important the goal was) predicted the frequency with which workers reported engaging in various paths. Finally, leader's considerate behavior was related to worker satisfaction. The results suggested that Evans might be on the right track. Followers' psychological states were indeed related to their perceptions of leader behavior, even if not exactly in the way that the theory predicted.

In 1971, Robert House offered an alternative path–goal theory of leadership that integrated situational variables as moderators of the effects of leader behavior, thus making his model a true "contingency" theory. House argued that Evans' approach neglected the characteristics of the followers and the followers' tasks. These situational variables should determine when and how the supervisor's behavior affects the motivation, performance, and satisfaction of the followers. Like Evans, House argued that the motivational function of the leader is to increase followers' perceptions of rewards for performance and to make the path to these rewards easier for the follower to travel by clarifying the appropriate behavior and criteria of performance and by removing roadblocks or barriers.

In specification of the situational variables, House (1971) included follower's ability and personality (e.g., locus of control, authoritarianism) and environmental factors, including the task, the formal authority system, and the nature of the primary work group (e.g., task interdependence). In reviewing the extant literature on leader behavior effects (e.g., Filley & House, 1969), House (1971) illustrated how conflicting findings might be reconciled by reference to the role that these situational variables play as moderators. For example, when group members work on highly interdependent tasks, consideration behavior might increase productivity by establishing a climate in which cooperation is maintained. Or, when a follower's level of authoritarianism is high, supervisory structuring behavior is more positively received than when the follower is less authoritarian.

Although the theoretical specification of situational variables was quite extensive, including both environmental and follower characteristics, a much more limited set of situational moderators was actually employed in subsequent research on the model (House, 1971; House & Dessler, 1974; House & Mitchell, 1974). Follower personality and ability factors were relatively ignored, and attention was focused on the nature of the follower's task, in particular, the extent to which the job was intrinsically interesting and fulfilling versus boring and aversive, and the extent to which the job duties were ambiguous and broad in scope versus highly structured and predictable.

The degree of structure in a task and the extent to which it is interesting and fulfilling are not conceptually identical, but they are related in practice. Tasks with greater scope, both in terms of complexity and autonomy, tend to have a higher potential for intrinsic motivation and interest (Hackman & Oldham, 1976). The theory hypothesized that when task strucuture is low, subordinates will respond positively to a leader's structuring behavior, which helps to clarify the task and the path to the goal. When the task is already structured, leader's structuring behavior will be seen as redundant and interpreted as overly close monitoring or heavy-handed production emphasis. Consideration behavior will have its most positive effects when the task is boring, aversive, or unfulfilling, typically when structure is high. When the task is intrinsically interesting, consideration behavior is irrelevant and should have no relationship to either subordinate motivation or satisfaction.

Many path–goal theory studies addressed the degree of ambiguity in the subordinate's job, operationalized either by subordinate ratings of task structure (Downey, Sheridan, & Slocum, 1975, 1976; Stinson & Johnson, 1975), by role ambiguity (Dessler & Valenzi, 1977; Valenzi & Dessler, 1978), or by task variety (Schriesheim & DeNisi, 1981). Other studies have inferred the degree of role ambiguity from formal structural variables such as administrative level (Sims & Szilagyi, 1975a, 1975b), group size (Schriesheim & Murphy, 1976), and organizational size (Miles & Petty, 1977).

Most of this research provides support for the model, some of it strong (House & Dessler, 1974; Schriesheim & DeNisi, 1981). In studies that failed to confirm the hypotheses, it was usually the case that consideration behavior was positively related to satisfaction regardless of the degree of ambiguity in the task or job (Downey, Sheridan, & Slocum, 1975), whereas initiation of structure effects were confusing and difficult to interpret (Dessler & Valenzi, 1977; Stinson & Johnson, 1975; Valenzi & Dessler, 1978). A comprehensive meta-analysis of path–goal theory research by Indvik (1986) indicated moderate, but mixed support for its major propositions.

Explanations of path–goal theory's mixed findings focus on two sets of issues. The first of these is methodological and reflects concern about the operationalization of the model's constructs. As early as 1970, Evans (1970) acknowledged a methodological "fly in the ointment" that would continuously call into question the validity of findings with path–goal studies. The problem was that all the measures of significant variables in the model (i.e., leader behavior, subordinate perceptions of instrumentality, satisfaction) were provided by the same person. Thus, the finding that consideration behavior is correlated with followers' satisfaction could mean that, indeed, leaders who are considerate make their subordinates more satisfied, or it may simply mean that when subordinates are satisfied, they perceive their leader as being considerate.

It is dangerous to equate perceptions of leader behavior with actual behavior. The problem is made especially problematic by the natural tendency for people to maintain consistency in their thoughts and attitudes. For example, the behaviors included in the Consideration factor are generally positive, such as, being friendly, considerate, and supportive. It is natural that subordinates who are satisfied with their leader will attribute those positive valence behaviors to him or her. A related problem is that the variables that are distinct from one another in theory may not be so easily separable in practice. The leader behavior factors may be correlated with each other, for example. Also, a subordinate's rating of how ambiguous a task is might already include the subordinate's assessment of the effects of the supervisor's attempts at structuring the task. In such cases, the leader's behavior and the conditions in which the behavior is manifested are confounded with each other. By equating perceptions of behavior with actual behavior and by not taking into account "halo" effects, single source methodologies may muddle attempts at causal explanation.

A second concern with path–goal theory is the relative neglect of subordinate characteristics in the research. For example, considerable research (e.g., Haythorn et al., 1956; Vroom, 1959) indicated that personality characteristics like subordinate authoritarianism affect reactions to leader behavior under a variety of conditions. Within the path–goal body of work, a study by Griffin (1981) suggests the powerful role played by subordinate personality. Griffin's study included a measure of the growth need strength (Hackman & Oldham, 1976) of the respondents. Growth need strength assesses an individual's desire for a job that allows for learning, personal growth, and autonomy. Griffin compared the reactions to leader directive, participative, and supportive behaviors by subordinates high and low in growth need strength, who held challenging or routine jobs.

He found that subordinates high in growth need strength responded positively to supportive behavior when their task was boring, but reacted negatively to directive behavior, even when the task was challenging. For subordinates low in growth need strength, the pattern was different. These workers did not show an especially positive response to supportive behavior when their task was routine because, we might assume, a routine task was not aversive, and they responded quite positively to leader direction under all conditions. Griffin's results point to the danger of neglecting follower personalities and needs in any analysis of the effects of leader behavior.

In recent years, research on path–goal theory has waned. The body of evidence that has been amassed, however, suggests that its major tenets are probably on target. The actions taken by leaders can have a powerful effect on subordinates' motivation and satisfaction. In most cases, leader behaviors that supply subordinates with needed information or desired support will be most effective, and those subordinates needs and desires will be influenced by personal and environmental considerations. A comprehensive theory of leadership must integrate the path–goal principles.

## Path–Goal Theory Sequelae

We can credit path–goal theory for awakening leadership researchers to the moderating role of environmental factors on the relationship between leaders and followers. Some other interesting theoretical ideas have evolved from this approach. Kerr and Jermier (1978) developed the "substitutes for leadership" concept. In the tradition of path–goal theory, Kerr and Jermier argued that the leader's function is complementary, that is, to provide for subordinates direction or support that is missing in the environment (e.g., structure for an ambiguous task). If the environment already supplies that resource, the leader's behavior becomes unnecessary and will have little effect on subordinate reactions. For example, explicit job descriptions or comprehensive training could reduce the value of the leader's structuring behavior for clarifying the subordinate's task. Similarly, supportive and closely knit work groups might substitute for the positive emotional effects of a supervisor's consideration. Also, features of the situation can have the effect of neutralizing any impact that the leader might have. For example, rigid organizational policies or technology-determined work patterns could render ineffectual any attempts at leadership influence.

An extensive test of the substitutes concept was recently completed by Podsakoff, Niehoff, MacKenzie, and Williams (1993). The substitutes measuring instruments were improved and administered to over 600 people, including MBA students and employees in three organizations (a university, an insurance company, and a gas transmission company). The results indicated that although some of the reputed substitutes (e.g., task characteristics, work team cohesiveness) did have strong effects on subordinates' psychological states, the effects of leadership were neither replaced nor neutralized. The strength of the relationship between leader behavior and subordinate outcomes was affected very little by the presence or absence of hypothesized substitutes.

A reasonable criticism of the substitutes for leadership concept is that it gives too little attention to the interpersonal and emotional aspects of the leader–follower relationship. For example, Chemers and Cunningham (1989) found that subordinates value the feedback that they get from their superior above all other potential sources, including feedback from the task itself. Workers in a medium-sized computer company were asked to rate the quality of positive and corrective feedback they received from their superior, from their peers, and from the task itself. Feedback from a superior had the strongest effect on a worker's job satisfaction, even in cases where intrinsic features of the task provided effective and timely feedback.

The substitutes' reasoning, however, should alert leadership researchers to the recognition that subordinate needs and reactions occur within and are affected by a group and organizational context. Despite the powerful impact of leadership on organizational functioning, it is important to recognize the limits of leadership effects.

Another important set of hypotheses instigated by path–goal reasoning were presented in House's (1977) theory of charismatic leadership. That work is discussed with related charismatic and transformational theories of leadership in chapter 6.

# THE CONTINGENCY APPROACH
# TO DECISION MAKING

The third major contingency theory in terms of broad impact is the normative decision model, first developed by Vroom and Yetton (1973). This model deals with decisions that affect a whole group or team, and was later expanded by Vroom and Jago (1974) to include decisions involving individual subordinates. The total body of work is referred to here as the Vroom–Yetton–Jago model. Vroom and his colleagues maintained that one of a leader's important prerogatives is controlling the process by which decisions are made. Their model aims to be both proscriptive (i.e., normative) in specifying the parameters that determine what kinds of decision processes should be used and descriptive, amassing data on the kinds of processes that leaders actually do employ.

One guiding principle of the model was provided by Maier's (1963) observation that high levels of subordinate participation in decision making increase commitment, but are costly in time and effort. A second general principle is that the quality of a decision is dependent on the quality of the information that contributes to the decision. From these starting points, the Vroom–Yetton–Jago model expanded to include a range of decision strategies to be considered against a set of situational parameters and to be guided by a list of rules designed to protect the eventual decision from various deficiencies.

The decision strategies range across the dimension of the degree of subordinate participation and fall into three general categories; autocratic, consultative, and group (democratic). The decision model for groups includes five strategies; Autocratic I, in which the leader makes the decision alone using available information; Autocratic II, in which the leader obtains information from subordinates, but makes the decision alone; Consultative I, in which the leader shares the problem with each subordinate separately, seeking information and advice, but reserving decision authority; Consultative II, which follows the same general pattern except that subordinates are consulted as a group; and Group II, in which the leader fully shares the problem with subordinates in a group setting and invites them to participate fully and equally in decision making. In the individual model, in which the decision affects only one subordinate, the Consultative II and Group II styles involving groups are dropped, and a Group I strategy, that is, participative decision making with a single subordinate is added. Also added in the individual model is a delegative strategy in which the superior gives the subordinate the relevant information and allows the subordinate autonomy in making the decision.

The situational parameters that must be considered in choosing the appropriate decision strategy are embodied in eight questions. These questions address whether the leader and/or the subordinates have the necessary information to make a high quality decision, whether the subordinates are likely to be supportive of the decision and committed to its successful execution, and whether there is conflict among the subordinates about the most desirable solution.

The conditions reflected in these questions are elegantly melded to the possible decision strategies by a set of rules and embodied in a decision tree/flow chart. (For a detailed explication, see Vroom & Jago, 1974). The 12 rules can be reduced to six general principles of leadership:

1. If you do not have enough information to make a good decision, you must get the information from somewhere.

2. If the information that you have is not sufficiently structured to facilitate a clear decision, you need to seek help and advice to clarify and structure the problem.

3. If you need the acceptance and commitment of followers to implement the decision and you're not sure that you have that acceptance, you must involve the followers in participative decision making to enlist acceptance.

4. If followers are not committed to the organizational goals embedded in the problem, they cannot be allowed to make the decision, although their advice should be sought and considered.

5. If followers are in conflict over the most desirable solution, they must be brought together to allow them to air their opinions before a decision is made.

6. Followers should be represented, that is, solicited and heard, about decisions that affect them.

The situational parameters subjected to the guiding rules yield what is called the "feasible set" of decision strategies. These are all the decision strategies that do not violate any of the rules. A particular situation might be such that several strategies are acceptable. The leader can then choose which strategy to use by choosing the most acceptable autocratic strategy if time and efficiency are important considerations, or the most democratic strategy if the development of subordinate talent takes priority over efficiency.

Vroom and his colleagues (1980; Vroom & Jago, 1974, 1978) reported descriptive data reflecting the actual usage of the decision strategies in varying leadership situations. Much of this data was collected in workshops in which attending managers were asked either to respond to standard problems or to recall a recent decision and describe its characteristics. Vroom (1980) recounted that managers reported choosing a decision strategy within the feasible set about two thirds of the time. When they did not choose an acceptable strategy, they were much more likely to violate the rules governing acceptance and commitment of subordinates than they were the rules governing information quality. In other words, they were more likely to fail to consider subordinate acceptance when they thought they knew what the correct solution was than when they were unsure of their information or structure.

## Predictive Validity

If leaders sometimes act in accordance with the prescriptions of the Vroom–Yetton–Jago model and sometimes do not, the question arises as to the relative effectiveness of the decisions made. A number of studies have been done to address the question of validity of the model, but all of them are characterized by relatively weak methodologies for addressing the question.

Vroom and Jago (1978, 1988) reported the results of a number of studies that involved asking managers to recall a past decision, to describe the situational parameters and the decision strategy chosen, and to rate the overall effectiveness of the decision. The recollections indicated that decisions that are in the feasible set have about twice the rate of success as decisions outside the set.

In a somewhat different approach, Margerison and Glube (1979) asked a group of managers to respond to the Vroom and Yetton (1973) standard problems and computed a score for how much each manager was in agreement with the model. The researchers then obtained supervisor satisfaction ratings of these managers by their subordinates. Managers' level of agreement with the model was positively correlated with subordinate satisfaction. A similar study by Paul and Ebadi (1989) divided a sample of service industry supervisors into groups whose answers to the standard problems were in high or low agreement with the model. The subordinates of the high agreement supervisors were found to have significantly higher productivity and job satisfaction than those of the low agreement supervisors. Although these studies do not assess actual leader behavior, the results do imply that better managers at least know the right answers.

In the most careful study to date, Field and House (1990) interviewed a group of managers about their most recent decision, collecting the managers' ratings of the key features of the model as well as ratings of decision quality, subordinate acceptance, and overall decision effectiveness. The research team also interviewed a subordinate of each manager. After the subordinate recognized the particular decision in question, they responded to the same descriptive and evaluative questions as the managers. The manager and subordinate descriptions showed relatively high agreement on most features. However, a few important discrepancies occurred.

The managers' ratings of decision effectiveness indicated that decisions inside the feasible set were significantly more effective than decisions outside the set, although the absolute level of difference was quite moderate. However, the subordinate ratings of decision effectiveness showed no advantage for the decisions inside the feasible set compared to those outside. One possible explanation for this effect concerns the relationship of subordinate participation to ratings of effectiveness. In the managers' ratings, participation and effectiveness were uncorrelated, as predicted by the contingency tenets of the model, that is, the effectiveness of participation depends on the situation. For the subordinates, however, participation was positively ($r = .30, p < .05$) correlated with the rating of overall effectiveness. Understandably, subordinates highly value their own input.

A similar result was reported by Heilman, Hornstein, Cage, and Herschlag (1984) in an experimental study. Subjects were asked to read Vroom and Yetton model case descriptions and to rate the probable effectiveness of the decision strategies used. Subjects were asked to take the perspective of either a superior or a subordinate of the manager in question. When in the role of superior, subjects' ratings of effectiveness closely followed the model's prescriptions, but when in the role of subordinates, the subjects rated participative behavior equal in effectiveness to the autocratic behavior prescribed by the model.

This disagreement between the model's prescriptions and the subordinates' perspective may be irrelevant. Autocratic behavior is only prescribed by the model under conditions where subordinate acceptance is assured or unnecessary. It may be quite an acceptable trade-off to tolerate a slightly disgruntled reaction among subordinates in order to garner the time and efficiency benefits offered by an appropriately autocratic strategy. On the other hand, subordinate reactions may be related to a long-term erosion of support for the leader that affects subsequent decision parameters and solution execution. The sort of retrospective or hypothetical methodology used in these studies without any objective data on actual effectiveness leaves the question moot.

Another important question about the Vroom–Yetton–Jago model and other prescriptive models concerns the extent to which leaders are able to vary their behaviors to match situational parameters. Models like this one and the path–goal theory assume that leaders can easily change their behavior in accord with situational demands. In contrast, Fiedler and Chemers (1974, 1984) represent leadership style as a personality trait or highly ingrained motivational pattern that is stable over time and not easily changeable. The empirical evidence is controversial. Vroom (1980) reported that only 10% of the variance in managers' responses to his standard problems was contributed to by differences between managers, and the variance contributed to by differences between the problems was 3 to 5 times as great. However, Hill and Schmitt (1977) reported individual differences in decision style.

A program of research by Bass and his associates (Bass & Valenzi, 1974; Bass, Valenzi, Farrow, & Solomon, 1975; Shapira, 1976) analyzed a large set of data relating decision styles to intrapersonal, interpersonal, and organizational variables. One important finding of that research indicated that managers had a propensity to use one style or set of related styles more than others, that is, they showed individual differences reflecting stable patterns of usage of particular autocratic or participative styles.

Further complexity is added to this question when one considers the trustworthiness of responses to questionnaires. Thompson and Chemers (1993) reported the results of two questionnaire studies in which managers were asked to report the likelihood that they would use particular decision styles or behaviors in various leadership situations. Half the managers were told that the purpose of the research was to examine common patterns of managers, whereas the other half was told that the study was about differences between male and female managers. The ratings given to various autocratic and democratic decision strategies or task- and relationship-oriented behaviors varied dramatically from one condition to another. Responses revealed that managers were more self-conscious when they thought that gender issues were being studied. An important question raised by these studies is whether managers' responses on a questionnaire taken while attending a seminar on decision making might not be very different from their actual behaviors in a "real-time work" situation. The ability of managers to change their behaviors at will remains an empirical question.

## ADDITIONAL CONTINGENCY THEORIES

Among the contingency theories, the big three (the contingency model, path–goal theory, and normative decision theory) have had the broadest impact on research and theorizing. Some other ventures into contingency theorizing, although not having as broad an empirical base or effect, have contributed to the development of more sophisticated theorizing.

### The Multiple-Influence Model of Leadership (MIML)

Hunt and Osborn (1980, 1982) offered an expanded contingency model that attempted to integrate theoretical refinements developed subsequent to the earlier contingency theories. The multiple influence model incorporates the work of several theorists into a model loosely based on Fiedler's (1967) contingency model.

To Fiedler's concept of leadership style, MIML adds the notion of *discretionary* leader behavior, based on Rosemary Stewart's (1982b) notion that organizations place demands and constraints on leader's behaviors, and the most important aspect of leadership is the way that the leader construes and reacts to the choices available. Hunt and Osborn (1980) discussed both the antecedents of leader discretion and its consequences. A number of environmental and organizational factors influence how much "clout" or discretionary authority a leader has. For example, a highly mechanistic organizational structure with centralized authority and rigid policies will reduce the discretion available to managers, except to those from the highest levels of organizational authority. Hunt and Osborn argued that whether a leader chooses to influence the work team in a group setting or in one-on-one interactions will depend on clout, that is, group influence attempts require greater discretionary authority than do dyadic superior–subordinate encounters.

The multiple influence model expanded the relatively narrow concept of situational control (based on leader–member relations, task structure, and position power) to include the role of hierarchical level (Katz & Kahn, 1966), environmental complexity (Melcher, 1979), technological complexity (Thompson, 1967), and organizational structure (Burns & Stalker, 1961; Tosi, 1982).

The multiple-influence model argues that it is the leader's job, at all organizational levels, to use knowledge and skill to bridge the gap between what is expected and what really happens. The nature of that gap is determined by the relative degree of complexity, contributed to by the organization's environment (i.e., markets, suppliers, competition), context (i.e., size and technology), and structure (i.e., vertical and horizontal coordination and specialization). Greater complexity in the leader's environment has the effect both of increasing the gap between expectations and reality and of limiting the manager's options (i.e., discretion) for dealing with the problem.

The multiple-influence model of leadership has not generated much empirical activity, so its predictive validity is moot. Nonetheless, some of the ideas it raises can be helpful in the development of a comprehensive theory of leadership. One very useful idea is the recognition that small group leadership occurs in an organizational context and that leaders at different levels in an organization may serve different functions. Further, the inclusion of the organization's external environment as part of the leadership situation provides a starting point for integrating microstructural, behavior analyses of leadership with strategic, macrostructural issues.

## The Multiple Linkage Model

An ambitious integrative contingency theory was presented by Yukl (1971, 1989). Yukl (1989) argued that good theory should have well-developed intervening variables that link together behavioral, situational, and outcome variables. The emphases in the multiple linkage model are on the intervening variables and the leader behaviors that affect them.

The process variables included in the model are:

1. Subordinate effort, that is, the extent to which subordinates are committed and responsible with respect to task objectives;
2. Role clarity and task skills, that is, subordinates' job related knowledge;
3. Work organization, that is, the extent to which personnel, equipment, and facilities are efficiently organized;
4. Cohesiveness and cooperation, that is, the extent to which group members function smoothly as a team;
5. Resources and support services, that is, the extent to which the group has the material and human resources that it needs for task accomplishment;

6. External coordination, that is, the extent of synchronization between the work group and other units in the organization. These variables are seen as interacting with one another to determine group effectiveness.

The model recognizes Kerr and Jermier's (1978) substitutes and neutralizers of leader behavior, but still gives a central role to the effects that the leader does have on the intervening processes. Yukl (1989) presented a taxonomy of managerial behaviors that categorizes the many ways in which leader behavior is related to effective group process. Eleven categories of behavior are included in the taxonomy including networking, supporting, managing conflict/team building, motivating, recognizing and rewarding, planning and organization, problem solving, consulting and delegating, monitoring operations and environment, informing, and clarifying roles and objectives. These 11 behavioral categories are aspects of four broad categories of managerial functioning; building and maintaining relationships, collecting and disseminating information, making decisions, and influencing people.

Yukl (1989) provided examples of how each category of behavior is linked to specific intervening variables and the conditions under which the behavior is likely to be most important. For example, supportive behavior which is the way that a manager shows concern and consideration for subordinates is likely to be most important when work is dangerous, tedious, or in other ways aversive, when groups members work under stressful conditions such as difficult deadlines or hostile clients, or when group members are insecure and lack confidence. For each of the 11 behavior categories, from three to seven conditions are listed that make that behavior category especially important.

However, the linkages are not comprehensive ı the sense that every behavior is explicitly linked to every intervening process. Indeed, if every linkage was specified, the model would be more encyclopedic than practical, but it would be helpful if some general organizing principles were provided to tie together the extensive lists of variables. What is especially useful about the model, however, is the emphasis on intervening processes as links between leader behaviors and group outcomes. Some theories, like Fiedler's model relate leader variables to outcomes without attention to process. Other models, like path–goal theory, focus on processes like motivation and satisfaction, but neglect tangible outcomes. Comprehensive leadership models would have to move in the direction taken by Yukl to bring together person, situation, process, and outcome.

## Situational Leadership Theory

Although the Vroom–Yetton–Jago model does consider short-term versus long-term considerations, and the contingency model allows for changes in the leadership situation as a result of leader experience, the contingency theories discussed thus far generally lack a consideration of temporal factors. It is not surprising that leadership theorists might be hesistant to add another layer of complexity to an already intricately, convoluted phenomenon. Nonetheless, it must be acknowledged that neither leadership situations nor the leaders and followers who function in them are static. When the growth and development of subordinates is considered, potential for change becomes a very significant aspect of leadership effectiveness.

The theory that directly addresses subordinate changes as an aspect of situational contingencies is situational leadership theory (Hersey & Blanchard, 1969, 1977). Perhaps the fact that situational leadership theory is primarily a training model, whose authors have not sought extensive empirical validation, made it possible to include change factors that are relatively costly to address in organizational research. In any case, situational leadership theory builds a prescription for supervisory behavior based on the stage of development (or maturity) of the subordinate who is the target of the leader's influence efforts.

The model classifies subordinate maturity on two dimensions; "psychological maturity," assessing the follower's commitment, motivation, and willingness to accept responsibilty; and "job maturity," which captures the follower's experience, knowledge, and understanding of task requirements. High psychological maturity reflects a willingness to undertake responsible tasks, whereas high job maturity reflects the ability to accomplish such tasks. Thus, a subordinate could be willing or unwilling and able or unable with the lowest level of overall maturity being the unwilling and unable subordinate, followed by the willing but unable, then the able but unwilling, and the highest level of maturity being both willing and able.

The superior's behavioral options include the now familiar task-oriented, directive, and structuring behaviors and the relationship-oriented, supportive, and participative behaviors. Treated as independent aspects of the leader's style, high levels of either, both, or neither behavior could be adopted by the superior. High levels of directive, task behavior combined with a low level of paticipative, relationship behavior is referred to as "telling"; high task and high relationship is "selling"; high relationship and low task is "participating"; and low levels of both task and relationship behavior is "delegating."

As the subordinate matures, the leader moves from telling to selling to participation and eventually to delegating where a capable and committed subordinate is encouraged to take responsibility for decisions and action. In practice, this model includes various rating scales for both superior and subordinate to assess levels of subordinate maturity. The model is used alone to improve leader–follower communications or in conjunction with other goal setting plans, such as management by objectives (MBO; Hersey, Blanchard, & Hambleton, 1980; Odiorne, 1965).

Although a popular training model, little is known about the validity of situational leadership theory. On the surface, the theory shares much in common with models like path–goal theory, which also attempt to prescribe appropriate leader behavior using some of the same parameters. Unfortunately, little empirical support for the theory's prescriptions has been accumulated. One empirical study of high school teachers (Vecchio, 1987) provided limited support for the theory. He found that teachers who were newly hired seemed to respond positively to structuring behavior from their superiors. Predictions were not supported for moderately or highly mature teachers, however. A major virtue of situational leadership theory, however, is the recognition that a centrally important aspect of a leader's role is the development of subordinate talent and capability.

# INTEGRATING AND RECONCILING THE CONSTRUCTS AND PREDICTIONS OF THE CONTINGENCY THEORIES

This chapter presented six contingency theories of leadership. Progress in leadership theorizing may result from the integration of commonalities and the reconciliation of discrepancies across these perspectives. Table 4.1 lists the six theories and compares them on the variables included in the models and their predictions concerning the relationships among those variables.

## Leader Variables

Of the six models, four are quite comparable in the specification of the important leader variables. The mulitiple influence model and the multiple linkage model include leader variables, but are not as specific or limited in the set of behaviors or orientations of interest. Among the other four theories, considerable agreement exists. All four theories focus on the extent to which the leader emphasizes task-relevant, directive, and structuring issues versus relationship-relevant, supportive, and participative behaviors.

The contingency model differs somewhat from the others in two ways. First, the leadership variable in the model (i.e., the LPC construct) is a value or motivational orientation rather than a set of behaviors, even though it is assumed that these orientations are related to the behaviors. Secondly, in path–goal theory, normative decision theory, and situational leadership theory, it is assumed that the leader is capable of employing whatever behaviors are required by the situation. In the Contingency Model, the leader's behavior is a product of stable, ingrained cognitive and emotional reaction patterns and is not as volitional.

## Situational Variables

There is considerable overlap across the theories on the specification of critical situational characteristics. All the models include a variable that could be integrated under the broad rubric of structure or predictability. The contingency model, path–goal theory, normative decision theory, and the multiple influence model are quite explicit in including variables that relate to the clarity and certainty of the task requirements and goal paths. A moments' reflection on the "subordinate task maturity" variable in situational leadership theory reveals that variable to have a very high similarity to the degree of structure in path–goal theory in particular. Both refer to how well the subordinate understands the correct actions to take in accomplishing the task. Variables like task structure are also included in Yukl's multiple linkage model, but are not highlighted relative to other situational variables.

It can be argued that the variable of follower support is prominent in several of the models, even when not explicitly referred to as support. Clearly, the contingency model and the normative decision theory are quite similar in their attention to how

**TABLE 4.1**
A Comparison of Parameters and Predictions of Several Contingency Models

| Theory Predictions | Leader Variable | Situational Variables |
|---|---|---|
| **Contingency Model (Fiedler & Chemers, 1974; 1984)** Directive in high & low control Participative in moderate control | Task versus Relationship Orientation | Follower support Task structure Authority |
| **Path–Goal Directive (House, 1971)** Directive in low structure Supportive in high structure | Structuring versus Considerate behavior | Follower Capability task Structure |
| **Normative Decision Theory (Vroom & Yetton, 1973)** Directive in high control Participative in moderate and low control | Directive versus Participative decision making | Follower support Task structure |
| **Multiple Influence Model (Hunt & Osborn, 1980)** Discretions limited by complexity and interdependency | Group versus one-on-one orientation | Complexity Interdependency |
| **Multiple Linkage Model (Yukl, 1989)** Enhance intervening variables | Extensive behavioral set | Extensive situational set |
| **Situational Leadership (Hersey & Blanchard, 1977)** Directive in low control Participative in high control | Directive versus Participative supervision | Follower commitment Follower capability |

much acceptance and support the followers are likely to give to the leader's influence attempts. In situational leadership theory, the variable designated as "subordinate psychological maturity" denotes the follower's motivation to work toward the organizationally defined goals and the willingness to accept responsibility. That variable, especially when assessed by the superior, pretty much amounts to follower support.

In path–goal theory, the follower's willingness to accept superior influence seems to be assumed. There is little attention paid to situations where the subordinate might resist influence, although the follower's reactions to leader behavior are not always highly positive. In the multiple influence and multiple linkage models, variables relating to group harmony, cohesiveness, and commitment are discussed, but are not explicitly integrated into a specification of a dimension or a prediction.

In the four theories that attempt to make explicit predictions relating person and situation variables (leaving out the Hunt and the Yukl models), the situational variables can be arranged along a dimension that roughly reflects the amount of predictability and certainty in the job environment. However, a major divergence among the theories relates to whose perspective is affected by this certainty.

In the path–goal and situational leadership theories, the degree of task structure is that which is experienced by the subordinate. In these two models, the supervisor is assumed to be completely knowledgeable and capable of supplying whatever direction or support is missing in the subordinate's environment. On the other hand, in the contingency model and in normative decision theory, it is the leader who experiences the relative degree of structure and predictability that impinge on the certainty of action. The entire team, including the leader, are confronted with a task of high or low ambiguity. This difference in the perspectives taken by the various theories is manifested in their predictions for effective leader action.

# Predictions

Again, the multiple influence model and the multiple linkage model do not fit well into a comparative analysis. The multiple influence model is really more focused on the characteristics of the macrostructural environment that affect a leader's discretion to exercise authority than it is concerned with or predictive of the specific behaviors that a leader should follow. The multiple linkage model provides a normative framework for leader action, but because it is aimed at integrating a large number of behavioral categories with a comprehensive set of intervening variables, it does not yield a limited set of specific hypthoses conducive to testing and comparison.

Among the remaining theories, agreement is very good. In the two supervisory theories (path–goal and situational leadership), a lack of capability of the subordinate to meet job demands is addressed by relatively high levels of structuring and directive behavior. Both theories suggest reducing structuring behavior when job knowledge and structure are high. Under conditions of high structure but low morale (read low commitment in situational leadership theory), high levels of supportive behavior are prescribed. The situation in which both structure and interest are high calls for delegation in the situational leadership model, whereas situations like that are not included in the path–goal model. The individual decision-making version of normative decision theory also recommends delegation in situations where subordinates know their jobs and are motivated to do them.

In the contingency model and in normative decision theory, where the dimension of certainty and predictability comes from the leader's perspective, we are confronted with models of problem solving rather than supervision. In these models, high levels of structure and control allow the leader to act directively because of extensive task knowledge without fear of follower disaffection, when levels of follower support and acceptance are also high. In situations where certainty is more problematic due either to a lack of acceptance or a lack of structure, both theories opt for more participative styles emphasizing consultation and power sharing.

The models diverge in the most extreme case (i.e., low control in the contingency model and low structure/low acceptance in the normative decision theory), with the contingency model recommending tough-fisted directiveness whereas normative decision theory calls for high levels of participation. This divergence may be attributable to a difference in temporal orientation of the two models. The contingency model was developed from data collected in vivo, using current productivity as the performance criterion, a set of conditions likely to emphasize short-term outcomes. Normative decision theory is a deductive model with its roots in research and theorizing on the long-term benefits of participation on subordinate commitment and development.

# SOME CONCLUSIONS

If we step back from these theories and squint one eye closed, we can blend them together well enough to make a few summary statements. It appears that the contingency theories agree that the dimension of greatest importance in leader action is the degree to which the leader involves the followers in problem definition and decision making. The situational parameters common across theories are those that contribute to a general dimension of clarity, predictability, and certainty. The relationship of leader action to situational demand depends on the perspective taken. The leader-oriented theories argue for greater consultation and participation when that will facilitate creativity and/or acceptance on the part of followers. The subordinate-oriented theories stress the importance of supplying followers with cognitive and emotional resources necessary to work effectively, but which are otherwise missing in the environment. Those resources include information, direction, counseling, support, and encouragement.

From these models, we see that leadership involves direction and guidance, motivation and encouragement, support and reinforcement, problem solving and creativity. Different environments and different people require a different mix of emphases among these functions.

# Chapter 5

## Transactional and Exchange Theories

The previous chapters dealt with theories that are primarily leader oriented. Some of these theories acknowledge the presence of followers, but the followers are regarded as targets of influence or sources of support. The sense of leaders and followers being engaged in an interpersonal relationship involving mutuality has not been an important aspect of those theories.

In this chapter, the theories presented are very much concerned with the nature of leader–follower relationships. The relationships are seen as reciprocal exchanges in which leaders and followers create a transaction that allows for mutual satisfaction of goals and needs. The theories included here are often discussed under a rubric of "transactional" or "exchange" theories of leadership.

## EXCHANGE THEORIES IN SOCIAL PSYCHOLOGY [1]

The social reinforcement and exchange theories are built on principles of behavioristic psychology, adapted to social interactions, and employ metaphors drawn from economics, such as, reward and cost, profit and loss. The major theories in this tradition share the notion that social interactions that are viewed by the participants as more rewarding than costly are likely to continue and to be evaluated and experienced in a positive way (Shaw & Costanzo, 1982). A brief review of the transactional/exchange approach is provided here, with special emphasis on theoretical issues most relevant to leadership exchanges.

---

[1]The material in this section draws heavily on the analysis presented by Shaw and Costanzo (1982).

# Homans' Theory of Elementary Social Behavior

George Homans (1961, 1974) argued that human beings, like all other organisms, seek to maximize rewards and pleasures and to minimize costs, pain, and punishment. When two people engage in social interaction, they exchange behaviors that either reward or punish each other. For each member of the exchange, the resultant combination of rewards and costs incurred will yield either a profit (i.e., rewards exceed costs) or a loss. Profitable relationships will be continued, whereas unprofitable ones will not. Each person's needs and desires, some of which are constant over time and some of which may vary, will determine the reinforcement "value" (i.e., the rewardingness) of any behavior.

Homans (1961) also described the concept of a fair exchange embodied in the principle of "distributive justice." Justice occurs when an individual who is engaged in an exchange with another person receives rewards that are proportional to costs such that the profits of each person are proportional to their investments. Investments are whatever assets, such as knowledge, skills, effort, or material resources, that each person brings to the relationship. The value of any investment is a matter of personal judgment, with each party to an exchange computing his or her own standard for a "just" exchange. When individuals get less than they deserve, they experience the emotion of anger. When they get more than they deserve, they feel guilt.

Judgments of when profits and investments are in fair and proportional arrangement depend on what the participants expect based on their previous experience, that is, their history of such exchanges. Thus, two individuals might differ greatly in the kind of reward–cost exchange rates they are used to, and they might also differ greatly in the value that they place on the contributions that each brings to the exchange.

# Thibaut and Kelley's Theory of Interdependence

John Thibaut and Harold Kelley (Thibaut & Kelley, 1959; Kelley & Thibaut, 1978) brought a distinctly social psychological flavor to Homan's (1961, 1974) operant conditioning orientation. Thibaut and Kelley integrated social psychological principles both as determinants of social reward value (e.g., similarity between the interacting parties as rewarding) and as outcomes of social exchange (e.g., norms, power and status, coalitions, etc.).

Particularly useful for leadership theorizing are the bases for determining the reward value of social interactions. Thibaut and Kelley (1959) discussed two classes of determinants; exogenous and endogenous to the relationship. Exogenous determinants are factors that exist outside the relationship, whereas endogenous determinants are those that arise within the context of interaction.

Exogenous factors are determined by the needs and abilities of the actors that affect the kinds of exhanges that would be particularly rewarding for them. Among the most important exogenous factors are abilities, similarity, proximity, and complementarity. People often choose to interact with others who have abilities that they themselves don't possess, so that each party to an exchange might benefit from the particular skills of the other. Similarity becomes rewarding because of the opportunity for social cohesion and support, which is more probable with people who share important values and attitudes. Physical proximity facilitates social interaction, reducing the costs of getting together. Complementarity is especially important because if the goals that are sought in an interaction are complementary, the costs of satisfying each other's interests are reduced. Jack Sprat ("who could eat no fat"), for instance, found it quite pleasurable to dine with his wife ("who could eat no lean"), because they weren't competing for the same rewards.

These exogenous factors would be very relevant to an exchange between a leader and follower. A leader's task-related or administrative skills and abilities would offer a good exchange for follower loyalty and effort as leader and follower strive to achieve their goals. Similarity of values and goals would enhance trust between individuals of differing power. Complementarity of purposes (i.e., the leader's desire for prominence and the follower's need for direction) could make the exchange emotionally as well as practically rewarding.

Endogenous determinants are those factors internal to the interaction that increase the amount of positive outcomes. Interactants may be able to adjust and synchronize their behaviors so that as each pursues his or her goals in the relationship, he or she facilitates or at least does not interfere with the other person's goals. Such adaptability enhances the rewards and reduces the costs of the relationship for both people. Good leadership, then, would entail fostering a group atmosphere in which individual and collective goals are compatible and mutually reinforcing. A highly inspirational leader might even be able to arouse collectivist motives in group members that would encourage them to subdue their individual goals and interests in favor of group goals, turning previously costly behaviors (e.g., self-sacrifice) into reward opportunities. In their analysis of transformational leadership, House and Shamir (1993) argued that the ability to arouse group-focused motives in followers is an important aspect of charismatic leadership.

Social interdependence theory addresses two other issues that are especially relevant to the study of leadership; the way in which relationships are evaluated and the nature of relationships based on unequal power. Thibaut and Kelley (1959) developed two evaluative constructs, the comparison level (CL) and the comparison level for alternatives (CLalt). The CL is based on the individual's history of social exchanges and represents the typical reward–cost outcome level expected in a relationship. Outcomes above or below the Cl will result in satisfaction or dissatisfaction. The CLalt is an evaluative standard based on the other exchanges available to the individual at the time. If a person has attractive alternatives, their dependence on any single relationship is diminished.

With respect to power, Thibaut and Kelley pointed out that when one person can affect the rewards and punishments received by another (i.e., their fate), unequal power exists. Fate control can usually be turned into behavior control in which one person can make it more desirable for another to engage in particular behaviors.

The use of power in relationships, however, usually entails costs to one or both parties. The loss of freedom is, itself, costly. Furthermore, in many relationships, including most leader–follower relationships, mutual fate control exists. A superior may have the power to reward and punish a subordinate, but the subordinate typically has the opportunity to affect the group's goal attainment, a concern of great importance to the leader.

Thus, leader–follower relationships characterized by gross inequalities in power and the frequent use of that power are likely to be compared quite negatively to alternative relationships, whereas exchanges based on feelings of mutual interdependency are likely to become increasingly cohesive and interdependent.

## Equity Theory

Homans' concept of distributive justice, and Thibaut and Kelley's comparison levels recognized that relationships are evaluated not only in terms of their absolute levels of rewardingness, but also in comparative terms. Either explicit or implicit in these constructs is the idea that relationships should in some sense be fair and equitable. Equity theory, first formulated and applied to motivation in work relationships by Adams (1963) and later extended to a broad range of social interaction by Walster, Berscheid, and Walster (1976), attempts to formalize the bases for and consequences of judgments of fairness in relationships.

The assessment of fairness in a relationship is made by comparing one person's ratio of outcomes to inputs to another person's ratio. Outcomes, as in Homans and Thibaut and Kelley, are equal to rewards minus costs. Inputs, similar to Homan's "investments," are each person's "contributions to the exchange which are seen as entitling him to rewards or costs" (Walster, Berscheid, & Walster, 1976, p. 3). Inputs might include resources like money, knowledge, task effort, leadership ability, education, and so forth. Thus, each person in a relationship asks, "Am I getting what I deserve?" and answers the question by comparing his or her relationship with those involving appropriate comparison persons.

A follower might judge whether her salary, benefits, and chances for interesting assignments are commensurate with her education, experience, and dedication, by examining what sort of exchanges a colleague or friend is receiving. When people judge that they are getting less than they deserve, they feel "inequitably underrewarded." When they perceive themselves as getting more than is just, they are "inequitably overrewarded." The state of inequity is aversive and energizes the individual to do something to restore equity.

One option for restoring equity is to try to change outcomes or inputs. An underrewarded worker, for example, might ask for a raise or work fewer hours or with less effort. An overrewarded follower might try to work harder, increasing the quantity or quality of their work. A less direct option for restoring equity might be to change one's perceptions of inputs or outcomes, deciding, perhaps, that one's job contains many rewards not readily apparent to others.

Applying equity theory to leadership relationships reveals that a follower's short-term motivation to accomplish a task or long-term commitment to a job or organization will depend on his or her perceptions of the fairness of the exchange. Path–goal theory (House, 1971), discussed in the previous chapter, argued that a leader's responsibility is to increase the rewards available to a subordinate and to clarify the paths to those rewards. The principles of the social exchange theories emphasize that the rewards must be seen as fair and equitable, and that a leader's responsibility includes sensitivity to a follower's perceptions of equity. Several leadership theories are directly or indirectly tied to principles of social exchange.

# TRANSACTIONAL LEADERSHIP THEORIES

## Hollander's Idiosyncrasy Credit Model

The first and most influential transactional leadership theory was developed by Edwin Hollander (1958, 1964). Hollander defined leadership as a social exchange, and legitimacy as the currency of that exchange. Central to Hollander's theorizing is the notion that leadership is a dynamic process involving on-going interpersonal evaluations by followers and leaders. In this transaction, the leader provides task-related vision and direction, as well as recognition of followers, and followers reciprocate with heightened responsiveness to the leader, essentially legitimating the leader's authority to exert influence (Hollander, 1993).

The concept of "idiosyncrasy credit" relates follower evaluations to leader legitimacy. Leaders earn credits that allow them to innovate, that is, to act in ways or suggest strategies that deviate from traditional pproaches of the group or organization, that is, they act idiosyncratically. Credits are earned through demonstration of competency in helping the group to achieve its goals and conformity to group norms, which attest to the leader's commitment to the values of the group. The leader, competent and trustworthy, provides a vehicle for the group to move forward.

When the leader's attempts at influence, especially innovative strategies, are successful, the leader gains more credits, status, and influence. Failures result in a loss of credits. A considerable body of research supports the predictive validity of the idiosyncrasy credit model (Hollander, 1960, 1961). Most of this research involved decision-making groups, in which idiosyncrasy credit was operationalized by the leader's willingness to deviate from group norms or to overturn the decisions of subordinates, or by the extent to which the leader influenced followers to go along with suggestions or support decisions.

An interesting feature of the idiosyncrasy credit literature deals with the effect of the source of the leader's authority. A number of studies compared appointed and elected leaders (Hollander & Julian, 1970). Elected leaders seem to feel greater legitimacy as shown by their willingness to reverse group decisions in a problem-solving task. However, elected leaders are also more vulnerable to criticism. Group members withdraw their support more quickly from elected than from appointed leaders.

One explanation of the greater vulnerability of elected leaders is that the followers have already given the leader a reward (i.e., the election), and therefore, expect a quick return in terms of successful performance (Jacobs, 1970). However, an alternative view of the legitimating process would place some emphasis on the followers' concerns, not only with getting a good momentary exchange, but also with trying to ascertain the wisdom of their commitment to the leader in the long run. Each success or failure has an immediate impact on the follower, but also may be predictive of future success. With an appointed leader, followers may place some trust in the organization or appointing authority, assuming that the appointment was based on a rationale and valid process. For elected leaders, followers have only their own judgment to rely on, a potentially fragile basis for choice. The leader's failure may be regarded as evidence that the followers' decision was a bad one that should be reversed as soon as possible. This may account for the fragility of leader authority in contemporary political democracies.

Hollander's work makes several points salient. First, that leadership is a process of give-and-take, in which the leader's ability to influence is based on a legitimacy that flows from followers. Followers are the leader's most important strategic audience, determining the leader's latitude to act (Hollander, 1993). Finally, the exchange between leader and follower must be seen as both just and expedient.

## Graen's Vertical Dyadic Linkage Model

George Graen and his associates (Dansereau, Graen, & Haga, 1975; Graen, 1976; Graen & Cashman, 1975; Graen & Scandura, 1987) have extensively studied the processes by which managerial superior–subordinate dyads develop a working role relationship and the consequences of the way in which that role relationship is defined and elaborated. Although the dyadic approach to managerial functioning has it roots in the writings of Chester Barnard (1938) and Herbert Simon (1957; March & Simon, 1958), Graen's vertical dyadic linkage (VDL) model is the closest fit to the social exchange principles (Thibaut & Kelley, 1959) of any of the contemporary leadership theories.

Broadly stated, the VDL model holds that a leader and subordinate go through a role-making process in which they negotiate the terms of their collaboration. This is particularly important for work on unstructured tasks for which job definitions and standard procedures are not sufficient to define all aspects of leaders' and followers' respective responsibilities. By sampling the possible ways in which they might interact around these unstructured tasks, leader and subordinate develop a pattern of reciprocal influence that moves the dyad toward greater or lesser interdependence, referred to as "coupling" in the role-making model (Graen & Scandura, 1987). The negotiated exchanges between superior and subordinate can be of a very high quality (mentor–protege relationship) or of very poor quality (overseer–peon).

Superiors may have a number of rewarding options available, including information, openness to influence, interesting tasks, latitude and autonomy, emotional support, and attention. These may be exchanged for the subordinate's commitment, loyalty, effort, and ingenuity. When exchanges of reciprocal influence develop, which are rewarding to both parties, the working patterns become more intricately and productively coupled.

Although the basic theoretical principles that underlie the vertical dyadic linkage model were well explicated by the social exchange theorists, their adaptation to leadership issues raises many important points. One such point is that the exchange relationship is based on more than simple liking between the leader and the follower. For example, the instrument used to measure the quality of the leader–member exchange (the LMX) has evolved from a 2-item scale that primarily measured negotiating latitude in the dyad (Dansereau et al., 1975) through several evolutions to its current 7-item form (Graen, Novak, & Sommerkamp, 1982). The development of the current measure revealed that the LMX's predictive validity for unit performance was improved by removing items measuring affective states such as satisfaction with supervision (Graen, Liden, & Hoel, 1982), implying that although the working relationship between leader and follower is related to follower satisfaction, it is not the same as follower satisfaction and is more closely tied to performance.

An extensive research program with the model shows that the quality of the leader–follower exchange is related to a range of outcomes including job-related communication (Schiemann & Graen, 1978), subordinate satisfaction (Graen & Ginsburgh, 1977), turnover (Ferris, 1985), and frequency of promotions (Wakabayashi, Graen, Graen, & Graen, 1988). A study by Graen, Cashman, Ginsburgh, and Schiemann (1978) indicated that the positive outcomes of high quality exchanges can cascade downward in an organization, with managers who have a good exchange with their superiors being able to generate more resources for exchanges with their own subordinates.

An important point of the theory is that exchanges may be highly differentiated within a working unit, with the superior having better exchanges with some subordinates than with others (Dansereau et al., 1975; Graen et al., 1982). This emphasis on the dyadic relationship is seen as making the model both more discriminating and more useful than approaches that treat the entire work group as a single unit and base measures on group averages. Graen and Scandura (1987) argued that "an average work group approach cannot reveal the variation in a unit's internal teamwork components" (p. 176). In conflict with Graen and Scandura's assertion, Ilgen and Fujii (1976) showed that individual ratings of leader behavior and group performance were much more likely to be less reliable than aggregated ratings. However, Graen and Scandura (1987) addressed the discrepancy as a question of "level of analysis." Group outcomes, such as overall team productivity, might be best predicted by aggregated average group measures, whereas performance or satisfaction outcomes specific to a particular individual can probably be better predicted by dyadic measures.

Consistent with our earlier discussions of the moderating effects of follower personality, attention must be paid to the specific characteristics of the particular subordinate. Graen and Scandura (1987) made the point that resources that are exchanged must be valued by the subordinate and that what often separates effective from ineffective managers is the former's attention to and understanding of subordinate needs. In a study that tested the effect of leader–member exchange model training on the productivity and satisfaction of dyads (Graen et al., 1982), overall positive effects across dyads were moderated by the specific subordinate's growth need strength (Hackman & Oldham, 1976). Subordinates who valued and desired growth showed greater gains in productivity and satisfaction than did less growth-oriented subordinates when superiors learned to create exchanges facilitating greater autonomy and influence.

Some longitudinal studies of role-making processes have revealed that the ultimate quality of the leader–follower exchange can be predicted very early in the relationship and seems to be based on the superior's initial impressions of the subordinate's likelihood of success (Graen, Orris, & Johnson, 1973). Liden, Wayne, and Stilwell (1993) conducted a well-designed study attempting to illuminate the factors that influence the early development of leader–member exchanges. That study deserves some attention, because it reveals both the promise and the difficulty of research on leadership.

Liden et al. studied newly formed managerial–subordinate dyads, assessing perceptions of the developing relationship within the first few days and then at 2-week, 6-week, and 6-month intervals. Measures were taken of leader's and follower's ratings of expectations for the relationship, perceived similarity, liking, and quality of the leader–member exchange, as well as measures of demographic similarity (i.e., gender, race, age, and education), and the leader's early appraisal of the subordinate's performance. The authors predicted that expectations, perceptions of similarity, and liking would be predictive of the quality of exchange, and that demographic similarity and performance evaluations would have strong effects on those perceptions and expectations.

The results revealed that early perceptions, within the first few days and weeks of the relationship, did indeed have strong implications for the quality of the leader–member exchange far into the future. Particularly, early expectations about the working relationship, perceptions of stylistic and attitudinal similarity, and interpersonal liking were quite predictive, but demographic similarity was unrelated to either the quality of the exchange or the early perceptions. Performance was only weakly related to expectations and only in the early stages.

A problematic aspect of the results may help to explain why performance effects are so transitory. Liden et al. (1993) reported that leader and follower perceptions of the leader–member exchange were only weakly related (average correlation across the three administrations of .16). Scandura, Graen, and Novak (1986) reported a similarly small and nonsignificant correlation of .24 between leader and follower perceptions of the leader–member exchange. This lack of convergence between leader and follower perceptions raises the possibility that, at least in some cases, leader–member exchanges may reflect perceptions and assumptions more than behavioral realities. In other words, if a leader or a follower holds positive expectations and impressions of their role partner, he or she will evaluate the quality of the relationship highly and will act accordingly, even if the objective quality of the exchange (or performance level) is quite different. The emphasis on perceptions of the rewardingness of relationships made so strongly by Homans (1958) and Thibaut and Kelley (1959) is very apt in this context.

The vertical dyadic linkage model makes an important contribution to leadership theory by illuminating the broad effects of social exchanges. Recognizing that the relationship between leader and follower is one involving reciprocal influence turns our attention to other models of influence that represent another aspect of the leader–follower transaction.

# PROCESSES OF INFLUENCE, MOTIVATION, AND CONTROL

A number of the theories presented in this and earlier chapters have described phases of subordinate development involving leadership behaviors that progressively increase subordinate autonomy, that is, from direction to participation to delegation (e.g., Dansereau et al., 1975; Hersey & Blanchard, 1977; Vroom & Jago, 1974). The development of subordinate autonomy involves a process of mutual influence in which leader and follower roles are negotiated.

The exchange theories of Homans (1961) and Thibaut and Kelley (1959) recognized that rewards play an important role in influence processes. Starting from a similar premise, but evolving along a different conceptual path, social learning theories of leadership also have their roots in the operant conditioning literature and place great emphasis on the specification and rewarding of desired behaviors.

## Behavior Modification Approaches

The recognition of the power of reinforcement to modify the expression of behavior has given rise to research attempting to integrate operant conditioning principles into the specification of effective leader behavior. Several theorists (Komaki & Desselles, 1990; Luthans & Kreitner, 1975; Podsakoff, Todor, & Skov, 1982; Sims, 1977) share the view that effective supervision involves "pinpointing" desirable target behaviors (i.e., specifying observable, quantifiable behaviors and the contexts in which they occur) and delivering reinforcement (i.e., rewards or punishments) in a contingent and timely fashion. Sims and Lorenzi (1992) found that rewards and punishments might be material (e.g., related to wages, bonuses, job security, etc.), symbolic (e.g., plaques, titles, etc.), social (e.g., praise, recognition, threats), or task related (e.g., enriched or diminished job duties, flexible hours, etc.)

The empirical literature on operant approaches is generally supportive of the notion that leaders who apply rewards contingent to subordinate performance are likely to be more effective (Hunt & Schuler, 1976; Podsakoff et al., 1982; Sims, 1977; Sims & Szilagyi, 1975a, 1975b; Williams & Podsakoff, 1988). The consensus of these studies is that performance contingent rewards are likely to increase subordinate performance and satisfaction, whereas contingent punishment has little effect on performance and may have somewhat negative effects on satisfaction.

Noncontingent sanctions, especially punishment, have quite negative effects on performance. The effects are most pronounced for high performing subordinates who are most likely to benefit from rewards that are contingent on their performance (Podsakoff et al., 1982). Podsakoff et al. (1982) pointed out that contingent rewards clarify path–goal relationships (House, 1971; House & Mitchell, 1974) and promote perceptions of equity and fairness, especially among the most productive group of subordinates (Hollander, 1978).

Judith Komaki and her associates (1986; Komaki & Desselles, 1990; Komaki, Desselles, & Bowman, 1989) developed a model emphasizing the delivery of clear and timely feedback to subordinates to increase the emission of target behaviors. Research with the Komaki model is characterized by careful and reliable observations of leader behavior, rather than reliance on subordinate self-reports, a much inferior measure. The essential features of the model include the necessity for the manager or supervisor to consistently monitor subordinate behavior and to deliver consequences frequently. Research with the model indicates that effective supervisors monitor their subordinates more frequently than do less effective supervisors (Komaki, 1986) and more frequently accompany monitoring with consequences (Komaki, Jensen, & Zlotnick, 1986).

In recognition of the fact that behavior modification techniques have been employed almost exclusively to affect the behavior of individuals, but that some of the most important work in organizations is accomplished by teams, Komaki, Desselles, and Bowman (1989) addressed the effects of monitoring and delivering consequences for behaviors involving team coordination. They observed and analyzed the behavior of 19 sailboat skippers as they prepared for and raced in a round-robin regatta. Skippers were coded for the amount of time they spent monitoring the performance of crew members, giving instructions, and giving feedback, and then these behaviors were broken down for those that addressed performances that either were or were not associated with team coordination.

The rate of monitoring and delivery of consequences for individual crew member behavior during races was strongly associated with both objective race performance (measured in times) and expert ratings of crew handling. However, those activities, when directed toward team coordination issues, were not significantly related to either race performance or expert ratings. The authors offered the explanation that activities requiring crew member interdependence, and thus coordination (i.e., spinnaker handling), occurred less than 10% of the time and occupied an even smaller percentage of the skipper's time, making their impact on racing outcomes less likely. However, this finding also highlights one of the basic problems of behavioral approaches to leadership. Many behaviors that are critical to effective organizational behavior are difficult to pinpoint and even harder to consistently monitor.

## Goal Setting Approaches

Behaviors might be difficult to pinpoint because the individual's task is not highly structured, and the specific desirable behaviors are not clearly known or may change from episode to episode. Important aspects of task behavior may not, in fact, be discrete. Tasks requiring alertness, attentiveness, or creativity demand a continuous orientation from the worker rather than a set of specific, discrete behaviors. Sometimes, the behaviors that are most relevant to task success occur so infrequently that monitoring their occurrence is difficult or inefficient.

One approach to overcoming difficulties in monitoring and rewarding specific behaviors is to focus on desired outcomes rather than on behaviors. By specifying the end state or outcome, the responsibility for regulating behavior is left to the individual worker who monitors and corrects his or her own behavior to reach goals.

The degree of employee participation in the goal-setting process may range from very low involvement (i.e., superior-set goals) through varying degree of subordinate input all the way to delegation. Goal-setting theorists disagree on the relative merit of subordinate participation in the process. Locke and Latham (1990a) asserted strongly that assigned goals are just as effective as participatively set goals, whereas Sims and Lorenzi (1992) based their "new leadership paradigm" on the importance of leading subordinates toward self-management.

Regardless of their views on participation, the goal-setting theorists are in general agreement about the basic principles laid out by Locke (1968). The overarching premise of goal-setting theory is that conscious intentions regulate actions, that is, people are more likely to do what they intend to do. Four specific principles underlie the general premise: (a) Specific goals result in higher performance than general goals or no goals; (b) difficult, but not impossible, goals result in higher performance than easy goals; (c) goals enhance the positive effects of incentives, feedback, and deadlines on performance; and (d) supervisor-set goals only have an effect on performance to the degree that they are consciously accepted by the subordinate.

Most of the research on which Locke (1968) based his theory was conducted with college students performing relatively simple laboratory tasks. In 1975, Latham and Yukl reviewed 27 organizational field studies of goal setting on performance, satisfaction, and organizational commitment. In several of these studies, goal setting was embedded in a management by objectives (MBO) program. Management by objectives is an intervention designed to facilitate superior–subordinate communication in order to clarify role requirements. Its purpose is to enhance organizational goal achievement through a process of participatively set performance goals combined with subordinate personal goals. MBO programs have many principles in common with goal-setting theory, but predate Locke's (1968) theory by many years (Drucker, 1954; Odiorne, 1965).

Latham and Yukl's (1975) review provides strong support for the principles of goal-setting theory, but also raises some interesting points that mesh well with contemporary leadership theories. With respect to the relative benefits of difficult goals, the authors raised the question concerning the assertion that goals must be accepted to be effective. They questioned the conditions that make subordinates likely to accept difficult goals set by superiors. Their answer was that employees will accept difficult goals when they perceive them to be reasonable, and when they perceive a strong contingency between goal attainment and desirable outcomes.

Once again, Hollander's (1978) emphasis on fair and reasonable exchanges seems relevant, as does path–goal theory's (House, 1971) stress on the leader's responsibility to clarify and strengthen the relationship between performance and desirable outcomes. Hard goals are more likely to be perceived as challenging rather than impossible when the subordinate has a high degree of self-assurance and a history of success.

With respect to the importance of participation in goal setting, Latham and Yukl (1975) waffled a bit and deferred to the contingency theorists (e.g., Morse & Lorsch, 1970; Vroom & Yetton, 1973; Yukl, 1971). They concluded, "Although most of the studies found some evidence supporting the superiority of participative goal setting, a significant difference is found only under certain conditions with certain types of employees" (p. 840).

In concluding a generally very supportive review, Latham and Yukl (1975) pointed out two deficiencies in goal-setting theory of the time. The first is the failure to specify the determinants of goal acceptance and goal commitment, and the second is the need to explicate the mechanisms by which acceptance and commitment result in higher employee effort and performance.

Locke and Latham (1990a, 1990b) set out to correct these deficiencies and provided an integrated explanation of the effects of goal setting on motivation, performance, and satisfaction in their "high performance cycle" model. The 1990 model added expectancy theory (Vroom, 1964) and social–cognitive theory (Bandura, 1986) notions to the basic goal-setting principles. Goal acceptance and commitment are determined by the subordinate's perception of the likelihood that effort will result in suitable levels of performance, with that perception largely affected by the subordinate's level of self-efficacy. Locke and Latham (1990b) further argued that assigned goals have a powerful effect on self-efficacy (equal to or greater than any effects of participatively set goals) because assigned goals reflect the judgment of a competent and legitimate authority; they show confidence in the subordinate's ability to meet the goal, resulting in an increase in the subordinate's feelings of confidence and self-efficacy; they provide a challenge that motivates the employee to prove competence; and they set a standard against which the subordinate can measure achievement and gain a sense of accomplishment and satisfaction.

The heightened sense of self-efficacy generated by the assigned goals as well as the standards set by the goals encourage the subordinate to internalize high personal goals. High assigned and personal goals in combination with high self-efficacy results in persistence, high effort, attention to the task and the feedback from the task, and more planning on how to achieve the goals. In other words, the subordinate is self-regulating behavior to align performance with goals.

The increased effort, persistence, attention, and planning yield higher levels of performance. Because goals are internalized, behavior is seen as self-directed, and high performance is attributed to internal causes resulting in enhanced self-esteem and satisfaction. The rewards that accrue for high performance also result in greater satisfaction with and commitment to the organization, perpetuating the high performance cycle.

Locke and Latham (1990a, 1990b) went to great lengths to establish the superiority of assigned over participatively set goals. The emphasis on superior assignment meant that they had to address the issue of leadership in goal setting. They asserted that "leaders play a major role in creating and maintaining the [high performance] cycle" (p. 245). However, Locke and Latham were not very explicit about how leaders accomplish those effects, except for a few gratuitous references to the use of vision as a means for setting overarching organizational goals (Bennis & Nanus, 1985) and turning those goals into specific objectives and action plans (Kotter, 1982).

It is not surprising that Locke and Latham (1990b) avoided an extensive discussion of leadership, because many of the unqualified assertions made about the superiority of assigned over participatively set goals depended on assumptions that remain quite controversial in the leadership literature. For example, to assert that assigned goals are universally associated with legitimate and competent authority is to ignore the extensive literature on leader legitimation (Hollander, 1993), expectancies (House, 1971), and acceptance of superior decision making (Vroom & Yetton, 1973). Furthermore, some contemporary behaviorally oriented leadership theories (e.g., Sims & Lorenzi, 1992) regarded subordinate participation and eventual acceptance of full autonomy (i.e., self-management) as the ultimate purpose of goal setting.

# From Goals to Self-Management

Locke and Latham (1990b) only gave "hand-waving" acknowledgement to the argument that goal setting can progress from directive supervision to self-management. Given Locke's (1968; Locke & Latham, 1990b) long-standing aversion to participation, it is not surprising that his version of goal setting placed scant attention on the benefits of delegation. However, Sims and Lorenzi (1992) regarded reinforcement schedules and assigned goals as stages along a subordinate development process culminating in self-management.

In self-management, the individual worker or manager sets and monitors his or her own goals, rewarding him- or herself when performance is achieved and taking corrective action when performance falls short of the goal. The process by which self-management is established bears a strong resemblance to Hersey and Blanchard's (1977) situational leadership theory, but with greater emphasis on teaching employees the behavioral and cognitive strategies of social learning theory. In the early stages of development, when the subordinate does not yet have the ability or interest to operate independently, the superior creates a learning experience that simultaneously maintains the subordinate's attention on set goals and provides the opportunity for successful experiences to build confidence. As the subordinate matures, he or she is encouraged to participate in setting goals and, eventually, has large aspects of the task and the decisions surrounding the task delegated to self-management.

Sims and Lorenzi (1992) saw the development of self-management as a potential substitute for leadership in which self-regulation replaces the role normally filled by supervisors. They presented Manz and Sims' (1980) "superleadership" training program for self-management as an example of how organizations can develop self-managing teams with performance outcomes that are superior to traditional organizational practices.

An interesting circle is closed by Manz and Sims' (1980) description of the characteristics of the leadership situation that make self-management an appropriate option: The subordinate's task is unstructured; the subordinate holds important information about the task; effective implementation of any task-related decisions require acceptance by the employee; and the employee shares organizational goals. The attentive reader will recognize that these are exactly the situational characteristics specified by normative decision theory (Vroom & Jago, 1974; Vroom & Yetton, 1973) for participative decision making in group tasks and for delegation with individual tasks.

The literature on behavior modification and goal-setting approaches to leadership mirrors earlier discussions of leadership theory, and provides an explication of how specific mechanisms (i.e., the nuts and bolts of influence) might operate. The behavioral and goal-setting approaches can, therefore, be quite useful in filling out an integrated understanding of effective leadership.

## Communication and Influence

The social learning and goal-setting literatures, like other approaches of supervision, recognize the importance of follower motivation for attaining task success. The emphasis in most of these approaches is on understanding the needs of the subordinate and creating an organizational environment that encourages the subordinate to seek the satisfaction of those needs through avenues that promote organizational success. These models are less explicit about the mechanisms of communication and influence. However, a small body of research directly addresses questions about the goals, directions, and strategies of social influence in leader–follower relationships. Although the processes of communication and influence are not solely confined to transactional aspects of leadership, their discussion here may help to clarify the role they play in many aspects of effective leadership.

In early work on the topic of influence strategies, Kipnis and Cosentino (1969) reported that organizational context affected the choice of strategies in downward influence attempts. For example, organizational type (i.e., military vs. industrial) mediated the use of coercive versus persuasive strategies. Also, the leader's span of control was relevant, with those having a greater number of subordinates being more inclined toward official mechanisms. Erez and Rim (1982) found that in large organizations where hierarchy was emphasized, influence attempts were more likely to be made upward to one's boss, whereas in smaller, less formal organizations, the same goals might be pursued through lateral influence attempts. Ansari and Kapoor (1987) found that a manager's choice of influence strategies was likely to provide a model for influence attempts by the manager's subordinate. Context and culture, then, play a role in choice of strategies.

The seminal work in the development of a taxonomy of influence strategies was done by Kipnis, Schmidt, and Wilkinson (1980). These authors asked MBA students to describe the kinds of tactics they had used in their work organizations in attempts to influence others. A questionnaire measure was developed from the descriptions and factor analyses yielded 8 prominent tactics including:

1. Ingratiation, making the influence target feel important;
2. Assertiveness, making demands or giving orders;
3. Rationality, explaining the reasons for a request;
4. Sanctions, using administrative means to gain compliance;
5. Eexchange of benefits, emphasizing trade-offs between the agent and target;
6. Upward influence, appealing to higher levels in the organization;
7. Blocking, preventing the target from achieving a goal;
8. Coalitions, enlisting the aid of others to influence a target.

The questionnaire asked respondents to describe the goal of the influence attempt (e.g., to get help with a project, to get someone to fulfill their job duties, etc.), the target (boss, subordinate, or peer), and the tactic chosen. Kipnis et al. (1980) reported differences in the tactic chosen depending on the goal and especially on the target of influence. Downward influence attempts were more likely to employ directive or coercive tactics, such as, assertiveness or sanctions, than was the case for upward influence. In fact, Kipnis, Schmidt, Swaffin-Smith, and Wilkinson (1984) posited the "iron law of power," holding that the greater the discrepancy in power, the greater the use of directive influence.

However, Yukl and Falbe (1990) identified a number of weaknesses in Kipnis et al.'s (1980) taxonomy and research methodology. They added two new categories (inspirational appeals and consultation) to the taxonomy, dropping the infrequently reported blocking and sanctions. Another criticism made by Yukl and Falbe of the Kipnis et al. work was that descriptions of influence strategies were obtained only through self-reports by the person exerting influence. Such reports may be quite susceptible to a variety of perceptual and reporting biases. Yukl and Falbe (1990) also asked targets of influence attempts to respond to their measure.

Their findings, although similar in direction to those of Kipnis et al. (1980), were much less pronounced. They did not find gross differences in the type of influence strategies used for different targets or different goals. They did find that the two most frequently used influence strategies reported were rational appeals and consultation regardless of the goal or target of influence. Consistent with findings about the nature of effective leadership exchanges (Graen & Scandura, 1987), the desirability of less coercive strategies was evident in this work.

In an extensive follow-up study, Yukl and Tracey (1992) studied the influence tactics of 128 managers. The focal managers' use of various influence strategies was rated by their three categories of associates; subordinates, peers, and superiors. In addition, the managers' superiors provided ratings of the focal managers' task-related performance, and all three targets supplied information about the level of task commitment that was engendered by the influence attempts.

Yukl and Tracey (1992) found that although there were significant differences in the use of specific tactics with different targets (e.g., exchanges of favors were rarely offered to one's superiors and coalitions were infrequently used to gain compliance from subordinates), such differences explained very little of the variance in the usage frequency of various tactics. In fact, the rank order of the tactic frequency was almost identical for all targets with the most commonly used tactics being rational persuasion, inspirational appeals, and consultation. The least commonly used tactics were exchanges, coalitions, and pressure tactics.

Perhaps not surprisingly, the most effective tactics for eliciting task commitment from the target and for gaining overall high performance ratings were the same high frequency tactics, with only minimal variability across targets. The implications of these results are quite clear. Practicing managers know what sorts of influence tactics are most appropriate and most likely to be successful, and they use them. These effective tactics seem to be, at least for the American managers sampled in these studies, noncoercive strategies that provide a rational and justifiable basis for attitude change, rather than manipulative or threatening attempts to gain compliance.

An interesting similarity exists between these findings on influence tactics and the research on the acceptability of the use of various power bases. Podsakoff and Schriesheim (1985) reviewed the literature on field studies of the effects of the use of French and Raven's (1959) five bases of power (i.e., reward, coercive, referent, legitimate, and expert). Podsakoff and Shriesheim reported that consistent positive effects on subordinate motivation and satisfaction were found only for power with referent and expert bases.

The relative undesirability of coercive and even reward-based power and influence suggests a limited role for behavioral and goal-setting leadership that does not recognize the needs and dignity of subordinates. In keeping with the tenets of path–goal theory, contingent reward leadership may have its most positive effects when subordinates have a strong need for structure and perhaps view rewards as a source of feedback.

A very interesting facet of the influence strategy literature concerns the effects of influence tactic on subsequent judgments and attributions by the person *using* the tactic. In an early study, Kipnis and Vandeveer (1971) reported that supervisors were more likely to emphasize rewards and punishments (i.e., sanctions) when dealing with a hostile subordinate. This indicates, as might be expected, that the perception of the subordinate affected the choice of the influence tactic. However, this also raises the question of whether the choice of an influence tactic might actually change the leader's perception of the subordinate.

Kipnis, Castell, Gergen, and Mauch (1976) developed an attribution theory of influence dubbed the "metamorphic effects of power." The theory predicted that if a power wielder obtains compliance from a subordinate through the use of strong and controlling means of influence, the power wielder will regard himself as the cause of the subordinate's compliance, resulting in more negative judgments of the subordinate. Kipnis, Schmidt, Price, and Stitt (1981) supported the prediction, finding that the use of noncontrolling influence tactics led the superior to ascribe greater self-motivation and more positive evaluations to a subordinate.

These findings indicate the possibility for a self-perpetuating cycle of power, influence, and attribution in which strong tactics lead to negative attributions eliciting subsequent use of strong tactics. If we consider the likelihood that the use of strong tactics will lead to negative reactions by subordinates, it is not difficult to imagine how a superior's coercion and a subordinate's hostility might contribute to the development of very poor leader–member exchanges (Graen, 1976). The role of judgmental processes in leadership, such as attribution, appraisal, and action, is developed more fully in a later chapter.

## SOME CONCLUSIONS

This chapter covered a lot of territory, viewing leader–subordinate transactions from a number of perspectives. The common thought that might be gleaned from all of these perspectives is that leadership influence rests ultimately on the followers' perceptions of the legitimacy of authority, just as Hollander (1958) argued almost 40 years ago. The empirical literature indicates that the best relationships between leaders and followers are built on high levels of mutual respect and trust (mentor–protege relationships). The most successful influence strategies are those that employ reasoned argument (rational appeals) and shared interest (consultation), and the most acceptable forms of power are those that rely on the leader's legitimate expertise (expert power) and the follower's trust and respect for the leader (referent power). Even the most specific forms of exchange, embodied in behavioral contingencies or goals, realize their greatest potentcy when employed in a program that allows the subordinate the autonomy for self-management with its potential for instilling instrinsic motivation and personal dignity.

The transactional theories of leadership are focused on how leaders can motivate followers by creating fair exchanges and by clarifying mutual responsibilities and benefits. In doing so, however, they direct our attention to the importance of a relationship between leader and follower that may, in fact, transcend the transaction. To gain an insight into a kind of leadership that seems to go beyond transactional considerations to create situations in which followers are induced to transcend their own self-interests and become truly committed to the leader's mission, we must address "transformational" leadership, which is the subject of the next chapter.

# Chapter 6

## Transformational Leadership

Although theorists acknowledge that leadership occurs at all levels of the organization and that the impact of all leaders contributes to organizational performance, a fascination has always existed with the larger-than-life, earth-shaking leaders who do more than transact the mundane concerns of everyday activity. These are the leaders who foment revolutions in politics or commerce and divert the streams of history.

Despite the glamour of heroic leadership and the long-standing interest of social philosophers in the subject, the scientific literature largely ignored the topic until quite recently. Conger and Kanungo (1987) explained the dearth of research by pointing to three problems inherent in this area of study. The theme, itself, has had mystical and quasi-religious overtones that did not fit well with the sort of down-to-earth empiricism of scientific psychology. Further, the constructs that defined heroic leadership (e.g., extraordinary levels of follower devotion, monumental changes in the existing order) were difficult to define and operationalize. Perhaps most importantly, heroic leaders were not easily available for study. Such figures, after all, appear infrequently and are usually too busy conquering the world to fill out the necessary questionnaires.

In the late 1970s and the 1980s, interest in so-called "transformational" leadership was given a boost by two coalescing factors. On the scientific front, researchers were becoming frustrated with the limitations of contemporary leadership models in explaining and predicting the powerful impact that leaders seemed to have on organizations. At the same time, increased levels of business competition stimulated interest among practicing managers in ways to improve personal and organizational functioning. Popular interest made it easier for researchers to gain access to top level leaders, and the demand for the findings of the research fueled the work of both empirical researchers and armchair theoreticians. Bass (1990) reported that in the 1981 edition of *Bass and Stodgill's Handbook of Leadership,* only 2 pages were devoted to transformational leadership, whereas in the 1990 version (Bass, 1990) over 100 pages of research results were reported.

Although we have seen a resurgence of interest recently, the roots of transformational leadership theory (so called because such leadership transforms the goals of followers from self-interest to collective achievement) were found in the writings of the turn of the century German sociologist, Max Weber.

## THE CONCEPT OF CHARISMA

In his seminal work, *The Theory of Social and Economic Organization*, Weber (1924/1947) distinguished among three types of leadership differentiated by the bases of legitimacy on which the leader's authority rested. Authority that derived its legitimacy on "rational" grounds was based on the collective belief that orderly organizations and other social systems were governed by a set of normative rules. These abstract rules defined positions in the system and the rights and responsibilities of position incumbents. Obedience was to the legal authority of those properly elevated to positions of responsibility by the social organization.

Authority that derived its legitimacy on "traditional" grounds was rooted in the sanctity and timelessness of the social order. Loyalty to the order and to the persons who typified the order (e.g., kings, hereditary chieftains, priests) evoked the obedience of followers.

However, a form of authority that rested neither on the technical competence of a position holder in a bureaucratic system, nor on the sanctified status of the heir of a traditional order, was the "charismatic" authority of a leader who had been "chosen" to fulfill a spiritual mission. The legitimacy of the charismatic leaders, from the Greek word meaning "gifted," rested on the followers' recognition of the sanctity, heroism, or exemplary character of the individual person as a sign of that person having been chosen by supernatural authority. Weber (1924/1947) described the gift as "a certain quality of an individual personality by virtue of which he is set apart from ordinary men and treated as endowed with supernatural, superhuman, or at least specifically exceptional powers or qualities" (p. 358).

Obedience was given as a moral duty embodied in the mission for which the charismatic leader had been chosen rather than to rules, social order, or even to the person. That is, if the leader failed to achieve or maintain certain behaviors or outcomes, the "gift of grace" would be seen to have left the leader, taking with it the grounds for authority.

The charismatic leader's special powers or capabilities, like the definition of the mission, were of divine origin. Followers were called to a duty rather than to a relationship of transactions. The charismatic leader created obligations, not exchanges. Rather than being rooted in a set of rational contingencies, the charismatic's appeal was irrational or even antirational. The goal was chosen not because of its expediency, but because of a moral imperative. Rather than deriving any legitimacy from traditional authority, charismatic leadership repudiated the past and was a revolutionary force for change.

If he were alive today, Weber might have difficulty recognizing his iconoclastic, revolutionary leader in the depictions of CEOs that appeared in the popular business literature of the 1980s. However, some of the first modern interpretations of charismatic leadership theory were quite reconcilable with Weber's ideas. For example, political scientist and historian James McGregor Burns (1978) studied the lives of several leaders who had profound impacts on the existing social order, such as Mahatma Gandhi, Franklin Delano Roosevelt, and Martin Luther King, Jr. Burns coined the terms "transactional," to describe leadership based on the exchange of benefits guided by self-interest, and "transformational," to depict leadership that transformed followers into leaders, and subsequently leaders into agents of change. Followers' responses to transformational leadership were based on the commitment to a higher moral responsibility rather than on self-interest.

The philosophical, sociological, and historical writings on charismatic leadership provide a rich and dramatic presentation of the concept. Alas, as Conger and Kanungo (1987) pointed out, such expositions do not provide an adequate basis for the empirical study of the phenomenon. However, at around the same time that Burns (1978) was developing a historical analysis, Robert House (1977) was searching for a more rigorous basis for the study of charismatic leadership.

## House's 1976 Theory of Charismatic Leadership

House's model, first presented in 1976 and published a year later, attempted to develop a set of empirically testable hypotheses about the nature and form of charismatic leadership. House compiled the descriptions of charisma in the sociological and political science literature and derived a set of verifiable propositions for empirical research. House began with the argument that charismatic leadership must be defined by its effects on followers. Following the work of Oberg (1972), and Etzioni (1975), he defined the evidence for charisma as the extraordinary levels of devotion, identification, and emulation that are aroused in followers. House maintained that the appropriate empirical strategy for the study of charismatic leadership is first to identify such leaders by their effects on followers, and then to assess the characteristics that differentiate charismatic leaders from leaders with more mundane impact on followers.

House (1977) extracted 12 characteristics or concomitants of charismatic leadership, which he grouped under three categories; (a) personal characteristics, (b) behaviors, and (c) situational determinants.

The personal characteristics that define a charismatic leader include extremely high levels of self-confidence; dominance over others; a strong conviction in the moral righteousness of his or her beliefs, and a high need to influence others. Thus, the charismatic is typified by a certainty in self and a willingness to impose that certainty on others.

Six behaviors were hypothesized to be directly related to the charismatic's ability to gain the devotion of followers and to successfully turn that devotion into high levels of performance or achievement. The charismatic leader usually employs *role modeling*, that is, demonstrating publicly the commitment to key values and beliefs in order to instill those thoughts and feelings in followers. Gandhi's willingness to live the life of an Indian peasant, even to making his own clothes and cleaning his own toilet, or Martin Luther King, Jr.'s courageous posture in the face of physical danger are examples of the power of modeling. Citing Bandura (1969), House said that a model's effectiveness depends on followers' perceptions of the model's attractiveness, nurturance, competence, and success.

Because the charismatic leader must be perceived as extraordinarily gifted (to say nothing of attractive, nurturant, successful, and competent), by virtue of traits possessed or outcomes achieved, the would-be charismatic must put a considerable amount of energy into *image building*, that is, creating in followers the perception of giftedness. Modern political advertising, with its emphasis on symbolic images of power, competence, and concern, clearly recognizes the pervasive role of image in leadership.

Central to all discussions of charisma is the importance of the vision or mission charged to the leader and followers. *Goal articulation,* in transcendant, ideological, and moral terms, is the call to a higher duty. That the goal is spiritual rather than pragmatic is what differentiates transformative from transactional leadership.

In addition to their lofty moral plane, the articulated goals must also be large in scope if they are to achieve the kinds of expansive effects associated with movements that revolutionize their times. Demanding goals require that the leader exhibit *high expectations* for followers and *confidence* in their ability to achieve them. High expectations and confidence buoy the self-esteem of followers and provide a frame of reference for their capabilities that induces an extremely high level of aspiration, resulting in challenging goals and a commitment to their accomplishment.

In order to help followers adopt an attitude that facilitates goal achievement, charismatic leaders adopt *motive arousal behaviors* that induce cognitive and emotional states consistent with the behaviors necessary to accomplish the goal. For example, if the task at hand demands an aggressive, hard-driving, and competitive posture, leaders may arouse power motives that elicit appropriate behaviors, for example, General George F. Patton's rousing histrionics on the eve of battle. If successful action requires group cohesiveness, supportiveness, and teamwork, the arousal of affiliative motives would be warranted.

Thus, the charismatic leader, by virtue of his or her own high levels of certainty and confidence, is able to instill confidence in followers and to direct them on the path to a clearly articulated goal through direct exhortation supported by modeling. Under what conditions, then, are potential followers most likely to accept this form of influence?

House (1977) pointed to two situational determinants that facilitate the rise of charismatic influence. Each of these is extremely useful, but not absolutely necessary. First, followers are most likely to be susceptible to charismatic influence when the surrounding situation if very stressful. People under stress are especially responsive to clear and definitive answers.

Second, because charismatic leaders must present a transcendant vision, situations that foster the opportunity to express goals in ideological terms are helpful. House offered the example that when people are engaged in routine tasks for

pragmatic benefits (e.g., assembly line workers in an industrial setting), the opportunities to define their work in ideological terms seems quite difficult. However, if
the industrial plant manufactures critical material during a major war, the picture
changes, and "Rosie the Riveter" becomes a heroic figure.

# BROADENING THE SCOPE OF
# TRANSFORMATIONAL LEADERSHIP

House's (1977) theory of charimatic leadership laid the groundwork for moving
the study of transformational leadership in a quantitative, empirical direction.
Theorists following House continued to refine the psychological and behavioral
characteristics of transformational leadership, broadened the definition of such
leadership beyond the constraints of charisma, and brought the effects of the
phenomenon into the pragmatic domain of complex, formal organizations. Because
of the business community's strong interest in transformative leadership for greater
competitiveness, a number of books on the topic were presented for popular
audiences.

## Popular Theories

*Leadership: Strategies for Taking Charge* by Warren Bennis and Burt Nanus
(1985), *The Transformational Leader* by Noel Tichy and Mary Anne Devanna
(1986), and *The Leadership Challenge: How to Get Extraordinary Things Done in
Organizations* by James Kouzes and Barry Posner (1987), were three of the most
popular books of this genre. They share a number of characteristics. Consistent with
Weber (1947), they were all interested in leaders involved in major changes,
operating from the top of the organization. All three studies utilized relatively small,
nonsystematic and nonrepresentative sampling (i.e., all Americans, very few
women, and almost no minorities), and nonsystematic data gathering techniques,
typically retrospective, self-reports obtained in unstructured interviews with the
leaders (although Kouzes and Posner added a large sample survey of followers).
The analysis of the interview data was similarly nonsystematic and idiosyncratic,
usually involving an attempt to find a consensus of points across the people studied.

What can we learn from this sort of research? The lack of a scientific methodology makes it hard for a reader to know how much confidence to place in the
findings. Without some sort of corroborative objective data, such as observations
of leader behavior, measures of productivity, or reports by subordinates, we must
regard these studies as compilations of what some leaders say is the key to
successful organizational transformation. However, some of the leaders in the
samples and some of their organizations have, since the books were published,
undergone reversals of fortune which call into question the very success of their
leadership styles.

The relatively high degree of agreement across the three books does indicate that a fair consensus exists among the leaders of contemporary corporations about what it takes (or perhaps what it "should" take) to create a transformational atmosphere. Interestingly enough, the major points of this consensus, although less specific, are not in gross contradiction to the principles included in theories that enjoy greater acceptance within the scientific community. At the least, the pervasive impact that popular books have had on models of training and development in contemporary organizations suggests that we should attend to their arguments and see how well they square with more trustworthy evidence.

Bennis and Nanus (1985) conducted interviews with 60 private sector and 30 public sector chief executive officers with reputations for being able to transform their organizations. They derived four strategies that these leaders shared. First, all were able to articulate a compelling vision. They knew clearly what they wanted their organizations to achieve. Secondly, they were able to communicate this vision in a way that allowed others in the organization to understand the vision at a visceral as well as intellectual level. They created a "shared meaning" around the vision. Third, the leaders were able to evoke strong perceptions of their trustworthiness among members of their organizations. The appearance of trustworthiness was enhanced by their undeviating commitment to the vision. Finally, all of these leaders were able to make the fullest use of their personal resources and capacities because they were extremely self-confident in their own abilities and optimistic about the outcomes of their actions. This confidence and optimism were contagious for the people who worked around them.

The findings reported by Kouzes and Posner (1987) are remarkably similar to those of Bennis and Nanus (1985). Kouzes and Posner listed five practices for outstanding leadership with two behavioral commitments under each practice. The first practice was "challenging the process," which includes searching for opportunities to do things in better ways and taking risks through experimentation. Next was "inspiring a shared vision" by developing a goal for the future and enlisting other people to sign on. The third practice was "enabling others to act," which is achieved by fostering participation and collaboration and by strengthening subordinates to enhance their ability to participate effectively. A fourth principle was "modeling the way" which can be accomplished by setting an example and by planning small wins that allow people to see how the vision can be realized. Finally, "encouraging the heart" provides the emotional momentum for motivation by recognizing each person's contributions to the collective effort and taking time to celebrate accomplishments along the path to the goal.

Interestingly, when 1,500 workers and managers below the level of CEO were asked by Kouzes and Posner to describe the characteristics of superior leaders, the first two choices were honest and competent, finshing ahead of forward looking and inspiring. Consistent with Hollander's (1958) idiosyncrasy credit theory, a follower first wants to establish that the leader has a legitimate basis for authority (i.e., competence and trustworthiness) before surrendering autonomy (Kouzes & Posner, 1987).

Tichy and Devanna's (1986) analysis of transformational leadership was focused on what leaders in large, well-established organizations do to create change, innovation, and entrepreneurship. They described the process in the metaphor of a 3-act play. The first act was entitled "Revitalization: Recognizing the Need for Change" wherein the leader uses various sorts of compelling imagery to make ordinary organization members give up their desire for security and resistance to change. The second act was about "Creating a New Vision and Mobilizing Commitment." The third and final act involved "Institutionalizing Change." Tichy and Devanna (1986) illustrate the dynamics of the drama through "war stories" about the 14 or 15 leaders that they studied. (One of these leaders was John Akers of IBM, who is described as a leader for the 1990s. Unfortunately, Mr. Akers didn't last far into the 1990s at IBM after market share and profits continued to drop under his leadership.)

Despite the dubious nature of their data-gathering approaches, these popular theories bear much in common with many of the theories that we have already studied or will study in the rest of this chapter. The emphasis on motivating subordinates through an inspiring vision, through fair and equitable exchanges, through trust and legitimacy, and so on reveal that many leadership practitioners have a pretty good idea of the basics of effective leadership.

The popular theories suffer from two major weaknesses, however. First, they tend not to be very specific in describing how a leader can develop the inspirational qualities and communication abilities necessary. The popular theories also tend to gloss over the contingent situational and subordinate factors that influence the feasibility or utility of a particular set of behaviors or course of action. They imply that the practices of effective leadership are universal across situations and relatively easy to learn and use. In this sense, such theories are oversimplified and oversold. The sections that follow also attempt to place charismatic or transformational leadership within the context of modern organizations, but try for a more rigorous theoretical and empirical approach.

## Conger and Kanungo's Behavioral Theory

Jay Conger and Rabindra Kanungo (1987) presented a model of charismatic leadership that had as its goal the demystification of the construct. They argued that charisma, like other leadership processes, should be definable in purely behavioral terms, that is, what is it that leaders do that results in follower perceptions of giftedness and willingness to give such leaders extraordinary levels of effort and loyalty? Conger and Kanungo further contended that once charismatic leadership was understood in behavioral terms, its manifestation in formal organizations could be understood.

Conger and Kanungo (1987) stressed that charisma is an attributional phenomenon, defined by the perceptions held by followers. The behaviors to be studied were those that evoke such attributions. An emphasis on charisma as an attributional process was also implicit in House's (1977) exposition, but the attributional orientation and terminology was less common in the leadership literature when House wrote. In fact, much of the theorizing in Conger and Kanungo (1987) remains quite close to the House work, primarily adding exemplars that expand the concept from the primarily political sphere to that of the complex business organization. However, Conger and Kanungo also diverge from House's model.

Conger and Kanungo (1987) theorized that attributions of charisma depend on four variables; (a) the degree of discrepancy between the status quo and the future goal or vision advocated by the leader; (b) the use of innovative and unconventional means for achieving the desired change; (c) the leader's success in assessing the environmental resources and constraints for effecting the change; and (d) the type of articulation and impression management used by the leader to inspire subordinates in the pursuit of the vision.

These variables and Conger and Kanungo's subsequent discussion reveal some departure from earlier discussions of charisma (Weber, 1947; House, 1977). For example, the emphasis on the successful assessment of strategic factors affecting the successful attainment of the vision places the model clearly within the contemporary management literature. Exemplars of charismatic leaders include Lee Iacocca and John DeLorean who risked personal finances and job security in order to enlist support for new corporate visions.

In the same vein, Conger and Kanungo (1987) placed great importance on the charismatic leader's technical expertise as a prerequisite for the perception that the goal can be attained. These authors saw the leader's power arising from this expertise and the attractive power of the vision. They wrote, "Charismatic personal power stems from the elitist idealized vision, the entrepreneurial advocacy of radical changes, and the depth of knowledge and expertise to help achieve desired objectives" (p. 644).

Here Conger and Kanungo seem to part company with Weber who argued that charismatic leadership did not have a rational basis and therefore, technical expertise was irrelevant. This point of contention may hinge on the differential origins of the "gift" that the leader carries. Because Weber's charisma was of divine origin, followers did not need to worry about the technical expertise of the leader. Competence was assured, because the leader and the moral duty were divinely chosen. The divine choice the agent of the moral duty carried with it was the assurance of capability. When the arena for charisma shifts to the corporation and the engaging vision concerns strategies to improve profitability, perceptions of technical expertise must be established and maintained.

Although Conger and Kanungo's demystification of charisma might be seen as cheapening the currency (e.g., DeLorean's risk of his job at General Motors compared to Martin Luther King, Jr.'s life on the line in Selma and Montgomery), it also broadens and makes the construct more useful for contemporary leadership theory. Lee Iacocca may, like Alexander the Great, be too busy to fill out our questionnaires, but at least he functions in a milieu that can be related to our experience. Charismatic leadership now seems not so much a uniquely separate type of leadership, but more along a continuum of effectiveness.

# Bass' Transformational Leadership Theory

The movement toward broadening the definition of charismatic or transformational leadership, making it more appropriate to the setting of complex, formal organizations, and answering the call (Conger & Kanungo, 1987; House, 1977) to develop quantitative tools to study it, was given an enourmous boost by the research program of Bernard Bass and his colleagues (Bass, 1985; Bass & Avolio, 1993; Hater & Bass, 1988; Yammarino & Bass, 1990; and others). Because of its scope and importance, that research is discussed at length here.

The initial impetus for the development of a theory and measurement tool for transformational leadership was an open-ended, informal discussion with 70 senior executives attending a leadership training workshop. Asked if they had ever encountered a leader similar to the transformational type described by Burns (1978), that is, a leader who aroused them to transcend selfish interests for the benefit of the mission, the executives described a number of characteristics of such leaders (Bass & Avolio, 1993). Subsequent discussions, critical incident interviews, and written protocols collected from administrators and military officers in several countries and from diverse types of organizations eventually resulted in the development of a survey instrument, the multifactor leadership questionnaire (MLQ; Bass & Avolio, 1990a).

Initial and confirmatory factor analyses of responses to the measure revealed a reasonably stable factor structure that included seven leadership behavior factors that became the basis for the model (Bass, 1985). The factors fall into three categories of transformational leadership, transactional leadership, and nonleadership factors.

## *Transformational Leadership Factors*

*Charisma.*   Charisma (idealized influence) reflects follower perceptions that the leader is extremely trustworthy and is capable of achieving an important vision. A sample item from this factor is, "Has my trust in his or her ability to overcome any obstacle."

*Inspirational Motivation.*   This factor overlaps with charisma, but is conceptually and sometimes statistically distinct from it. This factor reflects the quality and emotional appeal of the leader's vision rather than the degree to which the rater identifies with leader. This factor is similar to Bennis and Nanus' (1985) concept of "shared meaning" through which the follower is induced to share the leader's goal. A sample item from this factor is, "Uses symbols and images to focus our efforts."

A leader might be able to secure high levels of commitment from a subordinate to an inspiring vision, even if the leader is not seen as particularly gifted. Bass and Avolio (1993) compared the ability of the relatively less charismatic Lyndon Johnson and the more charismatic John Kennedy to elicit support for a visionary goal.

*Intellectual Stimulation.*   Intellectual stimulation assesses the extent to which the leader both encourages the follower to question past ideas and supports the subordinate for thinking independently and creatively. A sample item is, "Enables me to think about old problems in new ways."

Here we see a dramatic divergence from earlier charismatic models (House, 1977; Weber, 1947) in which it is the leader, exclusively, who breaks with the past and thinks creatively *for* his or her followers, not *with* them. Clearly, this is charisma for a modern era in which follower needs include growth and independence as well as security and meaning. A later chapter on cultural influences on leadership processes addresses the ways in which individualistic and collectivist cultural values affect follower needs and the acceptance of leadership.

*Individualized Consideration.* This factor measures the degree to which the leader treats each follower in a way that is equitable and satisfying, but differentiated from the way other followers are treated. This concern is similar to both Hollander's (1978) emphasis on equitable exchanges and Graen and Scandura's (1987) recognition that dyadic exchanges vary within a single work unit. Another aspect of this factor is that the leader's behaviors raise the maturity of the subordinate's needs by providing challenges and learning opportunities. A sample item is, "Coaches me if I need it." Factors 3 and 4 are reminiscent of the more effective leadership qualities discussed in the exchange models, that is, the emphasis on need-oriented coaching in path–goal theory (House, 1971), on developing subordinate maturity in situational leadership theory (Hersey & Blanchard, 1977), and on the development of self-management through targeted reinforcement and goal-setting paradigms (Manz & Sims, 1980; Sims & Lorenzi, 1992). Bass and Avolio (1993) acknowledged the relevance of transactional and exchange facets of leadership and argued that good theory building incorporates productive features of earlier models.

## Transactional Leadership Factors

*Contingent Reward.* Contingent reward assesses a positively reinforcing interaction with the leader and is quite similar in emphasis to the principles put forth by the behavioral theorists (e.g., Podsakoff et al., 1982). A sample item from this scale reads, "Makes sure that there is close agreement between what he or she expects me to do and what I can get from him or her for my effort."

*Management by Exception.* This factor reflects the extent to which the leader intervenes only when things go wrong. This may involve active monitoring of subordinate performance or just waiting for trouble to indicate the need for contingent punishment. A sample is "Takes action only when a mistake has occurred."

## Nonleadership Factor

*Laissez-Faire.* Laissez-faire behavior implies that leadership is absent, with the superior avoiding intervention and procrastinating decisions or action. "Doesn't tell me where he or she stands on issues" is a sample item. Factors 6 and

7 which represent managerial aloofness and withdrawal punctuated occasionally by negative interactions, bring to mind the "overseer–peon" style of leader–member exchange (Graen & Cashman, 1975).

Bass and Avolio (1993) grouped the first five factors, the four transformational factors and Contingent Reward, into a higher order factor reflecting active leadership, whereas Factors 6 and 7 comprise a passive leadership factor. The active leadership behaviors were hypothesized to be associated with effectiveness, that is, higher subordinate performance and satisfaction, whereas the passive behaviors were not. Bass (1990) argued that both active and passive, transactional and transformational leadership occurs at all levels in organizations, not just at the highest levels (e.g., Bennis & Nanus, 1985), and across many cultures studied (Yammarino & Bass, 1990). How good is the evidence in support of these assertions?

By and large, the empirical evidence is supportive of the theory. Leaders who receive high ratings from their subordinates on the active leadership factors are associated with high performing and satisfied units. Bass and Avolio (1993) reported data from 17 samples, including military officers, senior executives, middle managers, educational administrators, and other leaders from a broad range of organizations and nations. Correlations between ratings of the leadership factors and measures of performance and follower satisfaction ranged from .6 to .8 for the transformational factors (the highest being for charisma), .4 to .6 for Contingent Reward; +.3 to −.3 for Management By Exception; and −.3 to −.6 for Laissez-faire. Positive results were reported for a number of non-U.S. samples, including Japan (Bass & Yokochi, 1991), Singapore (Koh, 1990), Italy (Bass & Avolio, 1990b), Canada (Avolio & Howell, 1992), and Spain (Bass, 1988). These correlations provide support for the ideas that leader actions affect subordinate satisfaction and performance and that the transformational factors are more strongly related to those outcomes.

The data presented in support of transformational leadership theory are impressive, but some questions remain. One issue concerns how to integrate a transformational model that describes one style of leadership as universally effective across various situations and cultures with other strong evidence supporting contingency theories that specify different leadership behaviors and styles for different situations. A second question that Bass and Avolio (1993) addressed, but did not fully answer, concerns the role of cognitive biases in the specification of the behaviors associated with transformational leadership.

In the next chapter, I develop more fully the theoretical issues around leadership perceptions, but for the moment, it suffices to point out that descriptions of leader behavior may reflect an observer's learned assumptions about what good leadership "should be," rather than what behavior actually occurred. We encountered this anomaly in the discussion of the lack of agreement between leaders and followers in their ratings of the quality of a leader–member exchange (Graen & Scandura, 1987; Liden et al., 1993). If, for example, followers believe that good leaders allow their subordinates to participate in decisions, they may be likely to "remember" such participation from a leader they regarded as effective. The transformational leadership behaviors in the MLQ might reflect common assumptions about good leadership, rather than valid observations.

A third question, which may seem like just asking too much of a theory that has amassed as much careful data as Bass', is "How exactly do the leader behaviors work?" Why does an ideological vision make a follower give more effort to a task? In other words, is there a truly psychological explanation for the effects of charisma?

# House and Shamir's 1993 Self-Concept Theory of Transformational and Charismatic Leadership

It was House's (1977) paper defining charismatic leadership in behavioral and testable terms that provided the basis for the scientific study of the phenomenon. It seems fitting, then, that House is back, this time with Boas Shamir, to integrate the visionary, charismatic, and transformational leadership theories and to provide a framework to take their study to a more sophisticated level.

House and Shamir (1993) began, as in the earlier work (House, 1977), by describing the effects that transformational leaders have on followers

> ...such leaders transform the needs, values, preferences, and aspirations of followers from self interests to collective interests. Further, they cause followers to become highly committed to the leader's mission, to make significant personal sacrifices in the interests of the mission, and to perform above and beyond the call of duty. (p. 82)

House and Shamir (1993) theorized that charismatic leaders are able to accomplish these effects by engaging followers' self-concepts and linking valued aspects of those self-concepts to the leader's vision and mission, and by arousing unconscious motives relevant to mission accomplishment. In other words, the motivational bases for subordinate effort and commitment are made intrinsic (i.e., tied to the follower's self-concept) rather than extrinsic as they are in transactional leadership, based on the quid pro quo of effort for personal gain.

House and Shamir (1993) brought together path–goal theory (House, 1971) and self-concept theory to make their points explicit. The motivational basis of path–goal theory was rooted in expectancy notions, expressed in the following formula:

$$IV_b \xrightarrow{P_1} IV_a \xrightarrow{P_2} EV$$

where $IV_b$ is the intrinsic valence of relevant behavior or effort; $IV_a$ is the intrinsic valence of goal attainment or performance; EV is the valence of extrinsic outcomes; $P_1$ is the perceived probability that effort will lead to goal attainment; and $P_2$ is the probability that goal attainment will lead to desired extrinsic outcomes. Thus, followers are motivated to work hard when they think that they can successfully accomplish the required levels of performance, which will in turn result in the attainment of valued outcomes.

In path–goal theory, the leader affects subordinate motivation by enhancing the extrinsic valence of outcomes and by making the attainment of outcomes easier by clarifying paths to the goal and reducing roadblocks. The transactional leader provides coaching and guidance to improve the subordinate's perception of the probability of goal attainment and clarifies the relationship of performance to reward, for example, through goal setting and feedback.

What the transformational leader does that is unique is to attach the follower's self-concept to the vision. The leader does this by stating the vision in ideological terms, which place the goals in a moral or spiritual context, and by raising the salience of collective interests and group goals, thereby diminishing the salience of selfish interests and the quid pro quo assessment of personal interest.

The follower's desire to enhance self-esteem and to maintain a consistent personal identity raises the intrinsic value of effort and goal accomplishment and reduces or makes irrelevant the value of extrinsic rewards. The follower becomes "self-regulating," monitoring performance levels and adjusting effort to achieve goals, because it is the follower's own self-esteem and personal satisfaction and fulfillment that are at stake.

The leader also engages in selective motive arousal through the use of symbolic communication. The motives are selective in the sense that the specific motives (e.g., power, achievement, or affiliation) are those that are consistent with mission accomplishment. For example, General George Patton's use of patriotic symbols (such as a large American flag) combined with aggressive and belligerent verbal imagery was designed to arouse among his troops power motives consistent with attacking the enemy.

The enhancement of relevant motives further engages the follower's self-concept and increases the intrinsic valence of goal accomplishment. Goal-directed efforts not only seem like the right thing to do (i.e., morally correct), but they also feel right (i.e., result in motive satisfaction). Commitment to the mission and desire for participation are elevated.

When Martin Luther King, Jr. exhorted his followers to help America achieve the dream of a true democracy, he offered them an opportunity to become part of a mission with tremendous moral implications. Participation in that mission gave followers a chance to do and be something important. The participation and successful achievement of goals became the reward rather than a means to a reward.

House and Shamir's (1993) analysis brought together many of the transformational theories. The emphasis on an inspirational vision, on role modeling and on image building to establish trust in the leader and the vision, high expectations and confidence in followers, are concepts shared in various degree by all the theories presented in this chapter.

House and Shamir (1993) part company with most of the other theorists on a couple of points. They disagreed with Bass and Avolio (1993) in the role of intellectual challenge as a part of transformational leadership. In fact, House and

Shamir regarded the leader behaviors associated with the MLQ intellectual challenge factor as reflecting the leader's confidence in the followers' abilities. Likewise, individualized consideration was hypothesized to tap into the followers' trust in the leader and belief in their shared values. In this sense, House and Shamir appear to be downplaying the importance of follower needs for growth and challenge in their jobs. This may reveal a greater emphasis on the extraordinary levels of motivation associated with charismatic leadership rather than an emphasis on subordinate development and organizational transformation in the work of Bass and Avolio (1993) or Tichy and Devanna (1986).

Although these disagreements are really more matters of emphasis than substance, House and Shamir have a more essential disagreement on another point. Unlike Conger and Kanungo (1987) or Sashkin (1988) who argued that transformational leaders are extremely sensitive to the environment and adaptive to changing contexts, House and Shamir viewed the charismatic leader as neither flexible nor adaptive.

House and Shamir maintained that the charismatic leader's vision is not negotiable, nor are the basic features of the leader's personality and values changeable. They gave the example of leaders like General Patton or football coach Vince Lombardi, who had tranformational effects in one context (on the battlefield of war or sport), but who were unable to obtain the same effects in other settings. In this respect, House's roots in contingency leadership theory are manifested in House and Shamir's contention that the charismatic effects of a particular vision or motive-arousal behavior will occur only in receptive cultures and appropriate milieus. This argument offers the possibility that transformational and contingency approaches to leadership are not incompatible.

## ETHICAL CONSIDERATIONS

Discussions of charisma frequently turn to the question of the moral or ethical implications of such powerful leaders. Political charismatics, like Adolph Hitler, or cult leaders, like Charles Manson or Jim Jones, led their followers to acts of great destruction of self or others. When leaders have the power to bend others' wills to their own designs, the potential for evil as well as good is created. All leadership can have positive or negative effects, and charismatic leadership simply magnifies the implications.

However, other subtle questions about charismatic leadership are relevant. Jay Conger (1989) argued that the kinds of problems that all leaders may have are likely to achieve more extreme forms among charismatics. The expansive goals, limitless self-confidence, and heightened communication ability that make the charismatics such a formidable force can also be their undoing. Conger identified four ways in which charismatic leaders may have significant negative effects on their organizations.

The leader may allow his or her personal needs to dictate the vision, which is projected onto followers without respect to the followers' needs or interests.

Captain Ahab's obsessive search for revenge against the white whale in Melville's *Moby Dick* is an example. The three remaining flaws are related to Conger and Kanungo's (1987) specification of good judgment and strategic-planning skills as an element of charismatic leadership in complex organizations. The charismatic leader's zeal and self-confidence may encourage unrealistic assessments of the resources needed to accomplish the goal, of the availability of resources, and of the receptivity of the environment to the strategy. The charismatic's communication ability may allow the vision to be sold to followers even when such miscalculations are possible or even evident. Conger illustrated these points with examples drawn from the contemporary business world including follies or judgment errors by such well-known executives as Lee Iacocca, John DeLorean, and Edwin Land of Polaroid fame.

An interesting implication of the power of charismatic and transformational leaders is related to the effects on followers' empowerment. Deluga (1990) conducted a study of the influence strategies used by subordinates of transformational, transactional, and laissez-faire leaders. Deluga measured influence strategies with the Kipnis and Schmidt (1982) scales and leadership behaviors with the Multifactor Leadership Questionnaire (Bass, 1985). Deluga found that, due to the great referent power of transformational leaders, subordinates tended to use "soft" influence strategies (e.g., ingratiation) more than more direct approaches (e.g., rational appeals). Deluga aptly pointed out that ingratiation from subordinates might serve to inflate the transformational leader's already expanded self-image and cause denigrating perceptions of the followers, that is, the metamorphic effect of power (Kipnis et al., 1976). In this manner, the subordinates of transformational leaders, at least the strongly charismatic type, might be denied the empowerment necessary for growth and development. The organization loses the beneficial effects of participative decision making both in terms of future motivation and in problem assessment and creativity. The effects of transformational leadership cut both ways.

## SOME CONCLUSIONS

Although transformational leadership is usually treated as a separate and distinct, qualitatively different type of leadership, an argument can be made that many of the components of transformational leadership are present in other approaches covered in earlier chapters.

The sense of the leader as uniquely gifted and faithful to an important mission fits well with Hollander's (1958) idiosyncrasy credit notions in which leader legitimacy is based, in part, on the leader's competency to accomplish group goals and his or her loyalty to those goals. The leader's ability to project a high level of self-confidence resembles the confidence in self and followers that was reported as a result of leadership match (Chemers, Ayman et. al., 1991; Chemers, Hays, Rhodewalt, & Wysocki, 1985).

The extent to which the leader motivates and challenges subordinates and helps them to grow intellectually as unique individuals is present in the emphasis on subordinate development in several theories, such as path–goal theory (House & Mitchell, 1974), situational leadership theory (Hersey & Blanchard, 1977), and vertical dyad linkage theory (Graen & Scandura, 1987).

What is unique about the transformational perspective is the extent to which a transcendent vision is the source of motivation for followers and the degree to which followers can meld their personal identity with that mission. The power of the vision may emerge from a particular confluence of forces that include the leader's ability to articulate the vision clearly and compellingly and the followers' special susceptibility to the message, which might be caused by aspects of the environment (e.g., dangerous and unpredictable times) or strong personal needs (e.g., for a sense of life purpose or identity).

In the next chapter, we turn to the role of perception and judgment in leadership processes. One of the things that we uncover in that discussion is that sometimes "all that glitters is not gold" when it comes to leadership, even transformational leadership.

# Chapter 7

## Cognitive Approaches

In many of the theories discussed thus far, the actions of leaders or followers are determined by their expectations about the results of those actions. Examples include a leader's analysis of the relative utility of various behaviors to motivate and guide the work of subordinates (House, 1971), the choice of influence tactics (Kipnis & Schmidt, 1982), and decisions about how much autonomy a subordinate is capable of handling (Hersey & Blanchard, 1977). It is assumed that the expectations that the leader holds will determine the behaviors or strategies chosen. Research indicates that expectancies do, in fact, influence leader behavior (Matsui & Ohtsuka, 1978; Nebeker & Mitchell, 1974).

These leader expectancies are based on various kinds of judgments about subordinates, such as, needs, maturity, ability, and so forth. Although perceptions of leaders and followers are integral parts of many theories, until recently, very little attention had been paid to studying the processes by which interpersonal judgments are made. In fact, for the first 5 or so decades of research on leadership, it was simply assumed that reports and judgments were accurate reflections of reality. A rating of leader behavior on a measure like the Leader Behavior Description Questionnaire (Stogdill & Coons, 1957) was thought to be a more or less true representation of what behaviors the leader had actually performed.

In the 1960s, interpersonal perception and judgment, particularly attribution processes, became the dominant area of study in social psychology (Shaw & Costanzo, 1982). When organizational psychologists began to integrate attributional perspectives into the study of leadership, a shift in thought and orientation took place that was as profound as had been the acknowledgment of the contingency principle 10 years before.

This chapter examines the effects of perception and judgment on leadership processes from two perspectives; perceptions *by* leaders about their followers and perceptions *of* leaders by followers and others. I offer some analyses of the implications of cognitive effects for the practice and study of leadership.

# PERCEPTIONS OF FOLLOWERS
# BY LEADERS

## Attribution Theories

The impetus for the study of the dynamics of leader–follower perceptions came from the attribution theories developed in social psychology. Space considerations do not permit a full exposition of this extensive literature. This section briefly outlines some of the major principles of the theories that have been the most influential in leadership research.

Attribution theory is concerned with the processes by which people assign causes to the interpersonal events that occur around them. The origins of this work can be traced back to a paper on "phenomenal causality" by Fritz Heider (1944), which dealt with the ways in which perceivers make sense out of their social environment. Heider proposed that interpersonal relations are mostly determined by our perceptions of other people's actions, and that people have a very strong need to understand social events and actions so that they can predict future events and actions. Attribution theories are attempts to delineate the processes by which that understanding is accomplished.

Edward Jones and Keith Davis' (1965) "theory of correspondent inferences" explained how a perceiver uses another person's behavior to draw inferences about that person's intentions. In other words, under what conditions can one infer that an actor's internal dispositions correspond with the observed behavior. Several factors contribute to judgments of correspondence.

First, the actor must be seen as understanding the nature of the consequences that might ensue from actions, they must have the ability to cause those actions, and they must have the free choice to engage in the actions. Thus, behavior that occurs through either misunderstanding, accident, or the constraint of others does not reveal much about an actor's intentions. Along the same lines, behavior that is considered normative, expected, and therefore constrained by social role, is also less informative.

The consequences of the action also have effects on the perception of internal motivation. For example, do the positive and negative consequences that ensue from the act suggest that the actor would want to cause those consequences? Another way that consequences affect judgment is related to the essential egocentricity of human beings, that is, things that affect us directly have greater impact on our judgments than those that are irrelevant. Thus, when another person's act has positive or negative consequences for the observer ("hedonic relevance"), the observer is more likely to conclude that the act was intentional, with resultant positive or negative evaluations of the actor. This effect is enhanced if the observer also believes that he or she was the intended target of the action (personalism).

Finally, when predictions or expectations that the observer has about the actor are confirmed, dispositional inferences are stronger. Such expectations may arise from suppositions that the observer holds about the group to which an actor belongs, such as a racial or gender group (category-based expectations), or from prior knowledge or assumptions about the actor as an individual (target-based expectations). A manager might have the impression that one of her subordinates is not very smart and is likely to fail at intellectually demanding tasks. The manager will make confident attributions when those expectations are confirmed.

In summary, correspondent inference theory hypothesizes that we are likely to make dispositional attributions to an actor when we judge that he or she has acted with forethought and knowledge, constrained neither by another person's power nor by the force of social norms, but motivated instead by a desire to gain the positive consequences of the action. That judgment will be especially certain when the behavior is consistent with our expectations for the person and especially strong when the outcomes have relevance for ourselves.

Harold Kelley's (1967, 1973) "theory of external attribution" shares the similar goal of explaining the causes of a person's behavior, but takes a somewhat different perspective; it details the factors that influence judgments of causes external to the actor, that is, to an entity in the person's environment. External attributions are made when an actor's behavior is *distinctive* to a particular entity or object (i.e., occurs only when the entity is present); *consistent* across time and modality (i.e., occurs every time the entity is present in whatever form it is present); and typifies a *consensus* (i.e., other people treat the entity in a similar fashion). Thus, if a subordinate performed poorly on a task, but not on most other tasks; always did poorly with this particular task; and other workers also had difficulty with the task, we might assume that the cause of the poor performance was something about the task rather than something about the subordinate. By corollary, if a worker failed at most tasks over a long period of time, including tasks that other workers accomplished successfully, we would locate the cause of the difficulty in the subordinate.

Although such judgments would appear to be straightforward, consistent biases in attribution exist. One of the strongest of these (the "fundamental attribution error"; Ross, 1978) is the tendency to make internal attributions (i.e., to the person) even when evidence for an external or situational cause is present. This strong tendency to make personal attributions may reflect the need to ascribe causes to something that is more predictive of the future.

This sense of the attributional process simultaneously serving the need to predict the future and the need to enhance or protect one's ego is very relevant in explanations of attributions for success and failure. Weiner et. al. (1972) presented a framework for ascribing causes for success or failure that is very relevant to leadership perceptions. Weiner et al. (1972) proposed that we need to know the answer to two important questions about the causes of performance of ourselves or others. First, we need to know whether the cause is internal to the actor or external, that is, in the task or situation. Second, we need to know whether the cause is stable and therefore likely to occur in the future or unstable.

Arriving at the answers to these questions might involve the same factors suggested by Kelley (1967, 1973). Internal causes would probably be the result of low consensus and low distinctiveness, that is, the actor performs the same way on most tasks and most other people perform differently. Stability might be inferred from consistency information, that is, has this person performed this way in the past. The Weiner et al. (1972) two-dimensional breakdown results in four potential causes as presented in Fig. 7.1.

The choice of cause ascribed for subordinate performance can have dramatic implications for the leader's subsequent actions. A subordinate with low ability might be given training whereas one with low effort might be given incentives through rewards or goals. If the cause of performance is in the task, actions could be taken to address problems there (e.g., through job redesign), whereas a performance outcome that was caused by a random event might not elicit any action. In later work, Weiner (1979) added the dimensions of "controllability" to distinguish between controllable causes, such as effort, and uncontrollable ones, such fatigue or illness. The controllability dimension has not figured strongly in leadership research on attribution.

In the context of leadership, biases in the attribution process such as the fundamental attribution error, can be very problematic. As noted earlier, accurate judgments are assumed to provide the basis for the leader's choice of behaviors.

# An Attributional Model of Follower Performance

Terence Mitchell and his associates (Green & Mitchell, 1979; Mitchell & Wood, 1980) adapted attribution theory to the study of leaders' perceptions of followers. Green and Mitchell (1979) argued that when a supervisor is confronted with a subordinate's poor performance, subsequent remedial action is determined by the attributions that the leader makes about the locus and stability of causes. Following Kelley (1973), Green and Mitchell suggested that the factors of distinctiveness, consensus, and consistency will determine the supervisor's attributions.

Mitchell and Wood (1980) tested the model by presenting case studies involving poor performance by a nurse to a group of nursing supervisors. Consistent with predictions, they found that consistency, distinctiveness, and consensus affected internal attributions. They also found that internal attributions led to more punitive responses on the part of the supervisors. Finally, when the consequences of a subordinate's poor performance were more serious, supervisors made more internal attributions and more punitive responses. This effect was obtained even though the seriousness of consequences was manipulated independently of the Kelley factors. In other words, even a nurse with a good past record would be blamed for the outcome if it was serious enough.

|  | STABILITY | |
| --- | --- | --- |
|  | **Stable** | **Unstable** |
| **Internal** | Ability | Effort |
| **External** | Task Difficulty | Luck |

FIG. 7.1. Two-dimensional breakdown of stability and locus.

In a follow-up, Mitchell and Kalb (1982) studied further the effect of the outcome severity on the attribution process. Nursing supervisors were presented with cases in which a floor nurse had left the bed railing down on a postoperative patient. Half of the sample was presented with outcome knowledge (either the patient fell out of the bed, breaking a hip or another nurse put the railing up, before any problem could occur), while the remaining half of the sample received no information about outcomes. Those supervisors who had received negative outcome information assessed the outcome as more probable, saw the subordinate as more responsible, and made greater internal attributions for the cause, despite the fact that the nurse's behavior was the same in all cases.

Knowlton and Mitchell (1980) conducted a laboratory study in which undergraduate students ostensibly served as supervisors of other students, who were actually experimental confederates. After the confederates had performed either well or poorly on a decoding task, "supervisors" were led to believe that the performance was the result of either ability or effort. Subjects made more extreme evaluations of the subordinate when the attribution was to effort.

A similar finding was reported by Hamberg (1989) who asked managers to rate the appropriateness of various remedial actions for subordinate poor performance, including punishment, termination, training, social support, job redesign, and coaching. The highest ratings for punishment were given when the respondents were told that the cause of the poor performance was low effort. Apparently, "able, but not willing" is seen as more reprehensible than "willing, but not able."

Lord and Smith (1983) argued that attributional models place too much emphasis on carefully controlled processing of information. They believe that many of the judgments that leaders make about subordinates are the results of less conscious (automatic) processes that are not so rational and careful. Lord and Maher (1991) proposed that internal attributions probably occur quite spontaneously and without much thought, whereas external attributions may more often be the result of careful analysis. They based their argument partially on the work of Gilbert, Pelham, and Krull (1988) who described interpersonal perception as a three-step process. In the first step, we ask "What is that person doing?" (categorization). Then, "What is implied by that behavior?" (characterization); and finally "What situational constraints (i.e., external factors) might have caused the action?" (correction). Under the demanding and distracting conditions of ongoing interpersonal interaction, we frequently don't have time to do the careful processing necessary to answer the third question and so make internal attributions by default.

# A Model of Attribution to Groups

Karen Brown (1984) presented a model of the factors that might influence attributions surrounding the poor performance of whole work groups. Brown's theorizing placed significant emphasis on the ego-protective concerns of workplace leaders. She pointed out that poor performance by an entire work group poses problems far greater than those associated with poor performance by a single individual. For one thing, the consequences of group performance are more serious for the organization and may be associated with major problems, such as poor morale or inefficient systems. Because of the scope and importance of poor performance by the whole group, the potential reflections on the supervisor are correspondingly more serious and therefore more relevant.

Attributions about groups may be affected by some very insidious deviations from the more basic attributional processes. For example, in attribution scenarios typical for a social psychology study, judgments are made about an actor who has no special relationship to the observer. In real work groups, however, the leader's dependence on the subordinate to accomplish the group's task makes every situation one of high hedonic relevance. When an entire group is involved, that sense of dependency and relevance is heightened.

Because of the interdependence of manager and subordinate in the dyadic working relationship, a reversibility of perspectives occurs. The supervisor is the observer when regarding the subordinate's performance, which increases the likelihood of an internal attribution. However, supervisors are also actors with respect to their own responsibilities in the dyad, inducing a tendency for a supervisor to make external attributions for his or her own performance. The combination of these two perspectives strongly inclines the supervisor to attribute the causes for poor performance outcomes to the subordinates.

In traditional attribution models (Kelley, 1967), the effect of a whole group performing poorly should be a perception of high consensus and a lowered likelihood of internal attribution. Brown (1984) showed us that for groups, "it ain't necessarily so." First, earlier work on attributions to individuals suggested that consensus information is the most easily discounted (McArthur, 1972; Nisbett & Borgida, 1975). Group performance problems carry some special features that override consensus effects.

As already noted, the supervisor is inclined to avoid attributions to external factors that are supposed to be under his or her control, such as, training, coaching, work scheduling, and so forth, because such attributions reflect badly on the supervisor. One explanation more favorable to the supervisor is that of social influence. Perhaps the group contains one or two "bad apples" who are poisoning the group's attitudes about work.

Adding to the sense of relevance for the leader is that poor group performance quickly takes on the aspect of accumulated failures. Stevens and Jones (1976) found that accumulated failure increased defensiveness in the attribution process. The harrassed supervisor blames the failure on subordinates, setting up a cycle of recrimination and resentment which may, of course, lead to the accumulation of more failures.

As the administrative level of the observer or manager goes higher, the potential for misattribution increases. The manager several layers above the work group feels a distance from the workers that reduces the likelihood of identification with their perspective. Furthermore, the upper level manager is less likely to have much familiarity with the tasks and environment that occupy the work group. Mitchell and Kalb (1982) found that task experience reduced the observer bias. Thus, the upper level manager who is unable or unwilling to empathize with the work group several levels down the hierarchy is most likely to blame the group for its poor performance, rather than considering other possibilities such as inadequate training, poor task design, or inefficient support systems.

The dangers to effective managerial practice are obvious. Severe and relevant outcomes lead to highly certain, strongly negative evaluations and actions, often distorted by the need to protect self-esteem and a sense of control. The leader's inaccurate attributions become the basis for action toward the subordinate. Previous material has warned us, however, about the necessity, for both effective transactional and transformational leadership, to have accurate perceptions of the needs, desires, and capabilities of subordinates. Effective leadership is dependent on a leader's ability to overcome biases based on quick or ego-protective judgments.

## PERCEPTIONS OF LEADERS

Biases in leaders' perceptions of subordinates represent a serious problem for the effective *practice* of leadership. Potentially far more serious for the *study* of leadership, however, are biases and distortions in the perception of leadership. Perceptions of leaders are integral to leader–follower interactions (Hollander, 1993), and the study of perceptual processes helps to elucidate those relationships. Methodologically, however, biases in perception are more problematic. Many approaches to the study of leadership depend on reports about leaders and their behaviors (e.g., Bass & Avolio, 1990a, 1993; House & Dessler, 1974). If the reports of leader behavior are distorted in systematic ways, the validity of many leadership theories is called into question.

The theoretical view that perceptions and reports of leadership processes are determined more by perceiver preconceptions than by objective reality is referred to as the "constructionist" approach. A weak form of the constructionist argument holds that leadership and the effects of leadership on group and organizational performance are real and important, but that leadership processes are strongly influenced by cognitive processes that are inherently subject to bias and distortion. The strong form argues that the role of leadership in organizational performance, in fact the very concept of leadership, is questionable and of dubious usefulness (Calder, 1977). People see leadership and its effects, the constructionists maintain, only because they expect to see them.

The remainder of this chapter explores the processes that underlie leadership perceptions, first from the weak-form and then the strong-form point of view. The implications of the constructionist arguments for contemporary leadership theorizing are discussed.

## Revealing Biases in Leadership Perception: Early Findings

An important early study of leadership perceptions (Eden & Leviatan, 1975) asked subjects to fill out a survey, which included ratings of leader behavior, after being given extremely limited information about a fictitious production plant. Although no information about supervisory behavior was given, subjects were able to rate leader behavior. Subsequent analyses of the behavior ratings yielded factors quite similar to those typically reported in the leader behavior literature. The authors argued that subjects' ratings were guided by "implicit theories" of leadership that specified what behaviors are associated with effective leadership. Like implicit theories of personality (Hastorf, Schneider, & Polefka, 1970), which are a structured set of beliefs about how particular traits and behaviors are related, implicit leadership theories guide and organize perceptions and memories. Eden and Leviatan argued that ratings may be due more to these implicitly held assumptions than to the actual realities of leader behavior.

Around the same time, Barry Staw (1975) described the results of an experiment in which group members were given bogus feedback about performance effects for their groups. This manipulated information about group performance affected group members' reports of influence, cohesiveness, communication, motivation, and openness, revealing that subjects' causal beliefs (implicit theories) guided their ratings. Subjects who thought that they had been in high performance groups made more positive judgments of the group's dynamics. Downey, Chacko, and McElroy (1979) replicated Staw's (1975) experiment, varying the amount of time the group worked together, to see if actual experience working in a group could override the effects of false feedback. The results strongly supported Staw's original findings, indicating that such ratings are susceptible to performance feedback effects even when other information is available.

Leadership researchers began to zero in on the problems posed by implicit theory effects for studies using leader behavior ratings. Rush, Thomas, and Lord (1977) asked business students to rate hypothetical leaders described as effective or ineffective. Despite the fact that the students observed no leader behavior, their ratings yielded factor structures very similar to those found in most research. Furthermore, effective leaders were characterized as engaging in high levels of both structuring and interpersonally considerate behaviors, a pattern frequently reported for successful leaders (e.g., Bass, 1985). Mitchell, Larson, and Green (1977) reported similar results.

Salancik and Pfeffer (1978) presented a social information processing-approach to the study of job attitudes, such as satisfaction with leaders, arguing that a number of subjective influences affect the construction of such attitudes. One influence on an individual's attitude is the social reality that results from the consensus of friends and colleagues in the work group. Another influence is the individual's need to justify his or her behavior or actions taken. Thus, the respondent creates a coherent consistent understanding of the world and self by making sense out of what he and others do and say. The organizing principles for the consistent attitude network are the person's implicit theories linking tasks, people, and outcomes.

This is not to say that leader behavior ratings contain no valid information. Lord, Binning, Rush, and Thomas (1978) created videotapes in which actors portraying leaders demonstrated either high or low levels of structuring behaviors. Subjects rated the leaders' behavior after being told whether the group's performance was good or bad. The results indicated highly significant effects for both the performance cues and the actual behavior, but performance effects controlled a much greater percent of rating variance than did the actual behaviors.

In a similar videotape study, Phillips and Lord (1981) varied the salience of the leader by changing the camera angles used in filming the group. Performance feedback information was more strongly correlated with leader behavior ratings when the leader was made to appear more salient. Our implicit theories of organization place the role of leadership in a prominent and salient context, possibly exaggerating its importance.

# An Information-Processing Model of Leadership

As has been the case at many points in the history of leadership research, developments in other fields of psychology had a salutory effect on leadership theorizing. Cognitive, personality, and social psychologists (Cantor & Mischel, 1979; Rosch, 1978) were trying to understand the effects of cognitive structures on interpersonal perception. Already deeply interested in similar issues in leadership perception, Robert Lord (1985) adapted the information-processing findings to the leadership literature resulting in a very productive synthesis.

Lord and Karen Maher (1990, 1991) offered a model of leadership perception based on the interaction of two types of information, which could be processed in two possible modes (Shiffrin & Schneider, 1977). One way in which people process information is a *controlled* mode, which relies on a careful, rational analysis of information. Controlled processing requires high levels of attention. An alternate processing mode is referred to as *automatic* processing, involving less attentional demand on the cognitive system. As noted earlier in this chapter, Gilbert, Krull, and Pelham (1988) showed that when the social environment places concurrent attentional demands on an information processor, controlled processing may be replaced by automatic processes.

Automatic processes are guided by so-called "knowledge structures" (Galambos, Abelson, & Black, 1986). These knowledge structures are cognitive schemas (such as scripts, categories, implicit theories, prototypes, etc.), which are highly learned mental organizations that simplify the encoding, memory, and retrieval of cognitive material. Once a cognitive schema is accessed, the contents and structure of the schema guide what information is attended to, selected, and remembered.

One powerful class of schema that operates in interpersonal perception is prototypes (Cantor & Mischel, 1979; Rosch, 1978). Prototypes are knowledge structures about particular types of people and include the characteristic traits and behaviors associated with that category of person, for example extroverts, realtors, or musicians. When a set of stimuli bear sufficient similarity to a category, that is, when there is enough overlap in traits or behaviors between the particular stimulus and the more general prototype, the category is made salient. Then expectations and preconceptions about the nature of the category guide and direct processing of the particular case. For example, if we meet a person at a party, and the person's behavior (e.g., telling jokes, talking to many people) elicits the prototype for an extrovert, subsequent judgments of that person (e.g., deciding whether he might be a fun date) are guided by what we know about extroverted people in general.

Lord, Foti, and Phillips (1982) demonstrated that people hold prototypes for leaders. Like other prototypes (Rosch, 1978), leadership prototypes are hierarchically organized at three levels. At the highest, most general level, the prototype is differentiated from other categories, that is, leaders from nonleaders. At the next level down, basic level categories represent specific contexts, such as political leader, business leader, sports leader, and so on. At the most specific level, differentiations within a context are made, such as, liberal versus conservative political leader (Lord, Foti, & De Vader, 1984).

Lord and Maher (1991) argued that observers decide whether a person is a leader in part by matching the particular traits and behaviors of an observed individual to the prototype for a leader in the specific context. For example, if an observed individual acts in a decisive manner, giving instructions and directions to other group members, and encourages them to work hard, the individual may elicit the observer's prototype for a leader. The observer may use controlled processing, carefully analyzing the characteristics of the actor, or may use less effortful, automatic processes without really paying attention to the judgments being made. Lord and Maher referred to this use of observed behaviors to identify leaders as "recognition-based" processes.

Lord, Foti, and De Vader (1984) asked college students to read vignettes about a hypothetical manager. The three vignettes varied in the number of very prototypical leadership behaviors that were described, such as providing information, emphasizing goals, speaking frequently, and so forth. The degree of prototypicality of the vignette was strongly related to leadership perceptions. An important finding of this study was that when subjects were asked about behaviors that were not included in the vignettes but that were also prototypical of leaders, the behaviors received higher expectancy ratings if subjects had read the high prototypicality vignette. In other words, once the leadership category had been accessed, raters used the general contents of the category to organize information about the specific case.

However, observers of leadership may also hold another set of cognitive schemas that organize explanations and inferences about the causes for certain outcomes, such as success or failure. Implicit leadership theories are examples of such causal schemas. For example, an observer may believe that good performance in groups is caused by good leadership. When the observer believes that the group has performed well, an inference is made that leadership has occurred. Inferences about events and outcomes may be made in a relatively automatic or more controlled way depending on the amount of energy and attention that is employed.

The studies described earlier that showed how performance information affected ratings of leader behavior and group process (Eden & Leviatan, 1975; Lord, Phillips, & Rush, 1980; Rush, Phillips, & Lord, 1981; Staw, 1975) are examples of inferential processes at work. Note also that many possible causal schemas might be used to explain a particular event or outcome. The one that is actually accessed depends to some degree on the context. When Phillips and Lord (1981) used the camera angle to make a leader more or less salient in a videotape of a group, they were altering the context and affecting the likelihood of one causal schema (i.e., leadership) over others (e.g., talented group members).

Once a category is chosen to describe a person or to explain a situation, the associated knowledge structure guides subsequent evaluations and judgments. The category carries with it expectations for future behavior. When subsequent events or behaviors are consistent with expectations, they reinforce the certainty with which the category is applied. When events are inconsistent with expectations, they trigger more elaborate information processing to search for a potential explanation.

Wong and Weiner (1981) held that controlled processes are most likely to be employed during attribution when unexpected events occur. As long as events and behaviors are consistent with the observer's expectations, automatic processing will continue. However, social interactions can be anxiety provoking, placing high concurrent processing demands on the actors and observers (Gilbert, Krull, & Pelham, 1988). Under increased demand, the controlled process is most likely to be dropped in the interest of speed and conservation of limited attentional capacity.

These points add up to a significant inertia in perception once categorical labelling has occurred. Once the actor is identified as a leader, all the behaviors associated with the prototype will be ascribed to the individual. Further, subsequent behaviors or outcomes that are consistent with the leader prototype and script will be automatically processed will and strengthen the categorical assignment. Any behaviors or outcomes that are inconsistent with the prototype will trigger controlled processes that search for an alternative, external explanation for the inconsistency. In essence, as long as the individual is categorized as a leader, positive outcomes will be attributed to the leader's internal dispositions and failures to situational factors.

The impact of these processes on people whom the observer does not expect to hold leadership positions (e.g., women managers, minority group members, or other nontraditional occupants of leadership roles) is quite different. Such persons are less likely to be seen as leaders and their successes are more likely to elicit a search for explanations outside of the individual. The implications of this attributional pattern are discussed in a later chapter.

## Strong Constructionist Approaches

Lord and his associates argued that leadership is not always what it seems to be; that processes of leadership perception are distorted by assumptions, expectations, and limitations on our processing capacity. However, Lord and other theorists discussed thus far do not mean to say that leadership is not important or that the effects of leadership are insignificant. In the next section, some theorists are presented who take a more radical view with respect to the appropriate nature of leadership research.

# Calder's Attribution Theory of Leadership

In a paper that appeared earlier but that anticipated many of the points eventually made by Lord and Maher (1991), Calder (1977) took a much more extreme position on the implications of cognitive factors in leadership research. At one point, the essay offered the opinion that, "As a scientific contruct leadership is hopelessly ambiguous" (p. 186).

Calder based this dour assessment on his view that leadership research has never developed a scientific understanding of the leadership construct that takes it beyond the definitions that are used in everyday parlance. These "everyday" conceptions are based on commonly held social constructions, that is, prototypes. The failure to develop a means of measuring leadership independently from the prototype definition limits leadership research to restating common sense descriptions.

Calder argued that leadership is a disposition or internal quality that, in fact, cannot be measured but can only be inferred from observed behaviors or events. The particular behaviors or events could be interpreted in any number of ways, and it is the social context that determines when attributions of leadership will be made. Because leadership exists only in the form of such socially shared inferences, there is nothing to study about leadership except those inferences. Calder went on to develop a model based on attribution theory principles (Jones & Davis, 1965; Kelley, 1967) that shares many common features with Lord and Maher's (1991) analysis, the major point of divergence being Calder's assertion that it is only the perception of leadership, not the fact of leadership that is important.

# Meindl's Romance of Leadership Concept

James Meindl undertook an extensive research program that questioned the widely held assumption that leadership is the most important factor in organizational functioning. In fact, it is this assumption that Meindl (1990; Meindl, Ehrlich, & Dukerich, 1985) referred to as the "romance of leadership." He argued (1990) that "it is easier to believe in leadership than to prove it" (p. 161). People hold implicit theories about organizational functioning that attribute powerful effects to leadership. These implicit theories, operating in both automatic and controlled processing modes, explain a variety of organizational events and occurrences in terms of leadership, exaggerating the true effects of leadership and obscuring the contribution of other important factors.

Meindl, Ehrlich, and Dukerich (1985) analyzed fluctuations of interest in leadership by examining the number of articles appearing in business magazines and papers (e.g., the *Wall Street Journal*) and in dissertations and scholarly papers that were concerned with the topic. They found that the frequency of such articles was correlated with levels of the New York Stock Exchange. When the market fell, the number of articles about leadership increased. In difficult economic times, interest in leadership grows, implying a belief or a hope that good leadership might reverse negative economic trends.

In another study reported by these authors, business school students read scenarios describing an organization. The scenarios included information about a number of aspects of the organization including the leadership, employee characteristics, market trends, and government regulatory issues. Students were asked to rate the relative contribution of these aspects to overall organizational performance. When performance levels were described as extreme, either very good or very poor, students rated leadership as a significantly more important cause of performance than when performance was at moderate levels.

Arguing that leadership is such a highly valued construct in our implicit theories that it can change our evaluations of other aspects of an organization, Meindl and Ehrlich (1987) had students rate the overall performance of an organization after reading scenarios that discussed several aspects of the organization, including leadership. In some of the scenarios, the descriptions of the organization's leadership ware more salient and extensive. When organizational leadership was prominent in a scenario, students had a more positive overall impression of the organization's performance. In other words, not only does high performance imply good leadership, but strong leadership also implies good performance.

These explanatory causal models of organizations may function to give people a sense of control and predictability in much the same way that Heider (1944) viewed the role of dispositional attribution. If people think that leadership is responsible for organizational effectiveness, it provides a controllable, nonrandom focus for efforts to modify organizational functioning. In support of this view, Meindl and Ehrlich (1988) reported data on personality characteristics associated with the tendency to overrate the importance of leadership.

These authors developed a Romance of Leadership Scale (RLS) to measure stable, individual differences in this tendency. The scale includes items like, "It is impossible for an organization to do well unless it has high quality leadership at the top," and "With a truly excellent leader, there is almost nothing that an organization can't accomplish." Meindl and Ehrlich reported that one of the only personal characteristics significantly correlated with the RLS score was internal locus of control. Apparently, people who believe that they are in control of important events in their lives also believe that leadership is a primary determinant of organizational effectiveness. Perhaps strong beliefs in leadership provide a sense of control over organizational outcomes.

The implication of Meindl's (1990) approach is that these beliefs in the overwhelming importance of leadership are exaggerations. This may well be true, but is it necessarily the case? Although the subjects in Meindl's experiments clearly make leadership attributions that are excessive in light of the information provided in the scenarios, we cannot assume that those assumptions are invalid in everyday life. It is easiest to mislead people about a particular event when we tap into assumptions based on more general experience with a phenomenon. For example, we are disinclined to drink out of bottles labelled "poison" even when, unknown to us, an experimenter has filled them with a harmless substance. Could it be that the tendency to attribute organizational outcomes to leadership is widespread, because leadership does, in reality, often influence productivity and performance?

Meindl (1990) offered this explanation of the romance effect; "A working assumption here is that people, through their direct and indirect experiences in and around organizations, generate theories about what makes organizations more or less effective" (p. 163). A reader might ask whether the "direct and indirect experiences" that have led to those beliefs must be in error. The only personal characteristic, besides locus of control, that was significantly correlated with the RLS score was age. Older persons scored higher on the scale than younger. If we assume that older people have had a greater opportunity for direct and indirect experience with organizational life, that experience may have taught them the value of good leadership for organizations. The jury is still out on the final answer to the question.

Meindl (1990) saved his most biting, and most incisive, criticisms of "hyper-romanticism" for the transformational and charismatic leadership theories, arguing that the heroic depictions of leaders in these theories are most in line with romantic distortions. Meindl (1988) asked business students to imagine being the subordinates of Ronald Reagan and Lee Iacocca and to rate them on the Bass' (1985) Multifactor Leadership Questionnaire. Scores on the transformational leadership factors, especially charisma, were significantly correlated with the students' scores on the Romance of Leadership Scale. The more prone an individual was to romantic beliefs, the more likely they were to perceive leaders as having transformational qualities.

Meindl (1990) offered an alternative view of charismatic leadership that focused on the experiences of followers and the social processes that occur among them, and gave much less attention to the characteristics or behaviors of leaders. Meindl argued that rather than being caused by leader traits, charismatic attributes could be regarded as social realities created by and shared among followers. Meindl regarded charisma as a process of social contagion.

For example, a group of people might be in a state of shared arousal (e.g., caused by stressful circumstances) that creates a strong need for identification and action. This notion of a readiness or need that makes a group susceptible to charismatic leadership is also present in House's (1977) view of the situational concomitants of charisma. However, in traditional models of charismatic leadership, it is the leader who creates or coalesces the felt need and shared response. Meindl's approach maintains that the need might arise quite independently from a leader. In fact, the arousal might simply be the result of social facilitation effects (Zajonc, 1965), and the arousal is potentially capable of misattribution (Schacter, 1964). In other words, a large crowd, such as might be in attendance at a political rally, would be excited by the noise, music, and presence of so many people. That excitement might become attached to the most salient object, that is, the leader addressing the crowd. (The interested reader might examine films of Adolph Hitler's Nuremburg rallies for the deft use of romantic imagery and stirring visual and auditory effects.)

The arousal might even be generated from within the potential followers as some latent need for heroic self-identification (Meindl & Lerner, 1983). The shared need/arousal is given a collective force by a few instigators, that is, informal leaders who get the social contagion effects started and create a consensus around the

charismatic leader designate. Meindl (1990) argued that follower-focused alternatives to leader-dominant approaches have the potential of generating new productive ways of thinking about leadership phenomena, that is, alternatives to the
conventional wisdom and its intellectual straightjacket effects.

## Dachler's Organismic-Evolutionary Perspective

Peter Dachler (1984, 1988) offered some social constructionist notions that are
quite compatible with Meindl's approach. Dachler (1984) argued that contemporary leadership theories miss the fundamental nature of organizational life. Management, he argued, isn't about individual leaders or leader–subordinate dyads
working on discrete task and goals, but rather organizations are collectivities that
must be regarded as social systems.

Traditional models of leadership and management arise from a "rational-design
perspective." This perspective is rooted in the positivist assumptions that the world
is knowable in discrete cause and effect relationships. Leadership involves influencing subordinates in dyads or groups to work toward specific goals and organizational objectives.

An alternative model that Dachler (1984, 1988) proposed arises from an "organ-
ismic-evolutionary perspective." In this perspective, the focus is on the group and
the way in which the group engages social and political processes with the purpose
of making sense out of their environment. The group develops rules arising out of
the socially constructed realities of these processes. Organizational goals become
symbols that provide meaning for everyday activities. Such organizational myths
and symbols might be more important in determining organizational functioning,
including the forms of leadership displayed, than are the traditionally studied
variables, such as the amount of directive behavior the leader exhibits.

The essence of Dachler's arguments are that the strong positivist influence on
leadership theory limits our perspectives and our chances for expanding our
approaches. We expect group effects to be caused by leaders, so that is the only
place we look for them. As a result, leadership effects are the only ones we are likely
to find, perpetuating the limitations on the development of the field.

## IMPLICATIONS OF COGNITIVE AND CONSTRUCTIONIST APPROACHES

A number of arguments can be generated to diminish the critical implications of
the constructionist position, that is, that leadership is of dubious value in explaining
organizational outcomes. For one thing, the effects of leaders on group and
organizational performance can be established, even if the relative degree of effect
is disputed (Day & Lord, 1988). Some models of leadership such as the contingency

model (Fiedler, 1978; Fiedler & Chemers, 1984) employ research designs that are relatively impervious to cognitive or attributional effects because they are based on independent, often objective, measures of leader characteristics, situational variables, follower reactions, and organizational effects. Even in models where reports by leaders or followers are susceptible to distortion through knowledge structures (e.g., implicit theories, prototypes), evidence of powerful effects for individual leaders are evident. For example, Bass & Avolio (1993) reported data in which correlations between subordinate ratings of transformational leadership were between .6 and .8 with superior ratings or objective organizational productivity measures. Even if the specifics of the rated transformational behaviors are distorted by cognitive biases, the relative advantage of some leaders over others is apparent.

Nonetheless, the implications of the cognitive and constructionist approaches for both theoretical and practical aspects of leadership are quite important and deserve contemplation. Perceptual biases create problems for leadership theorizing, research design, and organizational practice. Theories that do not reflect the important role played by perceptions and judgments are inadequate to explain the full range of leadership effects. Research methodologies that regard reports by leaders and followers as accurate measures of behavior and outcome, ignoring the biasing effects of implicit theories, increase the likelihood of inappropriate conclusions. Finally, organizational practices, like leadership training, performance appraisal, goal setting and the like, that assume that leaders are capable of making unbiased judgments about subordinate characteristics and behavioral causation run the risk of institutionalizing problematic practices.

The work on attributions for subordinate poor performance (Brown, 1984; Mitchell & Wood, 1980) suggests that egocentric biases are an inherent part of the perceptual process. Leadership models and practical interventions that assume accurate leader perceptions of subordinate needs or maturity levels must consider and address that issue. The data concerning the role of prototypes in shaping reports of leader behavior suggest that the factor structure of leader behavior measures like the Leader Behavior Description Questionnaire (Schriesheim & Kerr, 1977) or the Multifactor Leadership Questionnaire (Bass & Avolio, 1990b) may be in error, and the specific items that are included in the measures may not be accurate reflections of the behaviors actually enacted. This represents a serious threat to the validity of theories that are based on such measures.

At the particular level, the behavioral ratings or work evaluations of any individual leader are likely to be biased by categorical moderators and attendent processes, leading to inaccurate and unfair evaluations. Leaders whose personal characteristics match prototypes (e.g., dominant culture/gender) tend to be overrated, whereas nontraditional leaders are likely to be underrated.

Inferential processes that attribute causes for group or organizational outcomes raise other problems. The degree to which any particular manager or leader was responsible for a specific event may be exaggerated. In the general case, the relationship among leadership variables (e.g., leader behavior and subordinate satisfaction or superior rated performance) might be inflated. Possibly spurious relationships may cause us to perpetuate unproductive theoretical orientations and may impede the development of new paradigms, neglecting potentially important areas of study, such as follower effects.

## Implications for Current Theorizing

Not all leadership theories are equally damaged by the questions raised in consideration of cognitive biases and constructions. The theories most seriously called into question are those based on general descriptions that are subject to prototypical responding and those research programs that employ single-source methodologies where relations among variable are heavily susceptible to implicit theories of causation.

Most of the popular theories of leadership (Bennis & Nanus, 1985; Kouzes & Posner, 1987; Tichy & Devanna, 1986) are extremely vulnerable to "romance of leadership" effects (Meindl, 1990). Attention is focused almost exclusively on heroic leaders who are assumed to cause everything that happens in their organizations. These theories were developed from unstructured, free reports, often self-reports, that are very likely to be guided by cultural prototypes of effective leaders. Because the respondents in these studies are very similar in background, sharing cultural expectations, the descriptions of effective leadership provided reveal a false communality.

Another area of research made dubious by cognitive considerations is the body of work on influence strategies (Kipnis & Schmidt, 1982; Yukl & Falbe, 1990; Yukl & Tracey, 1992). The high level of agreement across sources on the prevalence and effectiveness of different strategies may reflect prevailing cultural assumptions about the appropriateness of the strategies, rather than actual incidences of the use of the strategies. Without any objective measures of behavior, we are hard put to separate these competing explanations.

Wounded, but not mortally, are theories like Bass' (1985) transformational leadership theory, in which the basic constructs of the theories (e.g., charisma, inspirational appeals, etc.) are questionnaire based. We know that the specific behaviors reported in leadership questionnaires are influenced by prototypes and do not always accurately reflect actual behavior. Bass and Avolio (1993) presented a good deal of high quality data that strongly suggests that observers can indeed agree on highly effective leadership when they observe and respond to it. We can probably rest assured that transformational leadership exists, but we can be less sanguine about the accuracy of the descriptions of the specific behaviors.

Another group of charismatic leadership theories suggests behavioral correlates for testing the construct (e.g., Conger & Kanungo, 1987; House, 1977). These models have not reported empirical data in their support, and are not, then, susceptible to criticisms in methodology. House and Shamir's (1993) self-concept theory of charisma fares quite well with respect to constructionist critiques because it places heavy emphasis on follower psychological states as mediating processes and it recognizes the pervasive role of prototypes and social contagion.

The transactional models vary dramatically in the injury they suffer from cognitive biases. Hollander's (1993) recent writings easily accommodate attributional processes in the leadership perceptions that are the basis of leader legitima-tion. In fact, a reading of the early Hollander work (1958) reveals that attribution processes were anticipated by the theory.

Graen's LMX theory (Graen & Scandura, 1987) does not weather these criti-cisms so well. Most of the studies of the effects of leadership exchanges employ single-source methodologies quite susceptible to cognitive consistency bias. Schri-esheim, Kinicki, and Schriesheim (1979) revealed that individual differences in leniency bias (i.e., a tendency to give positive evaluative ratings) inflate the relationship among positively valent leadership variables. For example, the finding that subordinates who report good exchanges with their superior also report higher job satisfaction and organizational commitment may reflect such leniency biases. Furthermore, the low levels of agreement between managers and their subordinates in their ratings of the quality of exchange (Liden, Wayne, & Stilwell, 1993; Scandura, Graen, & Novak, 1986) increase the possibility that such ratings do not reflect accurate assessments.

The behavioristically oriented models (e.g., Komaki, 1986; Sims & Lorenzi, 1992) make less use of inference in either research methods or practical suggestions and should be less susceptible to problems of cognitive biases. Although ratings of supervisory behavior are potentially susceptible to prototype driven errors, the high levels of interrater reliability reported in these studies probably reduces that concern to a degree. The choices of which behaviors to observe are probably affected by cultural and theoretical preconceptions.

Among the contingency theories, the effects are varied. Fiedler's (1967) contin-gency model uses research designs in which cognitive biases are not too problem-atic. Although it may be argued that a leader's assessment of the degree of control in the leadership situation might be distorted, it is rarely the case that outcome measures in such studies (e.g., subordinate satisfaction, group productivity) are measured from the same source. The complex interactions of leadership style and situational control that the model predicts are not easily explained by biases in inference. In much of Fiedler's research, performance measures were based on objective data, such as, tons of steel poured during an 8-hour shift (Cleven & Fiedler, 1956). Such criteria are less susceptible to bias than are subordinate reactions.

One constructionist criticism that may be relevant to the contingency model is a lack of attention to followers, who are clearly regarded as adjunct in the heavily leader-oriented model. Another potential trouble spot occurs in the Leader Match training program that teaches managers how to use the contingency model to improve their performance (Fiedler & Chemers, 1984). The training program relies on the manager's judgments of situational parameters and subordinate performance, which might be biased by ego-protective and self-serving biases.

Fiedler and Garcia's (1987) cognitive resource theory is actually given an explanatory boost by the thrust of the cognitive theories. Cognitive resource theory predicts that under high stress, leader experience is correlated with performance, whereas under low stress, leader intelligence is the better predictor. Cognitive research suggests that interpersonal stress can act as a cognitive load interfering with controlled processing (Gilbert, Krull, & Pelham, 1988). Chi, Glaser, and Farr (1988) reported that experts (i.e., highly experienced persons) have more accessible, better articulated, automatically processed knowledge structures, supporting the notion that experienced leaders should do better under stressful conditions that interfere with controlled processing.

The credibility of Vroom and Yetton's (1973) normative decision model is damaged by constructionist criticisms in all three areas of theory, method, and practice. Most of the research that tests the model relies on retrospective, self-reports by managers on what decision strategies they used and how successful they were. If managers' implicit theories of leadership agree with the principles of the Vroom and Yetton model, their reports of their behavior would support the theory, even if their self-reports were quite inaccurate. The application of the Vroom–Yetton–Jago model in practice relies on the leader's ability to judge situational variables like degree of support from followers, followers' reliability, and other such distortable perceptions.

Path–goal theory (House, 1971) likewise was frequently tested with research designs that asked managers or workers to rate aspects of their work environment, their leaders' behaviors, and their satisfaction or motivation. Implicit theories, leniency biases, and other cognitive consistency biases may contaminate the results in such studies.

# A Cautionary Note

Before we turn away from a leadership field left in tatters by the spectre of cognitive bias, we should recognize that weaknesses in research design with the *potential* for error do not always result in flawed results and fallacious theory. The findings of the cognitive researchers and the constructionist criticisms that arise therefrom should cause us to question our results and to seek better research procedures, but do not call for the wholesale rejection of what we have found. Because an error might occur does not mean that it has occurred.

Many valid findings in the social sciences have resulted from less than perfect methods. Meindl's (1990) findings that the effects of leadership on organizations can be exaggerated does not mean that judgments of leadership are exaggerated in real organizations. The finding by Lord and others (Lord & Maher, 1991) that perceptions and ratings of leader behavior and leader effectiveness are influenced by prototypes does not mean that the results of all studies employing leader behavior ratings are invalid.

We must take the results of leadership research with the proverbial "grain of salt," but we must not reject a large body of very useful data. We need to add constructionist principles in our theorizing and analysis, but we needn't discard all other sources of information. Perhaps the best approach for leadership theorizing, as in other scientific disciplines, is to view the body of research as a whole and ask what general principles seem best supported across a range of approaches and theories. The leadership "baby" is too valuable to be thrown out with the bath water.

# SOME CONCLUSIONS

This chapter made clear the great importance of perceptual processes in judgments made by leaders about followers and by followers about leaders. The actions that a leader takes with respect to direction and support of followers are based on the leader's understanding of their needs and desires. Similarly, the degree of legitimacy and authority the leader commands with subordinates is determined by their judgments of competency and commitment. These perceptions reflect a combination of accurate observations combined with some common, systematic biases. A comprehensive and integrated theory of leadership must include attention to the role of perception and judgment.

Real and imagined differences between groups of people can have powerful effects on social perceptions, as we shall see when we turn to the examination of the role of culture and gender in leadership processes, the subjects of the next two chapters.

# Chapter 8

## Influences of Culture on Leadership Processes

The first seven chapters have presented the major theoretical approaches and empirical developments in contemporary leadership research. A careful perusal of the references cited in those chapters would reveal that most of the contributions to these dominant perspectives came from studies conducted in Western Europe and North America. Of course, leadership is not now and never has been the exclusive dominion of modern, western, industrialized societies. It is reasonable to ask whether the general principles or specific characteristics of leadership processes are affected by cultural or subcultural differences.

### CULTURE AND VALUES

An initial question concerns whether there is sufficient variation across groups to warrant a concern with the generalizability of our theories. In a chapter on cultural differences in values in the *Handbook of Cross-Cultural Psychology* (Triandis & Brislin, 1980) Marisa Zavalloni makes the point that the members of every group, organization, or society evidence variability amongst themselves. However, when the variability between groups is sufficiently greater than the within-group variability, it is reasonable to ask whether such group differences reflect important influences on psychological processes. Punnett and Ronen (1984) reviewed 25 studies that assessed national differences in work-related attitudes and values. They reported that 17 of the studies revealed significant national or cultural differences explaining between 15 and 63% of the variance in individual responses.

In the first chapter of this book, the critical functions of organizations were discussed. Be they small work groups, large industrial organizations, or national societies, social collectives must maintain an internal integration and adapt to their external environments. For most of world history, the greatest challenge facing human societies was successful adaptation to the external environment in terms of economic survival. Physical environments limited and influenced potential adaptative patterns. Rainfall, arable land, natural resources, disease vectors, and such factors helped to determine viable subsistence patterns, such as hunting and gathering, gardening, agriculture. In turn, the demands that these economic patterns placed on members of the society influenced the systems of internal integration.

Subsistence technologies based on hierarchical authority systems requiring reliable and obedient workers tended to develop religious and political systems consistent with the values that would support those demands. Over time, the adaptive patterns became traditions passed from one generation to another, stabilizing the institutions, norms, and values that maintain the system.

Geert Hofstede (1984) referred to culture as the "collective mental programming that distinguishes groups of people" and compares the role of culture in collectivities to the role played by personality in the individual, that is, the aggregate of characteristics that constitute the individual's response to the environment. Harry Triandis (1993) employed a similar analogy stating

> ...culture is to society what memory is to individuals. It is the institutional memory of what has worked in the past, what was adaptive; these memories are widely shared, and become unstated assumptions about what is right or wrong, about how people should think, feel, and behave. (p. 71)

Both Hofstede and Triandis emphasized, from slightly different though compatible perspectives, the adaptive role of cultural practices and their pervasiveness in thought and action.

The impact of culture on human behavior could be studied from a number of viewpoints, but psychologists have found the construct of values to be a most useful entry point. In fact, Thomas Znaniecki (1918) thought that values would serve as the central construct of a new discipline of social psychology that would eventually become a general science of the "subjective" side of culture. Echoing that orientation, Zavalloni (1980) maintained that values express the central features of cultures or societies and "...refer to orientations toward what is considered desirable or preferable by social actors. As such, they express some relationship between environmental pressures and human desires" (p. 74).

Culture can be defined at many levels. For our purposes the national level is most useful because most of the research has been done at that level. However, questions of culture in terms of commonly held values can occur at other levels, such as distinctive subcultures.

## FROM CULTURAL VALUES TO LEADERSHIP THEORY

Interest in cultural or national differences in work-related values and attitudes has been sporadic over the last 30 years. Early studies (England & Lee, 1971, 1974

Haire, Ghiselli, & Porter, 1966; Whitely & England, 1980) established that differences in attitudes did exist between managers in different countries and that those differences could be explained by a number of factors including religion, language, and level of industrial development.

An interesting series of analyses by Ronen and his associates (Ronen & Kraut, 1977; Ronen & Shenkar, 1985) subjected data from a large number of studies to a clustering procedure. Using a nonparametic, multivariate procedure known as "smallest space analysis" (Guttman, 1968), patterns of correlation between countries on chosen variables yielded clusters showing similar patterns. Figure 8.1 presents the clusters reported by Ronen and Shenkar (1985). Countries closest to each other are most similar. A careful study of the clustering reveals that language, religion, geography, and level of development are the strongest contributors to the resultant pattern. For example, countries that share a common language (e.g., English–the United Kingdom, the United States, and Australia; or Spanish–Latin European and Latin American) cluster together. The similarity of countries with comparable levels of development is revealed by the representation that shows that for each linguistic or geographical culture, the more economically developed countries share a common space at the center of the figure (i.e., Sweden, Argentina, France, etc.).

The cluster analysis provides two interesting insights; that we can indeed differentiate cultural groupings in a coherent and systematic way, and that forces of both convergence and divergence are acting on the world cultural stage. As

FIG. 8.1. Country cluster-based employee attitudes.

societies around the world develop more similar technological bases and more homogeneous economies, we can expect to see them become more alike in values and attitudes. On the other hand, factors such as religious differences, made more salient by the rise of religious fundamentalism in recent years, may act to maintain or even increase differences across cultures. What does seem safe to conclude is that considerable cultural variability in values exists at the present time and will continue at least long enough to warrant careful consideration in contemporary theorizing.

## Hofstede's Value Dimensions

Interest in the impact of cultural values on organizational dynamics was given a tremendous boost by the work of Dutch psychologist, Geert Hofstede. Although earlier work on values revealed that culture played an important role in the development of work-related cognitions, the research was not guided by a systematic theoretical framework, was not comprehensive with respect to the cultures studied, and did not clearly relate values to organizational concepts like motivation and leadership. Hofstede's (1980, 1983, 1984) work directly addressed those deficiencies.

In his role as a consultant to a large multinational corporation, Hofstede administered a work-related values questionnaire to a very large sample of middle managers (ultimately over 100,000) from first 40, and later, over 50 countries. The questionnaire was an extension and elaboration of other value surveys, including Gordon's (1975, 1976) Survey of Personal Values. Factor analyses of responses to the questionnaire yielded four dimensions of work-related values, which Hofstede labeled Power Distance, Uncertainty Avoidance, Individualism–Collectivism, and Masculinity–Femininity.

Power Distance refers to the degree to which a culture considers large differences in power between individuals to be normal and appropriate. The members of cultures who score high on this value (e.g., the Far Eastern, Near Eastern, Arabian, and Latin American clusters) would endorse the idea that an order of inequality exists in the world and everyone has their rightful place in that order; that differences in power are a basic fact of society and questions of the legitimacy of power are irrelevant; that superiors and subordinates are different kinds of people; that those in power are entitled to special privileges, and so on. By contrast, low Power Distance cultures (e.g., the Nordic, Germanic, and Anglo clusters) believe that inequality in society should be minimized; people should be interdependent; subordinates and superiors regard each other as "people like me"; and power should be exercised only on a legitimate basis. Organizations in high Power Distance cultures tend to be more highly centralized, with taller organizational pyramids, and more hierarchical and authoritarian management than organizations in low Power Distance cultures.

The Uncertainty Avoidance dimension measures the extent to which a society is threatened by and tries to avoid uncertain and ambiguous situations; by establishing formal rules, intolerance for deviant ideas or behavior, and belief in absolute and inviolable truths. Societies high in Uncertainty Avoidance (e.g., the Latin European and Latin American clusters, and to a lesser degree the Arabian, Near Eastern, and Germanic clusters) agree that conflict and competition can unleash aggression and should be avoided; that there is a need for written rules and regulations; experts and authorities know a great deal more than ordinary citizens; and deviant persons and ideas are dangerous. Countries low in Uncertainty Avoid-· ance, such as the Nordic cluster, some of the Far Eastern societies such as Singapore, Hong Kong, and India, and to a lesser degree, the Anglo cluster, are more willing to take life as it comes; believe in the commmon sense of the average person; and are more willing to tolerate uncertainty and accept the risks of everyday life. Organizational practices typical of high Uncertainty Avoidance cultures stress uniformity, bureaucratic routinization, risk avoidance, and foster managers who are quite task oriented and concerned with the details of everyday activity.

One of the value dimensions with the greatest implications for social relations is that of Individualism versus Collectivism. Individualistic cultures, of which the United States is the most extreme exemplar along with the other members of the Anglo, Nordic, and Germanic clusters, believe that in society, everyone is supposed to take care of himself or herself; one's identity is grounded in the individual and in that person's achievements; and that every person has the right and the responsibility to develop their own initiative and independent self-realization. Collectivistic values, evinced by most of the world's cultures, especially the Latin American and Far Eastern clusters, emphasize the responsibilities to and support from one's in-group; the individual's duty to others; and the desirability of harmonious interpersonal relationships. Organizational dynamics in individualistic societies stress calculative exchanges between the organization and employee; place a high value on individual initiative; and encourage managerial practices based on expertise and rationality. Collectivist-guided organizations see the individual's loyalty to the organization in moral rather than calculative terms; treat personnel as members of a "family," and favor managerial practices that show concern for subordinates.

The Masculinity–Femininity dimension reflects the degree to which the dominant values in the society are those associated with a stereotypically masculine perspective, such as competition, assertiveness, and acquisition, or those of a more stereotypically feminine nature such as concern for others. High Masculinity cultures (e.g., Anglo, Germanic, and Latin American clusters; and the highest scorer on this dimension, Japan) endorse the view that men should be assertive and women nurturant; performance is what counts; ambition and achievement are desirable; and big and fast is good. High Femininity societies (e.g., the Nordic cluster, Thailand) view male and female roles as more similar; value quality of life over achievement; emphasize service to others; and value small and slow over big and fast. Organizations in Masculine cultures accept higher job stress; place careers above private lives; and have fewer, but more assertive women in better paid jobs. Organizations in Feminine cultures try not to interfere in employee's private lives; favor job designs that foster teamwork; and have more women in managerial positions.

One major thrust of Hofstede's writing is that organizational theories developed in the West, primarily in the United States, are not always applicable to other cultures. With respect to the impact of cultural values on leadership processes, Hofstede (1983) highlighted the importance of Individualism–Collectivism and Power Distance. Pointing out that the United States occupies the most extreme individualist position among contemporary nations, Hofstede argued that American leadership theories are uniquely concerned with the centrality of individual self-interest, whether that self-interest is directed to material outcomes such as pay and promotion, or toward less tangible outcomes such as personal growth. He pointed out that the word "duty," implying obligation toward others and society, is not mentioned in any U.S. leadership theory. In collectivist cultures, leadership is more of a group-focused phenomenon, in which one of the leader's most important functions is to coalesce an "in-group" identity among team members, thereby eliciting from followers the selflessness and loyalty owed to in-groups.

The United States ranks at about the middle of the Power Distance dimension being far less autocratic than countries like France, Belgium, or Mexico, but at the same time, less egalitarian than the truly low Power Distance countries like Denmark, Sweden, or Israel. As many of the theories already discussed have pointed out, one of the most central issues in leadership is the degree of subordinate participation in decision making and control over job activities (e.g., Fiedler & Chemers, 1984; Hersey & Blanchard, 1977; Vroom & Yetton, 1973). In the United States, participative decision making is generally interpreted as giving subordinates a voice in analyzing a problem and suggesting solutions, with the leader retaining ultimate decision authority. This pattern is the decision style that Vroom and Yetton's (1973) normative decision theory refers to as "consultative," and is probably the most commonly approved style among American managers (Thompson & Chemers, 1993).

Hofstede indicated that in countries higher in Power Distance than the United States, subordinates neither expect nor desire to participate in decision making, and their behavior makes it difficult for their leaders to behave any way other than autocratically. On the other hand, in less autocratic cultures, subordinates often take the iniative toward upward influence and control, not waiting for their superiors to invite participation. The industrial democracy movements in the Nordic and Germanic cluster countries are indications of the widespread expectation of equal power in organizational governance.

A recent study by Welsh, Luthans, and Sommer (1993) supports Hofstede's observation. Welsh et al. reported on the results of the introduction of three organizational productivity interventions popular in the United States to a recently privatized Russian factory. The three procedures were enhanced use of extrinsic rewards, behavioral management (both of these being methods of control), and participative management. The first two procedures led to significant increases in worker productivity, whereas the participative management intervention actually caused a decrease in performance.

Hofstede and Bond (1988) described the ideal leader in a society that is low on Power Distance and high on Individualism, such as the United States, as a "resourceful democrat." In cultures with the reverse pattern of high Power Distance and high Collectivism, the ideal leader would be a "benevolent autocrat," similar to a good father. A study by Ayman and Chemers (1983) proved consistent with Hofstede and Bonds' prediction with respect to benevolent autocratic leadership. Ayman and Chemers focused on a group of Iranian middle managers, asking subordinates to provide ratings of leader behavior and satisfaction with their leaders, and asking superiors of the focal managers to provide ratings of leadership performance.

The instrument used to obtain leader behavior ratings was the venerable Leader Behavior Description Questionnaire (Halpin & Winer, 1957), but with a significant modification. An earlier study conducted in Iran by Chemers (1969) had secured leader behavior ratings from Iranian subjects and found, through subsequent factor analysis, that the ratings did not yield the two independent factors of Initiation of Structure and Consideration typical of ratings by American subjects. Rather, the two factors collapsed into a single evaluative dimension including both structuring and considerate items. Ayman and Chemers (1983) hypothesized that the single factor structure might represent the ideal Iranian leader, directive and caring, like a stern father figure, so they added two new items to the behavioral rating scale; "My leader is like a kind father" and "My leader is a good leader." Factor analysis of the Iranian subordinate ratings by Ayman and Chemers yielded a single factor containing most of the items from both the Initiation of Structure and Consideration factors, and the two new items loaded very strongly on this general factor.

Ayman and Chemers labeled the factor, "Benevolent Paternalism," and found that it was significantly correlated with superior ratings of leader performance and subordinate ratings of satisfaction, reflecting an ideal leader pattern for Iranian culture. An interesting ramification of this finding relates to the fact that the leaders in the Chemers (1969) study were U.S. citizens working in Iran and rated by Iranians, whereas the leaders in Ayman and Chemers' (1983) study were Iranian managers rated by their own Iranian subordinates. The implication of these results is that the structure of the leader behavior ratings may not have been determined by the actual behavior of the leaders, Americans in one case and Iranians in the other, but by the implicit theories of leadership held by the Iranian raters. This analysis provides a form of cross-cultural support for the arguments put forward by Lord and Maher (1991) discussed in the last chapter.

A recent series of studies resulting from a collaboration between Hofstede and Bond, reveals the dangers of ethnocentric research strategies and the benefits of international collaboration. In 1984, Hofstede and Bond reported the results of a reanalysis of data collected using the Rokeach Value Survey (Rokeach, 1973) from a number of samples in East Asia and Australia (Ng et al., 1982). Factor analyses of data from the Rokeach scale, developed in the United States, yielded considerable overlap with Hofstede's (1980) value dimensions, developed in Western Europe. Neither of these surveys had any signficant input from non-Western sources.

However, in collaboration with a number of Chinese scientists, Michael Bond developed the Chinese Value Survey (CVS), reflecting the cultural values of that society. The CVS was translated and administered in 22 countries around the world. Hofstede and Bond (1988) factor analyzed the CVS and found four major dimensions of values. Three of these corresponded to Hofstede's dimensions of Power Distance, Individualism–Collectivism, Masculinity–Femininity, but not Uncertainty Avoidance. Hofstede and Bond maintained that the central issue of the Uncertainty Avoidance dimension, the search for stable truth in the world, is a preoccupation distinctly associated with the religions of Judaism, Christianity, and Islam that purport to know the truth. East Asian religions, such as Buddhism, Confucianism, and Shintoism, do not believe that any person can know the truth, so people raised in these religious cultures are less concerned about issues of absolute truth.

The fourth dimension found by Hofstede and Bond, not present in the analyses of the earlier surveys, was a dimension they labeled "Confucian Dynamism." The authors explained that the central principles of Confucian teaching are the following;

(1) that the stability of society is based on unequal relationships between people; (2) that the family is the prototype of all social organization with its emphasis on harmony, dignity, and restraint; (3) that virtuous behavior toward others consists of treating them as one would like to be treated, which does not however include loving one's enemies; and (4) that virtue with regard to one's tasks in life consists of trying to acquire skills and education, working hard, not spending more than necessary, being patient, and perservering. (p. 8)

Hofstede and Bond's (1988) newly discovered value dimension included most of these Confucian teachings, but some were positively related to the factor whereas others were negatively related, the determining factor being the degree of "dynamism" and forward-looking nature of the principle. Thus, the positive pole of the Confucian Dynamism dimension included future-oriented concepts, such as thrift and perserverance, as well as acceptance of status differences and a sense of shame. The negative pole, less dynamic and more past and present oriented, included the principles of personal stability, saving face, respect for tradition, and reciprocation of favors and gifts. In data from 22 countries, the Confucian Dynamism dimension was found to be strongly associated with country-level economic growth over the period 1965–1985.

Hofstede and Bond argued that the values of Confucian Dynamism reflect a modern version of long-established Eastern, especially Chinese, values that are uniquely suited to an East Asian brand of entrepreneurship. The highest ranking countries on the Confucian Dynamism dimension were the so-called "Five Dragons" of Asian economic growth; Japan, South Korea, Hong Kong, Taiwan, and Singapore. The philosophically inclined reader will recognize that we seem to have come full circle on Weber's (1947) thoughts on "The Protestant Ethic and the Spirit of Capitalism," in which he argued that the virtues extolled by European Protestant theology (i.e., thrift, hard work, and the accumulation of wealth) were the antecedents of capitalism in the Protestant nations.

In a recent presentation made to the American Academy of Management and published in 1993, Hofstede summarized his thoughts on cultural differences in management. The Chinese work encouraged him to add a fifth dimension to his value survey reflecting a long- versus short-term time orientation. He also listed three major differences between American conceptions of management and leadership and those of other cultures. First, American approaches stress market processes, even in the description of interpersonal relations. Managers and subordinates make deals (i.e., contracts) by which self-interests are harnessed to organizational goals. This characteristic is reflected in our transactional and exchange theories of leadership and of interpersonal relations in general (Graen & Scandura, 1987; Thibaut & Kelley, 1959).

A second point of U.S. uniqueness is, of course, how individualistically focused all of our theories are with issues of individual gain, self-actualization, and personal growth. A third point is that American approaches are extremely focused on the leader as the primary determinant of subordinate motivation and performance. Hofstede illustrated the limitation of this viewpoint by identifying stronger influences than leadership in other cultures, such as peer group pressures in collectivist cultures such as Japan, and occupational training and pride in craftsmanship in Germany.

The views of Meindl (1990) on the overemphasis of attention to leaders and the underemphasis on the role of social groups as influence agents, of Dachler (1984) on the constraining role of leader-centered theories, and of Kerr and Jermier's (1978) substitutes for leadership concept assume a new relevance in this cross-cultural context.

Chemers (1991) recently argued that cultural values must be included as a moderating variable in any grand contingency theory of leadership. Factors like follower needs and expectations, leadership prototypes and behaviors, task characteristics such as uncertainty, have dramatically different implications in different cultural contexts. Despite the fact that culture adds yet another level of complexity to our theories, it also holds the potential for greater understanding and practical utility.

## Subjective Culture and Leadership

Harry Triandis (1972) was one of the first American psychologists to recognize the pervasive role of cultural differences in what we attend to, remember, value, and intend. In a recent chapter, Triandis (1993) turned his attention to the role of cultural values in leadership, providing several interesting insights on the topic.

Based on an extensive analysis of the individualism–collectivism value distinction (Triandis, 1990), Triandis made the important point that considerable variation can exist within a culture. It is important to recognize that "idiocentrics" (i.e., individualistically oriented persons) are present in collectivistic societies, just as there are "allocentrics" in individualistic groups. We would expect such "deviants" to be out of the mainstream in their societies and to seek out opportunities in the society compatible with their orientations. For example, allocentrics in an individualistic society might join a commune or other collectively organized entity. Idiocentrics in collectivistic settings might seek to disengage from the strong pull of the in-group, even migrating to more individualistic countries.

Ayman and Chemers (1991) studied leadership in a collectivist society (Mexico) and found that only the relatively idiocentric leaders in their sample showed a strong relationship between their inner personality and their outward relationships with others. In other words, it's hard to "do your own thing" in a society that expects everyone to follow the same rules regardless of their personal wishes. Triandis (1993) made the point that collectivists are context dependent and other oriented, and try to suit their behavior to the demands of the situation.

Hofstede's (1980) dimensions are not, of course, the only way to slice the pie of culture. Triandis (1978) presented empirical evidence that a common set of relational dimensions, rather than values, can be applied to relationships in every culture. These dimensions are (a) association versus disassociation, that is, is this a relationship I should enter?; (b) superordination versus subordination, that is, who is the dominant party in this relationship?; (c) intimacy versus formality, that is, what are the appropriate behaviors for this relationship?; and (d) overt versus covert, that is, is this a relationship to be publically acknowledged?

Alan Fiske (1991) built a taxonomy of relational orientations that incorporates the four dimensions described here, and Triandis (1993) related Fiske's orientations to leadership patterns. Fiske's relational orientations reflect the assumptions that underlie the way people structure social relationships in various contexts in different cultures.

One orientation is "community sharing," which emphasizes principles of association in a collectivist mode. Guiding aspects of this orientation are people's fears of isolation, loneliness, and abandonment. Societies with this orientation are characterized by strong in-groups with large amounts of generosity and concern for others. Decisions are made by consensus, and important social relationships, such as marriage, are determined by love rather than by tradition or financial advantage.

"Authority ranking" is an orientation based on asymmetrical power in relationships. It is similar to concepts in Hofstede's Power Distance and the Confucian idea of unequal relationships. Subordinates show respect, deference, loyalty, and obedience to the boss.

The third orientation, called "equality matching," emphasizes reciprocity, equality, equal distribution of rewards, and social justice. Interpersonal relations emphasize a diminishment of status differentiation.

"Market pricing" refers to a form of social relationship guided by profits and costs, much like exchange theories (Thibaut & Kelley, 1959). Important values undergirding this orientation are fairness and equity, individual achievement, rational decision-making, and individualism.

According to Triandis (1993), the ideal leader in community sharing would be the nurturant leader who says "we all work together until the work is done, then each takes what is needed." In authority ranking, it is the charismatic leader who expects the lower ranks to do all the dirty work and like it. In equality matching, all group members work together and share and share alike, whereas in market pricing, the best leader is the one who gives the most rewards to the biggest contributor to task success.

Formal studies linking the relational orientations to national cultures and leadership have not yet been reported. It is apparent, however, that although one orientation or another might dominate in a culture, all cultures will be a blend of different orientations in different contexts, or perhaps rankings of desirability of different orientations in specific contexts. For example, in the United States, marriage values are based on the community sharing principle, which is also present in our feelings about charity and the unfortunate, but the clearly dominant orientation is market pricing for most situations. In leadership, Americans probably favor market pricing relations in which people are rewarded on merit, but equality matching is acceptable and even desirable in situations that call for teamwork and the subordination of individual strivings. The star basketball player who is vigorously "market pricing" oriented in the privacy of the salary negotiation session becomes a paragon of "equality matching" in the championship postgame interview, for example, "It was a team effort, and I owe it all to my teammates/coach/parents/and so forth."

# Cultural Differences in Self-Construal: Implications for Leadership

Hazel Markus and Shinobu Kitayama (1991) epitomize the strong interest in cultural influences that has developed recently in social psychology. Markus and Kitayama focused on differences between individualistic and collectivist cultures in how the self is construed. Speaking about the "independent" self and the "interdependent" self, they addressed the implications of those differences in cognitive, emotional, and motivational processes. Although not directly concerned with leadership, many of the insights generated by their analysis are quite applicable to important issues in leadership theory.

*Cognition.* The cognitive processes involved in "self-relevant" information processing are likely to be quite different for the independent who focuses on inner dispositional states (e.g., how do I feel about this event) as opposed to the interdependent whose focus is on the feelings, desires, and expectations of significant others and the relationships with those others. That difference in focus is likely to have important consequences on cognition.

Interdependents are likely to be interpersonally sensitive and have a great deal of information about other people and the individual's relationship with them, whereas the independent is likely to be sensitive to his or her own feelings and to have extensive information about his or her own abilities, needs, and desires. For the interdependent, information about the self will be embedded in a social context. The self is, in fact, defined by the context, that is, a different self for the role of son from the self in the role of student, or friend, or colleague.

This sensitivity and empathy to others and the perception of the self in social context is likely to drastically reduce the tendency toward the fundamental attribution error (Ross, 1978). The interdependent person knows that behavior is context specific, so may look for the causes of behavior in situational contexts. As we saw in the work on attribution of causes for subordinate poor performance (Brown, 1984; Mitchell & Wood, 1980), the fundamental attribution error can be a very problematic tendency for a leader, one that may be less pronounced in collectivist cultures.

*Emotion.* Positive emotional states will result when one's view of the self is promoted and enhanced, but different construals of the self will involve different criteria for that outcome. The independent self is reinforced by personal and autonomous achievement, whereas the interdependent self is promoted through social acceptance in harmonious relationships. Thus, the conditions that elicit emotions may be different for different types of people and the ways in which emotion is expressed may also be different.

For the independent, "ego-focused" emotions, such as satisfaction, anger, and pride, will be commonly felt and expressed, but those emotions may be suppressed by the interdependent because their effects on others may disturb harmonious relations. For the interdependent, other-focused emotions, such as sympathy, communion, and shame, may be closer to the surface. Markus and Kitayama reported that in addition to the two major dimensions of emotion found in the West (i.e., pleasantness and activation), Japanese studies reveal a third dimension related to the degree of engagement and connectedness in relationships. The engagement dimension can have both positive and negative poles. For example, the emotion labeled *"oime,"* referring to a feeling of unresolved indebtedness to another, is felt as a more negative emotion than either sadness or anger.

Many theories of leadership, especially charismatic leadership, place considerable emphasis on the positive impact of emotional states that reveal confidence and optimism (e.g., House, 1977). However, the way that such feelings are experienced and expressed may be quite different for independent and interdependent leaders. Likewise, the expression of emotions of followers, such as dissatisfaction, anxiety, or hostility, important components of many leadership theories (e.g., Fiedler & Chemers, 1984; Vroom & Yetton, 1973) may be quite different or at the very least, more subtle in less egocentric cultures.

Meindl (1990), for example, argued that follower emotional arousal is a determinant of attributions of charismatic qualities to leaders. In a laboratory study, Mayo, Pastor, and Meindl (1992) had subjects rate the charismatic qualities of two videotaped leaders while under high- or low-arousal conditions induced by riding a stationary bicycle. In the high-arousal conditions, attributions of charisma were significantly more extreme. If culture helps to determine what conditions (e.g., crises or threats) are most likely to arouse followers, the manifestation of charisma will vary across cultures.

*Motivation.* Motivational factors are central to almost every theory of leadership theory. In many models (e.g., path–goal theory, House, 1971), the leader's main function is to affect the subordinates' motivational states. Independent

persons are motivated to fulfill personal needs, whereas interdependents are motivated to maintain relationships. Specific relationship-oriented motives would include familiar ones, like the need for affiliation, as well as those less common in
the West, like the needs for deference or the need to avoid blame.

A central motivational construct in Western social psychology is the need for
cognitive consistency, such as cognitive dissonance that arises from the need to have
public actions agree with private dispositions (Festinger & Carlsmith, 1959). However,
in a society in which one's public actions are supposed to be determined not by one's
own inner dispositions but by the expectations and desires of others, cognitive consistency, at least between thought and action, is not likely to be as important.

A motive of considerable importance in leadership theorizing is the need for
achievement. In the West, the achievement motive is satisfied by individual,
autonomous achievement. In more interdependent cultures, however, achievement
can mean having the group of which one is a part achieve, or it can even mean
achievement in terms of being accepted, that is, gaining subjective social approval
rather than some form of objectively defined success.

Jean Lipman-Blumen (Lipman-Blumen, Handley-Isaksen, & Leavitt, 1983)
developed a theory of "achieving styles" in which she defined nine different ways
in which people can seek achievement. The most highly valued routes to achievement for respondents in the United States are the "direct" styles, which involve
achievement through intrinsic features of successful task performance or through
competition with or domination of others. However, other styles of achieving
include social styles, such as networking or using connections, collaborating, and
contributing to another person's success, or more passive styles like relying on
others for help or experiencing achievement vicariously through the achievements
of a person with whom one shares a close relationship. Following Markus and
Kitayama (1991), we might expect the more passive and social styles to be far more
acceptable in some cultures than in others.

The cultural differences in the nature of motivation hold profound implications
for leadership. Leaders are supposed to increase the motivation of their followers
by recognizing what followers need and making it easier for them to meet their
needs (House, 1971), by modeling and arousing motivational states consistent with
task objectives (House, 1977; House & Shamir, 1993), or by encouraging new
motives (e.g., Bass, 1985). In most contemporary theories, the motives assumed to
be predominant in followers are personal growth and individual achievement
(Hersey & Blachard, 1977; Manz & Sims, 1980; Sims & Lorenzi, 1992) But an
interdependently oriented follower might desire a close communion with the leader
rather than personal growth, or may act out of loyalty to the leader and the group
rather than for personal achievement or material gain.

The discussion of attributions by leaders in Chapter 7 highlighted the importance
of the self-serving bias (Weiner et al., 1972), one of the most robust phemonena in
social psychology. Markus and Kitayama (1991) reported that the self-serving bias
may not be so common in Japan where a different sort of self is being served. For
example, whereas Americans often have inflated views of their own traits and
abilities (e.g., 70% of college students consider themselves to be above average in

leadership ability; Myers, 1987), Japanese students tend to see themselves as about average on most traits and abilities.

Markus and Kitayama raise the question of whether such modesty may be primarily impression management (i.e., acting modest is what is expected) or whether the lack of self-focus actually leads interdependents to be less concerned with and less prone to self-inflation. Markus and Kitayama reported on a study by Shikanai that found a "reverse" self-serving bias among Japanese students who attributed failure on an anagrams task internally (i.e., to lack of effort) and success externally (i.e., to an easy task).

It is interesting to contemplate the relative adaptiveness of such attributions for a work setting. An attribution of failure to a lack of effort should energize the person to try harder on the next opportunity, potentially resulting in better performance. An attribution of success to an easy task does not relieve the individual of the necessity to work just as hard to perform well the next time, especially because subsequent failure on a task declared to be easy may be especially shameful. Thus, the Japanese attribution pattern results in a modest self-presentation, unlikely to cause resentment in others, while at the same time not diminishing motivation to perform well in the future.

Another reason that task failure may not elicit ego-protective attributions, according to Markus and Kitayama, is that task success may not be the primary route to personal satisfaction for the interdependent. Markus and Kitayama alluded to Claude Steele's (1988) research on self-affirmation, which showed that an ego threat to one aspect of a person's self-esteem can be compensated for by affirming some other important aspect. Thus, the interdependent person who fails at a task, but who succeeds at maintaining harmonious relations, has affirmed an important aspect of the self.

Consistent with this analysis are two studies that reveal leadership orientation to be a moderator of personal satisfaction. In both a laboratory experiment (Rice, Marwick, Chemers, & Bentley, 1982) and a field study (Ayman & Chemers, 1983), task-motivated (low LPC) leaders showed a strong association between satisfaction and task success, whereas relationship-motivated (high LPC) leaders showed no relationship between task success and satisfaction, but relationship-motivated leaders did manifest a strong correlation between group harmony and personal satisfaction.

The Markus and Kitayama (1991) analysis provides a wealth of potential hypotheses on how cultural factors might affect the basic processes undergirding leadership relations.

## LEADERSHIP THEORY
## IN CULTURAL PERSPECTIVE

The previous section presented research on values, which has implications for leadership theory. This section discusses cross-cultural research that had its direct origins in the leadership literature.

# Misumi's Performance-Maintenance Theory of Leadership

Hofstede (1993) argued that leadership research and theory reflect cultural characteristics of the investigators as well as those of the subjects and the phenomena. An extensive program of research conducted in Japan by Jyuji Misumi (Misumi & Peterson, 1985) examined the structure and dynamics of effective leadership. The Far Eastern emphasis on patient, long-term approaches to organizational problems is reflected in the longevity and coherence of the Misumi research program.

Misumi was inspired by the early U.S. leadership studies of Lewin et al. (1939), Bales (1950), and Cartwright and Zander (1968). Misumi felt that there must be basic functions that are common to all leadership efforts, even if they manifest themselves differently across specific situations (Misumi & Peterson, 1985). The two functions identified were the performance function, which involves forming and reaching group goals, and the maintenance function, which involves preserving group social stability.

These two functions bear obvious similarity to the Initiation of Structure and Consideration factors of the Leader Behavior Description Questionnaire (Halpin & Winer, 1957), and the concordance between the constructs runs deeper than a surface similarity. Misumi (1984) developed a 24-item questionnaire measure and conducted a factor analysis of the responses of over 5,000 Japanese workers and managers. A clear two-factor structure was found. Examples of items that load strongly on the Performance (P) factor include: Is your superior strict about observing regulations? Does your superior urge you to complete your work by the time he has specified? Does your superior try to make you work to your maximum capacity? Does your superior ask you for reports about the progress of your work? The Performance factor embodies an emphasis on planning, guidance, and pressure for production. Exemplary items from the Maintenance (M) factor include: Is your superior concerned about your future benefits like promotions and pay raises? Does your superior treat you fairly? Do you think your superior trusts you? Generally, does you superior support you? Consideration, friendship, and easing of tension are the main components of this factor.

The performance–maintenance theory research program included both experimental studies in which leaders were trained to demonstrate specific behaviors (e.g., Misumi & Shirakashi, 1966) as well as field studies of existing work groups (e.g., Misumi & Tasaki, 1976). The consistent finding of these studies was that leadership that combines both Performance and Maintenance functions is superior, both in terms of work group performance and follower satisfaction, over either set of behaviors enacted alone and far superior to laissez-faire leadership that is low on both factors (Misumi & Peterson, 1985).

The superior effects of PM leadership are especially apparent in long-term relationships. Sometimes in the initial stages of group development and performance, the P factor in isolation yields results equal to PM, but over time, that effect changes and P leadership alone begins to engender negative outcomes. The positive effects of PM over time seem to reflect an interaction of the P and M functions.

Misumi and Peterson (1985) reported that the correlation of the Performance factor with group productivity is moderated by the presence of Maintenance behavior such that the correlation is considerably higher when M is present.

The finding that the best Japanese leaders combine task-directed behaviors with considerate, interpersonally directed behavior is consistent with similar effects reported for Iranian managers (Ayman & Chemers, 1983) and for Indian managers (Sinha, 1990). Many theories of leadership developed in the United States regard these two functions as independent of one another, if not actually mutually anti-thetical. The explanation for this divergence across cultures may lie in the different values that guide subordinate needs and expectations in these cultures.

In the extremely individualistic and moderately democratic culture of the United States, many subordinates have strong needs to participate in decision making and to have autonomy over their own job functions. Intrinsic motivation is thought to arise from the opportunity to gain meaningful self-esteem-enhancing feedback from autonomous activity (Deci & Ryan, 1980; Hackman & Oldham, 1976). An American leader's highly directive and controlling behaviors would preclude a subordinate's perception of the leader as also considerate and trusting. On the other hand, in the high Power Distance, collectivist cultures of Iran, India, and Japan, subordinates have less need for individualistic expressions of self through autono-mous achievement or participation in decision making, and a directive and demand-ing leader who is also friendly and considerate evokes the perception of both benevolent paternalism and the ideal leader.

The similarity of the main constructs of performance–maintenance theory to those of many American and European theories raises questions about the univer-sality of basic leadership constructs and the generalizability of their measurement. Smith, Misumi, Tayeb, Peterson, and Bond (1989) undertook a cross-cultural comparison of Misumi's (Misumi & Peterson, 1985) constructs. Smith et al. (1989) administered a questionnaire to shop-floor workers and their immediate supervisors in Britain, the United States, Japan, and Hong Kong. The questionnaire contained 20 items from the Performance–Maintenance measure (Misumi & Peterson, 1985) and another 36 specially developed items that described very specific behaviors dealing with the particular way in which the supervisor handled concrete problems, for example, "How much of the information available to your superior concerning the organization's plans and performance is shared with the work group?" or "When your superior learns that a member is experiencing personal difficulties, does your superior arrange for other members to help with the person's workload?"

The results are quite interesting. At the broadest level, factor analyses of the scales yielded the two-factor solution, with a task/performance factor and a consid-eration/maintenance factor, in all four countries. However, the specific items from the Performance–Maintenance questionnaire that loaded on each factor were not always the same in all countries. Some items, such as "Does your superior treat you fairly?" were common to the Maintenance factor in every country, and an item like "Does your superior urge you to complete work within a specified time?" loaded on the Performance factor in all countries. Other items, however, such as "Does your superior let you know about plans and tasks for your day-to-day work?"

showed much stronger loading on the Performance factor for workers from the Anglo cultures than for those from the Asian cultures.

Turning to the specific behaviors, the influence of cultural differences was more dramatic. Only 8 of the 36 specific behaviors loaded on the same factors in all cultures. It was more common for the behaviors to be associated more or less strongly with each factor in different countries, and sometimes for a behavior actually to be associated with different factors in different cultures. For example, in the Asian sample, a strong Maintenance behavior was found for the supervisor to discuss a subordinate's poor performance with other members of the group rather than to confront the subordinate directly. However, that behavior was a negative example of Maintenance for the Western cultures. The high M supervisor in China, for example, was one who tactfully resolved personal difficulties in an indirect manner, whereas the high M supervisor in Britain and the United States was one who shared task-related information with the subordinate.

In an analysis conceptually similar to the Smith et al. (1989) leader behavior survey, Schmidt and Yeh (1992) made a cross-national comparison of influence tactics. Schmidt and Yeh administered the Kipnis and Schmidt (1982) measure of influence strategy usage to samples of managers in England, Australia, Japan, and Taiwan. Factor analyses of the responses yielded a factor structure quite similar to that reported for managers in the United States. However, the particular tactics that loaded on each factor varied across cultures and reflected the differences in values between the countries sampled. For example, for the Asian samples, some of the more controlling tactics that normally load on the Assertiveness factor in American studies, showed up on the Reason factor. The authors quoted the Chinese aphorism of leadership advice, "Give benefit, but show authority," which reveals the acceptability and appropriateness of authoritarian aspects of leadership for high Power Distance cultures.

The implications to be drawn from this work on leader behavior and influence strategies may be that the basic functions of leadership are, indeed, universal. Leadership involves a job to be done and people with whom to do it. It seems obvious, then, that the leader must attend to both of these elements. There are enough common features in task effectiveness (e.g., the work must be accomplished in a reasonable amount of time) and in interpersonal relations (e.g., supervisors who are untrustworthy are unlikely to be appreciated by people who depend on them), so that when broad questions about effective leadership are asked, commonalities appear. It is also apparent, however, that cultural variability in values, needs, and expectations, ensures that the ways in which these two functions are most effectively executed will vary dramatically across cultures.

The cross-national comparisons on leader behaviors and influence strategies also suggest that the relative universality of a leadership theory depends on the level of analysis. At the level of the basic functions of leadership (e.g., task/performance and relationship/maintenance), cross-cultural generalizability seems warranted, but when we use a finer grained analysis (e.g., specific behaviors or influence tactics), cultural differences become more prominent. The contingency theories, with their emphasis on the situational context, might provide a productive point of analysis for examining questions of cross-cultural generalizability. Triandis (1993) made this point eloquently by saying, "Contingency theories, of course, acknowledge the role of situational moderators, and culture is the greatest of all moderators" (p. 168).

# CONTINGENCY THEORIES IN CULTURAL CONTEXT

In a recent paper examining the "cultural universality" of contemporary leadership theory, Chemers (1991) analyzed the significance of cultural parameters for the major contingency theories (e.g., the contingency model, Fiedler & Chemers, 1984; path–goal theory, House, 1971; and normative decision theory, Vroom & Yetton, 1973). Chemers argued that all the contingency theories are governed by the concept of match or fit between leader actions and situational variables. However, several different aspects of match are present in these theories.

For example, in the contingency model, there is the match between the leader's values, self-concept, or style with the amount of predictability and control in the situation that affects the leader's sense of ease, comfort, and confidence. In path–goal theory, the most important sort of match is between the leader's behavior and the subordinate's needs. In normative decision theory, the most significant aspect of match is between the group's decision-making pattern and the demands of the task environment. Each of these forms of match may be differentially susceptible to cultural influences.

## The Contingency Model

If leadership match is conceptualized in subjective terms, that is, leaders who have a good fit between their orientation and the situation will experience more positive emotional states (such as confidence, enthusiasm, an upbeat mood) that create an atmosphere conducive to productivity and satisfaction, match becomes a determinant of an internal psychological state. Effects on internal psychological states might have a universal applicability in that cultural norms may be less relevant to privately experienced states. Some evidence supports this view.

In a study of administrators in the United States (reported in chap. 3), Chemers et al. (1985) found that in-match leaders reported less job stress and stress-related illness than out-of-match leaders. Sanshiro Shirakashi (1991) closely replicated the procedures of that study with a sample of Japanese managers. The results were strikingly similar to those obtained in the United States, despite the tremendous disparity in cultural values between the United States and Japan.

The divergence between internal states and external effects of leadership has been investigated in a series of studies by Ayman and Chemers initially undertaken to test the cross-cultural validity of the contingency model. A first study (Ayman & Chemers, 1983) employed the traditional LPC and situational control measures (Fiedler, Chemers, & Mahar, 1976) with a group of middle managers in Iran. The effects of match were assessed via superior ratings of group performance and subordinate ratings of leader behavior and job satisfaction. Match effects were in the direction predicted by the contingency model, but were weak and nonsignificant.

Ayman and Chemers hypothesized that a collectivist culture like Iran would have very tight normative prescriptions for appropriate leader behavior (Pelto, 1968), and the expression of leadership orientation might have been inhibited in the interest of conformity to expectations. To test this possibility, Ayman and Chemers included the Self-monitoring scale (Snyder, 1974) in a series of follow-up studies (Ayman, 1983; Ayman & Chemers, 1991; Chemers & Ayman, 1985). The Self-monitoring scale measures the extent to which a person is sensitive and responsive to social expectations. Low self-monitors who are strongly guided by their personal attitudes and beliefs are more likely to allow their personal style and values to affect their leadership than high self-monitors who strive to meet social expectations.

In one study, Chemers and Ayman (1985) interviewed 100 managers in Mexican organizations, after collecting responses to the LPC and the Self-monitoring scales. Analyses indicated that low self-monitors revealed very clear differences between task-oriented leaders (who described an ideal leader as decisive, knowledgeable, and adaptive) and relationship-oriented leaders (who described the ideal leader as understanding, open minded, and concerned about subordinates). Among high self-monitors, no differences were found between task- and relationship-oriented managers, both of whom described the ideal leader in terms that included both directive and relational aspects. High self-monitors were providing the socially accepted prototype of an effective leader.

Using organizational surveys in several Mexican organizations, Ayman and Chemers (1991) collected data from 85 middle managers and their superiors and subordinates. The focal managers responded to the Self-monitoring scale in addition to the traditional contingency model measures. The effects of person–situation match on leader performance and subordinate satisfaction were found only for the low self-monitoring managers. High self-monitors were unaffected by the situation, performing at moderately high levels in situations hypothesized to be "in-match" or "out-of-match" for them.

A laboratory study with college students in the United States (Chemers et al., 1991) helps to tie these findings together. Results indicated that although match status did not affect the outward performance of high self-monitoring leaders, their internal reactions (i.e., mood, feelings of competence) were the same as those for low self-monitors. That is, in-match leaders, whether high or low self-monitors, reported greater confidence and more positive mood than did out-of-match leaders.

A tentative conclusion of these studies in the United States, Japan, and Mexico is that the internal states resulting from person–situation match are similar in all cultures, but the manifestations of those states are affected by values and expectations.

## Path–Goal Theory

In path–goal theory, the follower's task-related need for structure is hypothesized to moderate follower reactions to the leader's directive or considerate behavior.

However, Griffin (1981) demonstrated that subordinate personality (i.e., growth need strength) further moderated the effects of behavior. Hofstede (1984) and Triandis (1993) were quite clear that, like personality traits, cultural values can dramatically affect follower needs, expectations, and reactions. The effects of leader directiveness or supportiveness could be different depending on the values that influence subordinate needs.

For example, in high Power Distance cultures, subordinates expect high levels of autocratic, directive leadership and should be more willing to accept that type of behavior across a wide range of circumstances. In high Uncertainty Avoidance cultures, subordinates' greater need for structure and predictability would enhance their desire for direction from the leader.

Markus and Kitayama (1991) told us that in strongly collectivist cultures, people have a greater need for interpersonal harmony and close connections to others. Leader's consideration behavior, which shows concern and liking for subordinates, should be highly desirable in such collectivist cultures. Triandis (1993) echoed this point and said that some level of nurturant behavior from the leader is a component of good leadership in all collectivist cultures. We might also expect that the expression and acceptance of considerate and nurturant behavior would be more appropriate in the feminine cultures than would be the same behaviors for followers with a more masculine orientation.

The cultural values theories, then, make clear predictions about the relative effectiveness of supervisory behavior. The theoretical deductions also square nicely with the empirical evidence, such as Misumi's (Misumi & Peterson, 1985) findings regarding the higher effectiveness of Japanese supervisors who combine consideration behavior with high levels of directiveness. Japanese workers who are high in Power Distance, Uncertainty Avoidance, and Collectivism should indeed respond positively to that combination.

## Normative Decision Theory

Vroom and Yetton's (1973) decision-making model offers prescriptive advice on the appropriate decision strategies for teams to employ under varying conditions of task clarity and organizational support. One might assume that the objective characteristics of the task environment would have universal implications for appropriate decision strategies. The logic of this assertion resides in the notion that a complex, unstable, and ambiguous decision environment, as might be the case in highly competitive markets or in industries with fast-changing technology would require the same leadership and organizational approaches regardless of the cultural milieu in which they occurred. And yet, in contradiction to that logic, we observe that successful corporations in the United States and Japan compete in the same markets with the same products using drastically different managerial strategies and tactics.

One possible answer to this conundrum offered by Triandis (1993) invokes the logic of "level of adaptation" theory (Helson, 1964). Triandis hypothesized that cultures with particular values develop a set of practices and resultant expectations that provide a frame of reference for evaluating situations. For example, organizations in high Uncertainty Avoidance cultures may go to great lengths to increase task structure through rules and policies. Workers and managers socialized in such organizations might regard as relatively unstructured a task that in another culture would be seen as quite structured. Thus, the leadership orientations, behaviors, or decision strategies that will be most conducive to high performance may vary from culture to culture, even when the objective characteristics of the situation are quite similar. Common cultural practices might also affect the degree of support the leader receives, the amount of power and authority normally assigned to positions, and other factors relevant to contingency formulations. The effects of culture on the perception of situational parameters is an area ripe for future research.

## SOME CONCLUSIONS

All of the theorists discussed in this chapter who have analyzed the role of culture seem in agreement. The major functions of leadership and teamwork (i.e., task goal facilitation and morale maintenance) have universal importance, but the specific ways in which relationships are structured and behaviors are interpreted will be strongly affected by cultural variation.

The work-related values that people hold affect their reactions to leadership. Values determine the specific traits and behaviors that make up the prototype of an effective leader. They influence the needs and expectations that people bring to the leader–follower relationship. Finally, they affect the ways in which the characteristics of the organizational environment are perceived and addressed. The already complex puzzle of effective leadership adds yet another important component with the inclusion of culture.

# Chapter 9

## Women in Leadership

A question of considerable theoretical, practical, and political moment is whether women leaders differ from their male counterparts in terms of the likeliness of their becoming leaders, the patterns and styles of their leadership activities, and the effects of their leadership on group performance and subordinate satisfaction.

Careful scientific studies of women in leadership roles did not begin to appear until the 1970s. Many reasons may have contributed to this lack of attention. Organizational research methodologies and statistical techniques that were not sensitive to low base rate phenomena kept the small number of women in managerial roles relatively invisible. In laboratory research paradigms, the study of women in leadership was more feasible, but also more costly because of the necessary increase in the size of research designs. Perhaps more importantly, predominantly male researchers may not have been interested in questions of female leadership. Finally, the political posture of many academics was that there probably weren't any differences between men and women in leadership, so why open that sensitive area of investigation. The sum total of these and other forces meant that issues of female leadership were ignored by the scientific leadership community.

The "inattentive neutrality" of academic researchers was not shared by the public. Surveys of managers and business school students revealed a strong belief that women were unsuited for managerial roles and would make poor leaders (Bowman, Worthy, & Greyser, 1965). Popular writers, such as Hennig and Jardim (1977), offered quasi-theoretical justification for such beliefs, positing the notion that women lacked the skills and traits necessary for managerial success. Hennig and Jardim hypothesized, for example, that women's lack of experience with competitive team sports made them unsuited for the corporate boardroom.

The dramatic changes wrought in American society in the last 25 years by equal opportunity legislation, affirmative action principles, and feminist thought affected both scientific and popular interest in women managers. The increasing number of women in the workforce and in managerial positions has made the study of women's leadership easier to accomplish and of greater practical importance. Likewise, the increasing number of women entering the academic fields of social and organizational psychology and management have provided researchers interested in the topic a vehicle for raising the consciousness of other professionals. The greater number of women managers and of male managers with female peers has increased the audience for popular treatises on the topic.

In a recent article on gender differences in leadership style, Eagly and Johnson (1990) pointed out an interesting discrepancy between material written by scientists for academic audiences and by nontechnical writers for lay audiences. The popular books, employing interviews or personal impressions (e.g., Hennig & Jardim, 1977; Loden, 1985; Sargent, 1981) tended to report dramatic and meaningful gender differences in leadership and managerial style. The early books in this genre saw women as different from and inferior to men as leaders, whereas the more contemporary versions describe women leaders as different from, but superior to men in those roles. On the other hand, the scientific material, based primarily on either empirical observations or quantitative surveys, reported few differences.

Before we assess the empirical evidence relevant to the question of gender differences in leadership, it would be worthwhile to place the study of women's leadership within the broader theoretical context of gender differences.

## CONCEPTUAL APPROACHES TO GENDER DIFFERENCES

### Individual Differences and Social Categories

Kay Deaux (1984), a leading contributor to research and theory in the study of gender differences, commented on the relative utility of three common approaches to their study. Deaux categorized research into studies that treated gender as a subject variable, as a psychological construct, or as a social category.

In both the gender-as-subject variable and the psychological construct approaches, gender is regarded as an individual difference variable. Investigators attempt to discern how individuals with particular standing on the variable, that is, a man or a woman, differ in the ways that they think or act.

Gender-as-subject variable takes a more demographic approach and regards biological gender as the individual difference of importance. The second approach takes a more psychological than demographic tack. Gender-related characteristics, such as masculinity, femininity, and androgyny are addressed in a manner similar to personality traits. The gender-role identification of men and women is assumed to vary along the dimensions of masculinity and femininity, and it is the character of those identifications, rather than biological gender, that determines thought and behavior.

The third approach does not focus on actual differences between men and women, but rather on perceptions of and responses to the social categories, exemplified by men and women. The influence of the social categories on the stereotypes, expectations, and attributions of actors and observers are the points of interest.

The gender-as-subject variable approach has yielded very little meaningful information. Maccoby and Jacklin (1974) reviewed 1,400 published studies of differences between males and females on a plethora of attitudinal, behavioral, and ability measures. They found only four reliable differences. Males scored higher than females on measures of math ability and spatial memory; females scored higher than males on measures of verbal ability; and males exhibited higher levels of aggressive behavior than females. The magnitudes of these differences were extremely small and inconsequential, controlling from 1 to 5% of the variance in measurement. Furthermore, questions of adequacy in methodology and interpretation make dubious the certainty of even these small differences. For example, Eagly and Carli (1981) reported that the gender of the author of the published articles is a significant predictor of the differences reported, with authors tending to report outcomes that might be considered socially desirable for their own gender.

Deaux (1984) pointed out that most global differences observed between men and women can be significantly vitiated by moderator variables that interact with gender. For example, some studies reported that women, unlike men, were more likely to ascribe the causes of successful performance to external factors and failure to internal factors. Research by Deaux and her colleagues (Deaux & Farris, 1977; Deaux, White, & Farris, 1975) showed that such attributions, for both men and women, are moderated by expectations. People tend to make internal attributions when performance confirms their expectations, but assign responsibility to external factors, such as luck, when success or failure is unexpected. Furthermore, these studies indicated that women's expectations and subsequent attributions could be modified by the gender linkage of the tasks on which they performed. When women worked on ostensibly "feminine" tasks, their expectations and attributions for success and failure were similar to men's.

Deaux (1984) concluded that gender, as a dichotomous, biological marker with complex and unspecified connections to psychological characteristics, is too broad and undifferentiated a variable to have much utility as a predictor of human behavior. Recognizing that biology is not psychology, and that neither all men nor all women are alike, researchers began to study the effects of individuals' level of self-identification in traditionally masculine or feminine terms. Measures that were developed to measure gender-role identification include the Bem Sex Role Inventory (BSRI; Bem, 1974) and the Personal Attributes Questionnaire (PAQ; Spence, Helmreich, & Stapp, 1974).

Respondents to these measures are asked to rate the degree to which they are accurately described by terms with traditionally masculine connotations, such as competitive, assertive, analytical, and competent, or by feminine traits, such as empathic, sensitive, caring, and emotional. Bem (1974, 1977) proposed that a combination of masculine and feminine traits, a pattern referred to as "androgyny," was superior to other characteristics and was hypothesized to result in an individual who was flexible, adaptive, and well adjusted. Little empirical evidence supports the hypothesized positive effects of androgyny (Deaux, 1984).

Moving away from a broad definition of these scales as reflecting masculine and feminine personalities, Spence and Helmreich (1978) offered a narrower view of the masculinity scale as a measure of instrumentality and the femininity scale as a measure of expressiveness. They argued that these traits should predict specific behaviors that are highly indicative of instrumentality or expressiveness, but should be much less strongly associated with other more general domains of gender-related behavior. This last point is particularly relevant to the question of the role of gender in leadership behavior and performance, because leadership would not be expected to bear a simple and direct relationship to either instrumentality or expressiveness.

The social category approach to gender differences regards the effects of gender not in terms of what men and women think or do, but rather the beliefs, perceptions, and expectations that people hold about members of the social categories, "men" and "women." Social categories are presumed to affect beliefs about characteristic traits and behaviors, judgments of competency, expectations for and reactions to success and failure, and so on. These categorical assumptions and presumptions affect the reactions of male and female actors and observers. The choices that individuals make, from careers to leisure activities, might be influenced by how they relate to gender-relevant schemas.

Furthermore, expectations and reactions set up confirmatory sequences (Darley & Fazio, 1980). For example, a woman student who attempts to exercise leadership influence in a small group working on a classroom project might meet with unsupportive reactions from other students who don't expect leadership behaviors from a woman. Her subsequent attempts to lead may be withheld or may become more tentative, reinforcing expectations about women's leadership motivation or capacity. In this example, the reactions of the actor and others in the situation are guided by the stereotypes they hold about women in general, rather than by their reactions to the specific behaviors of the actor.

The research emphasis in the social category approach is not so much on identifying differences in the behaviors of men and women as it is on the differences in categorical perceptions, cognitive processes, and resultant effects.

# Cultural Versus Structural Influences in Gender Differences

In an analysis of individual differences that takes a slightly different perspective from Deaux (1984), James House (1981) distinguished between a "cultural" and a "structural" explanation of gender variation. As was pointed out in the previous chapter, a culture is a set of cognitive and evaluative beliefs about what is and what ought to be that is shared by members of a social system. These shared values and beliefs are transmitted to new members. A cultural analysis regards differences between the behavior of men and women as caused by these learned, internalized values and beliefs.

A social structure, on the other hand, is a "persisting and bounded pattern of social relationships among units in a social system" (House, 1981, p. 542). A structural analysis posits that an individual's behavior is determined by the position that he or she holds in the social structure. It is the external constraints of the position rather than the internalized beliefs that are causal.

A cultural approach to gender differences would hold that women are socialized differently than men because of traditional expectations for the roles that they are expected to fill. The socialization of women would include traits associated with constructs like expressiveness or what Eagly (1987) referred to as communal, taken from Bakan's (1966) term "communion." Communal qualities are those associated with a concern for the welfare of others and include traits, such as sensitivity and compassion, that might make a person more able to address such communal responsibilities. Men are socialized for an "agentic" role that encompasses assertive and controlling tendencies that allow men to be instrumental in accomplishing task-related objectives.

In the cultural explanation of gender differences, gender-role socialization is thought to be so pervasive and powerful that behavior in domains outside of traditional roles remains consistent with gender-role socialization. Nieva and Gutek (1981) referred to the idea that women's traditional role behavior is carried into workplace behavior as "gender-role spillover."

The structural approach emphasizes situational constraints associated with the individual's role in the social structure. House (1981) asserted that "contemporaneous situational contingencies exist that motivate behavior" (p. 543). Factors external to the individual's personality, such as the amount of power and authority one holds or the role demands of a particular job, determine the individual's behavior. If a person's position in an organizational structure is partly or wholly determined by their gender, differences in behavior engendered by the constraints of the position might incorrectly be attributed to gender.

For example, research on influence strategies (Kipnis & Schmidt, 1982; Yukl & Falbe, 1990; Yukl & Tracey, 1992) suggests that upward influence attempts, that is, attempts of a less powerful person to influence a more powerful person, are likely to use strategies different from those used in downward influence attempts. If there are more women in low power positions in an organization, and if people in such positions tend to use, for instance, indirect or ingratiating influence tactics, women will be perceived as more likely to use such tactics. Situational power differences between men and women are ignored, and the fundamental attribution error results in the inference that women use different influence tactics from men. The structural explanation illuminates why people with similar internal beliefs, attitudes, and motivation might act very differently if their positions in a social system diverge.

House's (1981) concept of cultural influences is similar to the individual differences perspective in Deaux's (1984) analysis. In both analyses, differences are caused by internal dispositions of the actors. House's notion of structural constraints goes beyond Deaux's social category approach but is not incompatible with it. The expectations and stereotypes held for social categories or social roles and the expectancy confirmation sequences they engender may be some of the mechanisms by which structural constraints operate. Roles are, after all, sets of normative expectations that direct the behavior of position occupants.

Whether cultural or individual differences or the structural and social category explanations of gender differences are more valid, or if, indeed, gender differences in leadership exist at all, are questions of theoretical and practical significance. It is to those questions that we now turn.

# GENDER DIFFERENCES
# IN LEADERSHIP:
# PERCEPTION AND REALITY

## Stereotypes

A number of negative stereotypic beliefs have existed about women and their suitability for managerial positions. Whereas women are seen as acceptable in the service or assistant roles, such as nurse, secretary, administrative assistant (Kanter, 1977; O'Leary, 1974; Schein, 1973), perceptions of their capabilities in leadership positions have often focused on their lack of experience or training for such roles (Hennig & Jardim, 1977; Trahey, 1977).

Bass, Krusell, and Alexander (1971) conducted a factor analysis of 176 male manager's responses to a survey of attitudes toward women at work. The resultant factors included women lack career orientation; women lack leadership potential; women are undependable; and women are emotionally less stable.

Broverman, Vogel, Broverman, Clarkson, and Rosenkrantz (1972) asked college students to indicate on which characteristics, attitudes, and behaviors, men and women differed. The female stereotype that emerged found women to be less aggressive, more dependent, and more emotional than men. A woman was believed to be easily influenced, submissive, excitable, illogical, and a number of other traits not particularly associated with positions of leadership in our society.

Do such attitudes still exist in the general population, after more than 20 years and many social changes? A series of studies on stereotypes regarding women and leadership have attested to the staying power of such beliefs. Virginia Schein (1973, 1975) asked male managers to describe the attributes of men in general, women in general, and of successful middle managers. She found that the stereotype of a man was quite close to that of a successful middle manager, whereas the stereotype for women overlapped very little with that of a successful manager. In 1979, studies by Powell and Butterfield and by Massengill and DiMarco indicated that the masculine nature of managerial prototypes had changed very little.

Heilman, Block, Martell, and Simon (1989) conducted a careful replication and extension of the Schein (1973) study. However, in addition to rating men and women in general, the stimuli also included "men managers," "women managers," "successful men managers," and "successful women managers." Heilman et al.'s (1989) findings for the stimuli included in the Schein (1973) study were almost identical to those of the earlier study. However, the stimulus "women managers" was rated as more similar to successful middle managers than were women in general, but not as closely as was "men managers." "Successful men managers" and "successful women managers" were both described very similarly to "successful middle managers" with the men given only a slight edge.

Thus, when subjects were specifically told that the women were successful in the managerial role, they assumed that the women shared the traits of other successful managers. This finding is consistent with the conclusion reached by

Heilman, Martell, and Simon (1988) that "when provided with unambigous and undeniable information about performance effectiveness, undervaluation of women and their work does not occur" (p. 107). Locksley, Borgida, Brekke, and Hepburn (1980) also found that individuated behavioral information about a target individual wiped out gender-stereotypical influences on raters. Apparently, however, stereotypes about women and managers are sufficiently ingrained that counter-stereotypic information has to be extremely pointed to have an effect. Simply identifying a woman as a manager did not make Heilman et al.'s (1989) respondents see her as similar to a successful manager, whereas they did see male managers in that light.

The perception of women in general and women managers as gender stereotypically feminine, communal, and unlike ideal depictions of managers, is strong, pervasive, and resistant to change. How accurate is that perception? Do women leaders, indeed, exhibit patterns of behavior different from male leaders?

# Gender and Leadership Style

In the early 1970s, empirical studies of gender in relation to leadership motivation, behavior, and decision styles began to appear in the scientific literature (e.g., Bartol, 1976; Brief & Aldag, 1975; Brief & Oliver, 1976; Terborg, 1977). By 1981, enough information had accumulated for Bass (1981) to conclude that "the preponderance of available evidence is that no consistently clear pattern of differences can be discerned in supervisory style of female as compared to male leaders" (p. 499).

The empirical studies and reviews have continued to mount up, and aided by the meta-analysis strategy, Eagly and her associates (Eagly & Johnson, 1990; Eagly & Karau, 1991; Eagly, Makhijani, & Klonsky, 1992) conducted a number of meta-analyses of gender effects in leadership and other behaviors. These analyses were guided by a social-role interpretation (Eagly, 1987), which held that behavior is likely to be influenced by global, gender-role stereotypes to the extent that other, more specific role demands are not made salient. Gender-role expectations were expected to affect leadership actions in situations, such as laboratory experiments and assessment center settings, where clear role expectations are not present, and with individuals, such as college students or people not actually in leadership positions, for whom other role demands (e.g., organizational role expectations) are absent.

Eagly and Johnson (1990) provided the definitive review of data from 162 studies that compared men and women on measures of leader behavior (e.g., the LBDQ), leadership style (e.g., LPC), or decision-making style. Guided by the distinction between agentic behaviors associated with male role expectations and communal behaviors associated with female role expectations, gender effects were expected to show that males scored higher on measures of structuring, task-oriented behavior, and more directive and controlling (e.g., autocratic) decision styles, whereas women leaders were expected to be characterized by considerate, relationship-oriented behavior and more participative (e.g., democratic) decision styles.

Data were compared from studies done in organizational settings, assessment centers, and laboratory experiments. A number of other variables, such as the sex of authors, year of publication, type of measure, and so forth, were also coded in the analysis, including one very interesting and revealing set of moderators. Eagly and Johnson asked students to rate all the leadership positions included in the 162 studies on the degree to which the positions seemed more "congenial" to men or women as leaders, that is, the extent to which men or women would be likely to seek out such positions and to do well in them.

The meta-analysis revealed that on measures of leader behavior and leadership style, overall differences between men and women were very slight, with no differences at all found in the organizational studies. Significant differences were found on measures of decision style, in all settings. Women were found to be more democratic in their style than men, as predicted. However, a number of moderators tended to weaken or eradicate the effect. For example, in lower managerial levels, men were reported to be more task oriented, but at the middle management level, the effect reversed. A very revealing effect was found for congeniality of situation. In leadership positions that were seen as appropriate and congenial, both men and women evidenced higher levels of task orientation. Also, the tendency for women to employ a more democratic or less autocratic decision style than men was erased for positions high in congeniality. The authors concluded, "These findings suggest that being out of role in gender-relevant terms has its costs in terms of some decline in their tendency to organize activities to accomplish relevant tasks" (p. 248). In other words, when both men and women were in positions hypothesized to be comfortable for them, their behavior was similarly task oriented.

Another set of effects raises the possibility of artifact clouding the interpretability of some of the results. The one place that reliable differences between men and women were found was on the measures of decision style, which are at once the least specific of the measures used and the most susceptible to social desirability demands. A significant gender-of-author effect was found on this measure with authors more likely to report higher use of democratic decision style for their own gender. Terms like "autocratic" and "democratic" are clearly value laden in American society.

In general, then, male and female leaders showed very slight differences in their approach to leadership, with even the decision style differences subject to strong moderation effects. It would appear from this analysis that an extremely limited factual basis exists for the strongly held stereotypes about women's leadership style. Despite their inaccuracy, stereotypes can have a powerful effect on opportunities for women to gain access to leadership positions and on the evaluations they receive once they are in those positions.

## Leadership Emergence: Experimental Studies

A number of studies have been done to test for gender differences in leadership emergence in leaderless groups. Almost all of these studies have been conducted in academic settings using one of two research paradigms; (a) subjects in an experiment are brought together for one short meeting to discuss an issue or solve a problem, or (b) students in an ongoing class are formed into groups for a specific task, such as writing a report or participating in a business simulation. In both paradigms, the groups start out without a leader, and emergence is operationalized by group members' ratings of leadership contribution or through process analysis of behavior, by assessing task-oriented behavior or simply by amount of participation by each group member.

The review of this literature is made more accessible, because Eagly and Karau (1991) presented a meta-analysis of the findings in this area, following an approach quite similar to the Eagly and Johnson (1990) analysis just described. The social-role interpretation (Eagly, 1987) was especially apt for this group of studies, because all of them were done in academic rather than organizational settings. Eagly and Karau's reasoning was that if stereotypes about the appropriateness of men and women for leadership positions are made salient, social expectations will reduce the likelihood that women's attempts to lead will be reacted to positively or that women's contributions to group success will be recognized.

Eagly and Karau also hypothesized some moderating variables. Men are expected to have the stronger advantage on measures of task-related leadership, whereas women may be favored for social leadership, for example, maintaining group morale. Further, the shorter the time the group is together and the less specific and ability-related the task, the more likely it is that gender-role stereotypes will be used and males will be favored for leadership emergence. Because the class projects methodology involves a longer time of interaction (several meetings across a school term vs. a single short meeting) and also involves a task with clearer criteria for judging task-relevant competence and quality of contribution than does the ad hoc experimental groups method, gender effects were expected to be lessened in the former approach.

The results clearly supported Eagly and Karau's hypotheses. Women emerged less frequently than men on task-related or unspecified measures of leadership, but more frequently on social leadership indices. The differences in rates of emergence were dramatically lessened in situations with longer time of interaction and with tasks allowing clearer judgments of competency. However, the differences in emergence rates between men and women were still significant.

These results suggest that the more the situation resembles a real-world organization, the weaker are the effects of gender-role biases. This is heartening in that it means that women in managerial roles can expect that, over time, their task-relevant competencies will be recognized and accepted. On the other hand, the pervasiveness of gender stereotypes and their resistance to change suggests that whenever gender roles are made salient in a group context, women may be at a disadvantage for achieving leadership positions.

# Gender Differences in Leadership Evaluation

Another significant question is whether gender-role expectations bias evaluations of women who are functioning in leadership roles. Are the contributions of women devalued relative to those of men? This question has been investigated in two ways. An experimental approach involves presenting randomly chosen subjects with a sample of behavior or performance, either in the form of a written vignette or a confederate-enacted presentation, with only the gender of the rated target varying between conditions. An alternative approach involves the use of organizational surveys to obtain ratings of male and female leaders by their superiors and subordinates or through objective performance measures. The experimental approach, although somewhat artificial in setting, has the virtue of controlling for any real differences between leaders and assessing the pure effect of gender biases. The organizational survey approach provides a more realistic setting and studies people who hold actual leadership positions.

Like much of the research on gender differences in leadership that we have discussed, individual studies of gender effects on evaluation have yielded very mixed results. Some reviews of the area (e.g., Osborn & Vicars, 1976) maintained that the research setting moderates divergent results, with experimental studies being more likely to find gender differences than organizational studies. Unfortunately, methodology does not cleanly cleave the effects. Some field studies have failed to find gender effects (e.g., Day & Stogdill, 1972; Osborn & Vicars, 1976; Rice, Instone, & Adams, 1984), but other field studies have reported gender differences (e.g., Petty & Lee, 1975; Petty & Miles, 1976). Likewise, some laboratory studies have found differences (e.g., Bartol & Butterfield, 1976; Butterfield & Powell, 1981; Haccoun, Haccoun, & Sallay, 1978; Rosen & Jerdee, 1973), and others have not (e.g., Bartol, 1974; Cohen, Bunker, Burton, & McManus, 1978; Lee & Alvares, 1977).

Nieva and Gutek (1980) attempted to bring some order to the interpretation of these conflicting findings by emphasizing theoretical rather than methodological differences between the studies. Their review came to the following conclusions about gender differences in the evaluation of leaders.

Evaluation bias appears to be strongest when the judgments made required the greatest amount of inference. Studies in which raters were asked to make causal attributions for the success or failure of a target or were asked to predict how well a target's qualifications fit a future leadership position revealed more gender effects than when raters were simply asked to evaluate past performance where information was specific, clear, and complete. Several arguments support this analysis. Terborg and Ilgen (1975) suggested that bias and stereotyping are most potent when little information about the target is known. The same argument was made by Locksley et al. (1980) with respect to gender stereotypes outside the leadership area. Berger, Conner, and Zelditch (1972) held that status characteristics, such as sex or race, create expectations that influence judgments. Kiesler (1975) referred to this effect as "actuarial prejudice." Raters use the base rates of success by some social category, for example, women, to estimate the likelihood that a particular woman might succeed in the situation being rated. Thus, base rates of women in corporate executive positions are used to judge the capability of women to achieve success in that venue.

Nieva and Gutek (1980) also deduced that gender-role congruence between the person and the position affects evaluations and judgments. They cited the work of Levinson (1975) who had male and female students apply for strongly gender-typed jobs (e.g., delivery boy, receptionist, file clerk). Gender-incongruent applicants, both men and women, were turned away in very high percentages.

The third moderator identified by Nieva and Gutek (1980) was the level of performance about which attributions or judgments were made. Expectations for men to be successful and for women to fail were greater the higher the level of qualification or performance being studied.

Eagly et al. (1992) provided a comprehensive meta-analysis of the experimental research on gender effects on leadership evaluation. The findings of this analysis were consistent with the earlier analyses of gender-role effects (Eagly & Johnson, 1990; Eagly & Karau, 1991). Specifically, the tendency to undervalue women is extremely slight, overall, and the percentage of comparisons in which men are favored (56%) is not significantly different from no advantage. However, several moderator variables were significant effect predictors, and their results were similar to Nieva and Gutek's (1980) analysis.

The bias in favor of men was somewhat greater on measures of competency or satisfaction than on judgments of behavioral style. Consistent with the gender-role expectation hypothesis, women were devalued most when they were depicted as acting in "masculine" (i.e., task-oriented, autocratic) style. The opposite effect, however, was not found, that is, male leaders were not devalued for acting in a relationship-oriented or democratic manner.

Another important set of moderators was the degree of gender-typing in the setting and the type of person making the judgment. The greatest gender bias was shown in settings dominated by male leaders and the most biased ratings were made by high school students and nonmanagerial workers. No bias was found for college students or for real managers. The high school students in these studies were predominantly male varsity basketball players rating the competence and acceptability of male and female basketball coaches. Eagly et al. (1992) concluded that this meta-analysis reveals gender bias in these ratings to be a "very weak overall effect," especially when compared with effect sizes in other meta-analyses of this type.

Another approach that has been followed in only a few studies, but that has revealed an important theoretical moderator involves the psychological characteristics of the raters. Rice, Bender, and Vitters (1980) constructed experimental problem-solving groups of male and female cadets at the United States Military Academy at West Point, at a time when women were first being admitted to the Academy. Rice et al. measured the attitudes of the male cadets toward women as leaders. In groups composed of male subordinates with progressive attitudes about women, there were no differences in group performance or follower satisfaction between male and female led groups. However, when subordinates held traditional attitudes hostile toward women leaders, the female cadets performed more poorly than male leaders and had less satisfied subordinates. Similar results were reported by Garland and Price (1977).

The literature on gender differences in leadership behavior, emergence, and evaluation reveals that actual differences between men and women are either slight or nonexistent. However, stereotypes about women's leadership are persistent and pervasive. Under some circumstances, those stereotypes have very little effect on leadership processes. Specifically, when leaders and followers know each other well and interact on specific tasks for which performance feedback is available, men and women are rated as quite similar in leadership style and leadership performance. Unfortunately, whenever a gap between knowledge and inference opens, stereotypes seem to slip into the interstice, biasing judgments and evaluations.

If individual difference explanations of gender effects do not appear very useful in understanding gender differences, perhaps structural and social category approaches will be more revealing.

# STRUCTURAL EFFECTS
# ON WOMEN'S LEADERSHIP

Karl Weick (1969), the astute analyst of organizational dynamics, once said that what the concept of energy was to the field of physics, the construct of power was to organizational theory. Likert (1961) and Pfeffer (1981) supported that view and argued that managerial power is a primary determinant of effectiveness. Subordinate perceptions of managers are linked to power (Pelz, 1952; Trempe, Rigny, & Haccoun, 1985). Liden and Graen (1980) argued that good leader–follower exchanges depend, in part, on a manager's power to secure rewards for subordinates.

There are good theoretical reasons to ask whether power in organizations is affected by the gender of the manager. Some research has shown that the possession of power is incompatible with stereotypes of women managers (Frieze, Parsons, Johnson, Ruble, & Zellman, 1978). Leaving aside psychological explanations, the discussion of status rigidification in chapter 1 made the point that those in positions of power and privilege are usually loathe to share access to their power. We might well expect that the latest arrivals on the managerial scene, that is, women and minority group members, might have difficulty gaining and using power in organizations.

The implications of power and its relationship to gender effects in leadership formed the basis of the research program of Belle Rose Ragins (Ragins, 1989, 1991; Ragins & Sundstrom, 1989, 1990). She asked the question of whether women and men differ in their access to power in organizations, in their use of power, and in the effects of the use of power. The results of that research program are quite informative.

Ragins and Sundstrom (1989) completed a comprehensive review of the literature on gender differences in power in organizations. They concluded that

> for women, the path to power contains many impediments and barriers and can be characterized as an obstacle course. In contrast, the path to power for men contains

few obstacles that derive from their gender and may actually contain sources of
support unavailable to their female counterparts. (p. 81)

Power in organizations develops across the course of a manager's career and is
affected by events that occur at labor market entry, organizational entry, and
promotion up the hierarchy. Women seem to be at a disadvantage at every stage of
transition.

Gender-role stereotypes and socialization may affect job opportunities and job
choices. Biased recruitment, selection, and tracking may shunt women into positions with less status and power. Biases in performance appraisal affect promotions
and other opportunities for gaining power. Work relationships, such as networks,
coalitions, and mentoring, are more difficult for women to utilize effectively.

Structurally, then, women face the tasks of leadership and management with
fewer resources than the men with whom they compete. Do women also use power
differently than men and with different effects as would be suggested by the popular
literature on gender differences, or are the sometimes observed differences between
men and women more attributable to differences in their power than to differences
in their style?

Ragins undertook an extensive study of power effects for men and women
resulting in three revealing analyses. The three analyses (Ragins, 1989, 1991;
Ragins & Sundstrom, 1990) employed the same carefully developed sample of male
and female managers at three government-operated research and development
organizations. Fifty-five pairs of male and female managers were matched for
organizational rank, area of specialization, age, and tenure with their subordinates.

The first study (Ragins, 1989) tested Johnson's (1976) theory of gender congruency in the use of power. Johnson argued that of French and Raven's (1959) five
bases on social power (i.e., reward, coercive, legitimate, reference, and expert
power), reward power was most congruent with a feminine leadership role, whereas
coercive, legitimate, and expert power were congruent with the male role. Referent
power, with its emphasis on personal identification, was thought to be gender
neutral.

Ragins (1989) asked subordinates to evaluate their leaders and to rate them on
type of power used. Results indicated that subordinate perceptions of the supervisor's use of expert and referent power were strongly associated with postive
evaluations, regardless of the gender of the supervisor or the subordinate. Leaders
employing the same power bases received the same kinds of evaluations regardless
of gender. The finding that expert and referent power were the most potent
contributors to positive subordinate evaluation is consistent with similar findings
by Podsakoff and Schriesheim (1985), and is also consistent with idiosyncrasy
credit theory (Hollander, 1958), which identified task-relevant competence and
trustworthiness as the bases for leader legitimacy.

In the second study, Ragins and Sundstrom (1990) asked whether subordinates
perceived differences in the power available to male and female leaders. Results
revealed no significant differences in the overall level of power between men and
women. In other words, men and women of similar organizational rank were seen

as having similar levels of power. The only exception to this finding was that female subordinates gave higher ratings on expert power to female supervisors than to male supervisors. One possible explanation offered for this effect was that, if women experience barriers to gaining power in organizations (Ragins & Sundstrom, 1989), they may place more emphasis on gathering expertise, the only power base that is under their direct control.

In the third analysis, Ragins (1991) employed the structural perspective to address the question of gender differences in leadership evaluations. She pointed out that although some reviews suggested that the laboratory/field study distinction could account for the presence or absence of gender effects in evaluation (Dobbins & Platz, 1986; Osborn & Vicars, 1976), they do not in fact do so. Both laboratory and field studies have reported both positive and negative results. However, a review of 21 studies of gender differences in evaluation revealed that, in eight studies controlling for the power of the target person, no gender effects were found, whereas among 13 studies that did not control for power, gender differences were found in 7 of these studies. Turning again to her sample of managers, Ragins found that although power was strongly correlated with effectiveness ratings for expert power ($r = .82$) and for referent power ($r = .77$), no significant variance in effectiveness was explained by gender differences.

In other words, leaders with appropriate and desirable bases of power were positively evaluated regardless of their gender. The Ragins studies indicate that men and women in organizations have differential access to power, but that men and women of comparable rank in organizations possess and use the same types of power with the same effectiveness.

## A SOCIAL CATEGORY APPROACH
## TO WOMEN'S LEADERSHIP

The research discussed so far in this chapter reveals, as Deaux's (1984) analysis suggested, that real differences between the genders in leadership behavior are very slight. When women managers possess power comparable to their male counterparts, the women act and are evaluated similarly to male managers, especially when performance information and clear criteria for judgment are available. Yet, the continuing prevalence of stereotypical beliefs and organizational barriers inimicable to female managerial success supports Deaux's (1984) argument that a social category approach to gender differences might be a more productive avenue of investigation. It may well be that it is the persistent stereotypes that create and reinforce organizational barriers.

Lord and Maher's (1991) information-processing approach to leadership is well suited to examine the role of categorical perceptual and attributional influences on leadership. Their analysis posits two types of processes that influence judgments of leaders. Recognition-based processes affect the observer's perception that a person is acting in accordance with prototypical behavioral patterns indicative of effective leadership. As we have seen, such prototypes are much more compatible with stereotypes associated with the social category of "men" than with that of "women." The second process by which leaders are judged are inferences about the causes of performance outcomes associated with a particular actor. When successful outcomes are attributed to the causes internal to the leader (e.g., ability or effort) rather than to external causes (e.g., luck or someone else's ability), leaders are evaluated more positively. We know that expectations influence such attributions, with expected outcomes (e.g., male managers will be successful) resulting in stronger internal attributions.

In general, then, commonly held assumptions and expectations about women should put them at a disadvantage relative to these perceptual processes. Lord and Maher (1991) were more specific in their analysis and examined the effect of organizational level on perception of women leaders. They suggested that women are severely disadvantaged at entry and lower levels of management, because little information is available about their performance and judgments are likely to be more influenced by stereotypes. Furthermore, the people who are judging these leaders (i.e., their subordinates) are also less experienced and knowledgeable, and therefore, are more likely to rely on stereotypes than on well-developed knowledge structures.

At middle management levels, the biases against women should be at their weakest. More information about the manager's work and performance history and more complete samples of her behavioral repertoire are available. Also, subordinates, peers, and superiors have a greater base of expert knowledge on which to judge the manager.

However, at the uppermost managerial levels, the forces turn against women leaders again. High-level leaders, such as chief executive officers or governmental agency heads, have broader constituencies with whom they interact. Many segments of these constituencies observe the leader from quite a distance (e.g., corporate shareholders, voters), having less access to actual behavior and being more susceptible to stereotypical processing. Furthermore, the prototypes for high level managers are more demanding and may be more difficult for a woman to fulfill convincingly. The effective middle level woman manager who presents an image of a hardworking, results-oriented, and well-organized leader may find it quite difficult to pull off the impression of the charismatic warrior or the uncompromising tough guy affected by many male upper level managers.

Beginning from a position similar to the analysis by Lord and Maher (1991), Roya Ayman (1993) brought attention to the effects on actors and observers of raising the salience of situationally inappropriate social categories. Ayman pointed out that as long as the managerial situation is defined in role-appropriate terms, the female manager can function quite effectively. However, when gender roles are made salient, for example by comments about a women's clothes or physical characteristics, the multiple-role expectations engendered cause considerable strain, confusion, and discomfort.

This is especially true, of course, because the stereotypically feminine role of passivity and deference is so inimical to the demands of the managerial role. The female manager caught in this "double bind" may be well aware of the fact that if she behaves according to the female role expectation, she will lose her power and effectiveness, but if she persists in the male-oriented managerial role, she runs the risk of being labeled in deviant and socially undesirable terms, such as a "dragon lady."

Actions that raise the salience of gender-based social categories may be a potent tactic by which male managers weaken the power and effectiveness of their female counterparts. Good evidence suggests that real differences in leadership behavior, power, and effectiveness are small. On a "level playing field", women managers make contributions to organizational performance equal to their male colleagues. However, stereotypical responses, whether the errors of automatic processes or a conscious tactic of competition and control, restrict the opportunity for women to function effectively in organizations. Psychological impediments and structural barriers to women in management create stress and burnout for individuals and a serious loss of talented and committed employees for organizations.

## A BRIEF COMMENT
## ON MINORITY LEADERS

The empirical literature on ethnic minority leaders (such as African-Americans, Latinos, Asian-Americans, Native-Americans, Jewish-Americans, etc.), is very sparse. However, in a recent review of the available literature, Chemers and Murphy (1995) reached conclusions similar to those presented here for women leaders and managers. There is little indication that minority leaders differ dramatically from dominant culture leaders in behavior, performance, or subordinate satisfaction. Nonetheless, negative stereotypes about minority leaders are prevalent, and such leaders have a more difficult time moving up the corporate ladder.

## SOME CONCLUSIONS

This chapter evaluated the empirical evidence for gender differences in leadership style, emergence, and effectiveness from three explanatory perspectives; cultural, structural, and social category. The sum total of the data indicates that although actual differences between men and women are slight, strong stereotypical expectations persist. These expectations make it more difficult for women (and minorities) to gain access to power, with attendant structurally caused differences in behavior and effectiveness.

## LOOKING TOWARD INTEGRATION

The first nine chapters comprehensively analyzed leadership theory and research. We are now ready to see if these broad-ranging perspectives can be integrated into a coherent and meaningful general model of leadership effectiveness.

# Chapter 10

## A Function and Process Integration

A common criticism of contemporary leadership research and theory, both from within the leadership area and from other organizational theorists, has been that the literature is fragmented and contradictory. A lack of both coherence across theoretical approaches and reliable empirical findings is said to characterize the field of leadership studies (McCall & Lombardo, 1978; Quinn, 1984). Because logical consistency and empirical reliability are the sine qua non of theoretical validity, if these criticisms are accurate, they compromise the basis for a valid science of leadership.

One of the most obvious controversies is reflected in differences between popular and scientific approaches; a clear example being the popular theoretical assertions of powerful and pervasive differences in the leadership styles of men and women contrasted with the scientific findings of extremely limited and pragmatically inconsequential variations.

A second area of disagreement is between contingency approaches, which argue that no one style or set of behaviors will be effective in all situations, and "one best way" approaches, which delineate a leadership pattern of universal application. For example, Bass' transformational leadership theory (Bass, 1985; Bass & Avolio, 1993) with its emphasis on the four dimensions of outstanding leadership, seems incompatible with Fiedler's contingency model (Fiedler, 1967; Fiedler & Chemers, 1974, 1984), which stresses the importance of situational factors in the determination of appropriate leadership.

At the broadest level of analysis, dispute arises about the relative importance of leadership at all. The constructionists, such as Calder (1977), Meindl (1990), and Dachler (1988), view leadership and its supposed effects as primarily perceptual constructions. The more positivist theoreticians, who might include Vroom and Yetton (1973), Bass (1985), House (1971) and most of the rest of the field, regard leader actions and situational characteristics as factual entities with relatively tangible effects on real organizational outcomes.

In this chapter, I endeavor to present an integrative framework that transcends the apparent contradictions. One integration adopts a functional perspective that posits that apparent divergences between theoretical approaches result from attempts to use one theoretical orientation to explain separate and distinct leadership functions with different processes and effectiveness criteria. A second integration ties together the central processes that underlie team leadership in an attempt to provide a coherent understanding of the dynamic qualities of effective leadership. These integrations also suggest avenues for future research.

# FUNCTIONAL ASPECTS OF EFFECTIVE LEADERSHIP

A first step in sorting out the commonalities and contradictions among leadership theories is to recognize that leadership is a multifaceted process. Leaders must analyze information, solve problems, motivate subordinates, direct group activities, inspire confidence, and so on. If we try to explain all facets of the leadership process from a single point of view, we are bound to fail, and when we use a single perspective to compare theories that explain different aspects of the leadership process, we further increase the confusion.

Frequently, theories that share a particular principle, such as contingency theories (e.g., path–goal theory, House & Mitchell, 1974; normative decision theory, Vroom & Yetton, 1973; the contingency model, Fiedler, 1978), are grouped together and compared. Discrepancies in predictions made by the different theories are used as the basis for accusations of incoherence across leadership theorizing. However, as discussed in chapter 4, although these theories all ascribe to the notion that one leadership pattern will not be effective in all situations, they differ in other important ways. Some contingency theories attempt to explain the effects of supervision on subordinate motivation and commitment; others are concerned with team performance; whereas still others are focused on how leaders obtain and implement high quality decisions.

Another potential source of misunderstanding is created by grouping theories that share a common process, but that apply that process to different aspects of leadership functioning. For example, attributional processes provide an explanatory basis for theories that address the ways that followers judge and react to subordinate performance. However, attribution theory is also applied to processes that underlie perceptions about leaders and their effectiveness. Even though these attribution-based models share many features, their applications are better understood and evaluated when studied in the appropriate context.

The integrative model presented here maintains that the functional aspects of leadership can be grouped into three facets. These facets, although not totally independent of one another, illuminate quite separate and distinct features of leadership. Within each facet, contemporary theories do reach relatively consistent conclusions about the effective management of groups and organizations.

The three facets are labeled *image management, relationship development*, and *resource utilization*. Image management recognizes that individuals who wish to function in a leadership role must present themselves in ways that legitimize their authority. They must, in effect, look and act like effective leaders. Relationship development refers to the necessity for leaders to motivate and direct the activities of followers. The resource utilization facet acknowledges that team and organizational performance ultimately depend on the leader's ability to apply effectively the resources of self and followers to task accomplishment.

## Image Management

The primary goal of image management is to establish a legitimate basis for the leader's attempts to influence others. Hollander's (1958) idiosyncrasy credit model established that the central criteria for leader legitimacy are competence and trustworthiness. Likewise, Kouzes and Posner's (1987) survey of subordinates reached similar conclusions reporting that the two most highly cited characteristics of an outstanding leader were honesty and competence.

These legitimacy criteria make good sense. The acceptance of leadership from another person involves an implicit contract in which followers sacrifice some level of personal autonomy and pledge loyalty and effort to the leader. The leader's side of the exchange is to facilitate the group's or followers' progress toward their goals. The followers must be sure that the leader has the competency to lead effectively and the trustworthiness and loyalty to the group and its goals to lead in the direction promised.

Judgments of leader capability and trustworthiness are perceptual processes that are guided by information-processing principles. Lord and Maher (1991) showed that candidates for leadership establish competency through the two processes of recognition and inference. Individuals who display characteristics consistent with the followers' leadership prototypes are assumed to possess the characteristics associated with the prototype, that is, competence. In other words, they are "recognized" as good leaders.

One of the most prototypical of leadership traits appears to be confidence. Both popular (e.g., Bennis & Nanus, 1985) and academic (e.g., House, 1977) theorists describe a highly confident demeanor as typical of outstanding leaders. Confidence may in fact imply competence if followers infer that the leader's confidence is engendered by mission-relevant knowledge and ability.

Inferential processes affect perceptions of leader competency through attributions about the causes for a group's successful or unsuccessful outcomes. When positive outcomes are ascribed to the leader's abilities or efforts, perceptions of competence are enhanced.

Several leadership theorists with an information processing orientation argue that the inferential processes that underlie attributions of leadership competence are facilitated by powerful cognitive biases (Calder, 1977; Meindl, 1990). Observers hold implicit theories of organizational functioning that assign responsibility for organizational outcomes (perhaps excessively) to the efforts and abilities of leadership. Such "romantic" views of leadership strengthen attributions that link the leader's actions to group outcomes.

The tendency to attribute outcomes to leadership is increased by the natural proclivity to assign causation to actors, that is, the fundamental attribution error (Ross, 1978). Anything that increases the salience of the leader with respect to other possible causes will further this tendency (Phillips & Lord, 1981). One strategy that leaders use to manipulate the link between salience and attribution is to prominently announce successes, but to allow someone else to give the news of failures. For example, White House Rose Garden signings of popular legislation provide U.S. presidents with an opportunity to be attached to successful outcomes.

A leader seeking to manage his or her image effectively will seek to appear prominently in group activities, to display prototypically consistent behaviors, and to be attached to successful group outcomes. The essential nature of image management is not lost on political leaders. Because political figures rarely interact directly with their constituents, such leaders are especially dependent on the impressions they convey.

In his analysis of the success of American presidents, Simonton (1987) employed attribution theory as a central explanatory construct. Political candidates go to great effort to have their image projected in ways that are consistent with leadership prototypes, including the characteristics of strength, confidence, and decisiveness. Zullow, Oettingen, Peterson, and Seligman (1988) found an extremely high correlation between the degree of confident imagery in the nomination acceptance speeches of American presidential candidates and the likelihood of their winning the election.

The electorate entrusts great power and responsibility to political leaders, so voters are also quite concerned about the leader's trustworthiness. Kissing babies, saluting the flag, and other shows of virtue help to establish the candidate's trustworthiness. Financial and romantic scandals can scuttle a campaign or propel a politician from office. Voters reason that a leader who does not share their moral values may not be leading in a direction they want to go.

When image management is particularly successful, the leader may be described as charismatic. Inferences of competence and trustworthiness are taken to an extraordinary level. The perception of a supremely gifted leader driven by a moral vision fulfills the romantic expectations of followers. The heroic corporate warriors of popular management books and the transformational leaders identified in empirical surveys (Bass, 1985) share these characteristics of a compellingly articulated, highly moral vision, a loyal and trustworthy character, and a confident and optimistic demeanor.

Because image is very dependent on the perceptions of others, it is the facet of effective leadership that is most susceptible to constructionist influences. A leader may be perceived as capable, honest, and visionary, because he does, in fact, possess those virtues. However, as the followers of Adolph Hitler, Charles Manson, and Jim Jones eventually found out, it may be too late before the truth underlying those perceptions is known.

# Relationship Development

The very concept of leadership is defined by the relationship between the leader and the led. The preponderance of leadership research focuses on the factors that influence that relationship. As the social exchange theories make clear, relationships are built on mutually rewarding exchanges, involving the satisfaction of the needs of both parties.

Effective leaders must build a relationship with subordinates that results in highly motivated, mission-oriented, and goal-directed team members. The key features of productive leader–follower relationships are coaching, judgment, and transactional exchange.

*Coaching and Guidance.*    One of the leader's most important responsibilities is the development and direction of subordinates' goal-oriented capabilities and activities. The literature sometimes appears scattered on how the leader can best accomplish this function. However, greater clarity can be gained through the recognition that the leader–follower relationships are dynamic over time and that no two relationships are the same. The supervisory behaviors that work for one subordinate may not work for another or even for that subordinate at another stage of development.

The behaviorally oriented theorists (e.g., Komaki & Desselles, 1990; Podsakoff et al., 1982) propose that subordinates perform most productively when key work behaviors are identified and rewards are delivered contingent on the performance of those behaviors. Contingent punishment is of more dubious merit, and noncontingent rewards and punishment are clearly ineffective in terms of motivation, productivity, and satisfaction.

Although effective in the proper situation, contingent reward supervision is limited by the nature of both the task and the characteristics of the subordinate. In order for behaviorally oriented interventions to be productive, tasks must have sufficient structure and clarity to allow for careful pinpointing and surveillance of desirable behaviors, without the encouragement of unwanted behaviors or the suppression of desirable behaviors not rewarded. Secondly, the contingency theories of supervision (e.g., Hersey & Blanchard, 1977; House & Mitchell, 1974) indicate that although high levels of leader directiveness can be helpful when subordinates are confronted with tasks beyond their current capabilities, such close monitoring and instruction can become counterproductive when subordinates find their tasks within their capabilities. In addition to task-relevant ability and knowledge, subordinate needs and personality also moderate the desire for highly structured work and the effectiveness of close supervision. Subordinates high in both independence and a need for challenge are likely to respond less positively to close supervision regardless of the task (Griffin, 1981).

The virtues of pinpointed, contingent reinforcement include channeling the attention of workers to critical features of their tasks and providing feedback mechanisms to help in regulating work activity. Those virtues can be preserved and the negative effects of close surveillance reduced by shifting from an attention on specific behaviors to a focus on goals and objectives (Locke & Latham, 1990b). Goals and specific objectives provide a mechanism for subordinates to regulate their own activities, adjusting their behavior when performance feedback falls short of targets. The goal-setting process is also an opportunity for interventions related to subordinate development and autonomy.

An essential element of good leadership is not only the direction of subordinates, but their personal development as well. Coaching and guidance become more important than direct targeted supervision as the subordinate becomes more capable. Increasing subordinate participation in the definition of objectives and the setting of goals shifts the subordinate from extrinsic motivation to an intrinsically focused, self-regulation.

The descriptions of charismatic or transformational leaders (e.g., Bass, 1985; House & Shamir, 1993) place great emphasis on the outstanding leader's ability to encourage self-motivation and mission orientation. Bass (1985) argued that this shift in subordinate orientation is accomplished through an inspiring vision and an intellectually challenging task. House and Shamir (1993) emphasized the importance of substituting collective goals for individual objectives. In both analyses, employees achieve outstanding levels of commitment and motivation by tying personal satisfaction to team achievement.

The leader's success in moving a subordinate toward greater autonomy and intrinsic motivation depends on the leader's ability to recognize the form of supervision needed at a particular time in the subordinate's development and the subordinate's readiness for graduation to the next level.

*Attribution and Judgment.*    How does a leader know when a subordinate is ready for a more difficult task, greater participation in decision making, or delegation and autonomy? Conversely, what determines the advisability of increasing directiveness or providing encouragement and support through a difficult experience? A multitude of factors affect the answers to such questions and reflect the complex interaction of the subordinate's ability, training, and knowledge with needs and personality, in the context of a particular task and organizational environment. As in any social relationship, these judgments require attention and sensitivity.

Solid empirical evidence (e.g., Green & Mitchell, 1979; Mitchell & Wood, 1980) suggests that judgments of a subordinate's capabilities, needs, and personality follow the logic of attribution theory (Jones & Davis, 1965; Kelley, 1967). Leaders try to act as "naive scientists," assessing the subordinate's current and past work behavior, comparing it to that of others in the group or organization, and arriving at a course of action based on judgments of the role of internal and external factors in performance.

Unfortunately, a wealth of forces intrude on the leader's unbiased judgmental processes. A dynamic and demanding environment places a cognitive load on the harried leader that diminishes the capacity for careful analysis (Gilbert et al., 1988). The relative importance of the performance outcomes on the leader's own peforance evaluations may lead to more extreme judgments. The reciprocal interdependence of leaders and followers can create defensiveness in the leader resulting in an inaccurate and unfair assignment of responsibility or blame to subordinates (Brown, 1984).

The influence literature suggests that the way in which a leader uses power and influence can affect the leader's interpretation of the causes of a subordinate's behavior and performance. A study by Kipnis et al. (1976), for example, found that superiors who used more power-oriented influence tactics ascribed more of the responsibility for their subordinates' behavior and performance to their own leadership than did supervisors using less coercive tactics. A supervisor who concludes that a subordinate is unmotivated may use threats to increase the subordinate's efforts. Any change in the subordinate is then attributed to the supervisor's actions.

Inaccurate attributions are likely to lead to inappropriate remedial actions that engender confusion or hostility in the affected subordinate. As we have seen, the developing relationship between leader and follower can be one of increasing interdependence and mutuality or it can be a downward spiral of enmity and withdrawal. Sensitivity and understanding may not be the most prominent features of the American leadership prototype, but they may be among the most important.

*Transactional Exchange.*     Subordinate guidance and development occurs in the context of a personal relationship. The personal and emotional basis for the leader–follower relationship should not be understated. In a study of substitutes for leadership, Podsakoff et al. (1993) reported that although features of the subordinate's environment, such as peer relationships or organizational climate, may have a strong impact on the subordinate's satisfaction and motivation, such factors do not lessen the strength of the leader's effects on the follower. Similarly, Chemers and Cunningham (1989) found that feedback from one's superior had the strongest effect on overall job satisfaction, regardless of what other feedback sources were available. The relationship of leader and follower appears to be one of sufficient emotional weight that, regardless of other factors operating in the situation, the leader's acts will have great import for a subordinate.

Hollander (1978, 1993) attested that leadership legitimacy relies on perceptions of competence, but within a relationship based on honesty, fairness, and mutual loyalty. Graen and his colleagues (e.g., Graen & Scandura, 1987; Liden et al., 1993) described the range that the quality of leader–follower exchanges may encompass, from the unrewarding and unproductive "boss-hired-hand" relationship to one of shared objectives and mutual respect.

What is the currency of good exchanges? Research on power and influence tactics (e.g., Kipnis & Schmidt, 1982; Podsakoff & Schriesheim, 1985; Ragins & Sundstrom, 1990; Yukl & Falbe, 1990) suggests some common relational features. The most highly valued and effective power usage relies on the bases of expert and referent power, that is, power based on the leader's competence or attractiveness and trustworthiness. Similarly, the most highly rated influence tactics are rational appeals, consultation, and inspiration, that is, sources of influence based on the agent's competence or vision, with respect for the intelligence and autonomy of the influence target.

As we move up the ladder from transactional to tranformative exchanges, we observe an intensification of the principles already established. Bass (1985) told us that outstanding leadership involves challenging and inspiring the subordinate in the context of consideration and understanding. The transformational leader, by understanding where the follower is and where he or she is capable of going, helps the follower to expand abilities and adopt intrinsic motives to achieve a meaningful goal. House and Shamir (1993) illustrated that true transformational leadership occurs when followers adopt mission objectives as part of their own self-concept and pursue their own personal fulfillment by achieving collective purposes. Whereas transactional leaders exchange salaries, bonuses, and promotions for subordinate effort and loyalty, transformational leaders offer an exchange of self-esteem and personal fulfillment for selfless commitment and limitless effort.

It is important to recognize that both what is exchanged and how the transaction is managed will not be the same for every leader and every subordinate. Vertical dyad linkage theory (Graen & Scandura, 1987) emphasizes the uniqueness of each managerial dyad, as does the "individualized consideration" factor of Bass' (1985) transformational leader's behavior.

The work of the cross-cultural theorists (e.g., Hofstede, 1984; Markus & Kitayama, 1991; Misumi, 1984; Triandis, 1993) reminds us that the type of exchange that will be satisfying and inspiring depends on the needs that leader and subordinate bring to the exchange. In collectivist cultures, for example, it should be much easier to induce team members to forego personal goals for organizational objectives. In cultures high in power distance, subordinates may react positively to relatively autocratic leadership across a range of situations. The important point to remember is that the appropriateness and rewardingness of a leader's acts and their resultant effect on the quality of the leader–follower relationship depend on the values, needs, and expectations of both parties.

*Summary.*      Effective leader–follower relationships are built on a foundation of mutual understanding. Leaders guide subordinates in the accomplishment of task objectives while recognizing the broader needs and personal goals that the subordinate brings to the work environment. Mutual understanding is built on nondefensive perception and communication and leads to exchanges that make followers more productive by making them more intrinsically motivated and more personally capable. In essence, the bases of the relationship proceed from quid pro quos to expanded horizons.

# Resource Utilization

The third function of leadership in groups is the coordination of the team's collective resources (material, intellectual, and energetic) for task accomplishment. From the point of view of organizational survival, this is also the most important function of leadership. As noted in chapter 1, status systems recognize and elevate capable group members to positions of responsibility and supply those individuals with enhanced authority to carry out the tasks of critical importance to group and organizational viability. The resources available to a group include those that are associated with the leader individually, and those that are held by the team collectively. The utilization of the leader's personal resources follows a somewhat different process than that of team resource coordination. I deal with the leader's personal resources first.

*Leader Self-Deployment.*    The leader possesses physical and intellectual resources garnered from personality, training, experience, or other origins. The resources become useful when they are successfully deployed in helping the team to accomplish its task or mission. A number of empirical and theoretical findings suggest that a leader's emotional states, particularly confidence and optimism, play an important role in the utilization of those personal resources.

Bennis and Nanus' (1985) interviews with successful organizational leaders revealed that a common feature of their orientations to their jobs was a sense of confidence in their own abilities and optimism about the outcomes of their actions and the efforts of their followers.

In an extensive study of managers undergoing an assessment center evaluation, Staw and Barsade (1992) analyzed the effects of positive affective states on both impression formation and objective performance. Students in a graduate management program were measured on scales assessing emotional traits such as self-esteem, depression, and so forth. In an in-basket exercise, the more emotionally upbeat subjects integrated more of the available information and reached more complex and accurate decisions. In a leaderless group exercise, positive affect was associated with higher perceptions of leadership ability, both by other participants in the exercise and by trained evaluators.

A study by Chemers, May, and Watson (1996) found that leadership ratings of R.O.T.C. cadets by their military science professors were highly correlated with the cadets' scores on a measure of confidence in their leadership ability and a measure of optimism (Scheier & Carver, 1985). Multiple regression analyses indicated that other less specific measures of positive affect, such as self-esteem (Brockner, 1988), attributional style (Seligman, 1991), or hopefulness (Snyder et al., 1991) did not contribute to the effect. A follow-up study with the same group of cadets indicated that confidence was also highly predictive of high performance and high ratings by peers and superiors at a 6-week leadership training camp.

In addition to positive emotional traits, such as dispositional optimism, more temporary, state-like emotional influences also seem to affect leadership. Bavelas et al. (1965) provided positive feedback to selected members of a leaderless discussion group. The individuals who received the reinforcing feedback increased the frequency of their influence attempts and were rated highy on measures of leadership by other groups members. In a study by Gruenfeld et al. (1969), confederates acting as followers were trained to give positive or negative responses to influence attempts of appointed leaders in a laboratory experiment. Subsequent leadership behavior was strongly affected by those follower reactions. In a similar experiment, Watson and Chemers (1996) found that leaders high in confidence and optimism (termed *mettle*) were more resilient under stressful conditions characterized by negative feedback from subordinates.

An experimental study by Chemers, Ayman, Sorod, and Akimoto (1991) assigned either task-motivated or relationship-motivated (i.e., low or high LPC) undergraduate students to act as leaders of groups given highly structured or unstructured tasks. Leaders were also asked to report their perceptions of their support from followers and the degree of task structure (i.e., situational control in the contingency model, Fiedler & Chemers, 1984). Leaders were classified as "in-match" or "out-of-match," based on contingency model predictions. Postsession questionnaires asked leaders and followers to report on their moods, their perceptions of the leader's contribution to group activities and task outcomes, and the amount of harmony and cooperation among group members. In-match leaders gave significantly more positive self-reports of mood and of their own contribution to group activities than did out-of-match leaders. Followers of in-match leaders reported higher scores for leader's contributions and for group harmony than did the followers of out of match leaders. Observers who viewed videotapes of the group sessions gave higher marks to the in-match leaders on all variables.

Chemers et al. (1985) analyzed the effects of contingency model "match" on self-reported stress and stress-related illness for a sample of university department chairs. Out-of-match administrators reported significantly higher levels of stress and stress-related illness than did in-match leaders. A follow-up study of a large sample of secondary school administrators replicated these effects of match on stress and illness (Chemers et al., 1986).

Recent research with cognitive resource theory (Fiedler, 1993a; Fiedler & Garcia, 1987) provides strong evidence that job stress drastically reduces leaders' ability to utilize their intelligence to solve problems and to direct group activities. Cognitive resource theory concludes that the anxiety and distraction associated with job stress interfere with the leader's ability to manipulate abstract and complex ideas.

In summary, a variety of theoretical perspectives point toward the conclusion that a leader's capability for effectively using task and interpersonal skills and knowledge may be dependent on maintaining a positive emotional state. These affective orientations, such as confidence and optimism, may be part of a leader's personality, or they may result from contemporary aspects of the situation, such as social support or situational match.

*Team Resource Utilization.* The ultimate test of leadership is how well the group and organization perform on the tasks related to the organizational mission. Although creating a positive impression and building mutually rewarding relationships may be essential parts of the leadership phenomenon, performance and productivity are its goals. As we move the analysis toward criteria of productivity and effectiveness, the objective features of the organizational environment play a greater role in determining good leadership. A leader might try to be everything to everybody, but the strategic harnessing of group resources requires hard decisions that propel the group in particular directions. Any strategy chosen involves a trade-off of advantages and disadvantages. Situational variables, such as task clarity or information uncertainty, will make some trade-offs more advantageous than others. When specific strategies meet specific environmental parameters, the contingency principle reigns.

Both the attentional energies of the leader and the time available for group activity are limited commodities. Leaders cannot pay attention to every aspect of the interpersonal and task environment. Explicitly or implicitly, they must prioritize the targets of their attention. Likewise, groups must efficiently use the time available to them. Task groups usually function in competitive environments in which other groups are trying to accomplish similar tasks or penetrate the same markets. Even when time pressure is not intense, faster and more efficient units will function more competitively than those that dissipate their time and energies.

A common feature of contingency-oriented leadership theories is an emphasis on the degree of follower participation that is permitted in the leader's strategies for processing information, making decisions, and executing plans. The relative distribution of authority is an essential aspect of intragroup relations. The greatest advantage of directive strategies is speed. The greatest weaknesses associated with such autocratic approaches is that they limit the amount and complexity of information in the system, and they reduce intrinsic motivation among followers. In terms of trade-offs, the advantages of directive leadership strategies are most useful and the disadvantages least harmful when the task environment provides the leader with a predictable and reliable basis for decision making, planning, and execution.

Poorly understood tasks or changeable and unpredictable situations reduce the leader's control and with it, the advantages of centralized, directive leadership. Under more complex or unpredictable conditions, decision making is enhanced by the integration of more diverse information and perspectives. Participation of followers in problem identification and solution increases both the sources of information available and the capacity for processing that information. Further, the intrinsic motivation engendered by participation increases self-regulation. Self-regulation, in which employees monitor and adjust their own behavior to achieve task objectives, is especially useful when complex or unpredictable situations require spontaneous reactions.

The foregoing principles are the underlying logic of the contingency theories of team leadership. They are quite explicit in Vroom and Yetton's (1973) normative decision theory. In that model, the leader's choice of relatively more or less participative decision-making strategies is made against a background of situational parameters that assess the quality of information available for making the decision and the probable subordinate enthusiasm for executing the solution. The same principles are more implicitly organized in Fiedler's (1967, 1978; Fiedler & Chemers, 1984) contingency model. The variables included in the dimension of Situational Control (i.e., follower support and cooperativeness; task clarity and structure; and the leader's authority to enlist compliance from subordinates) focus on the same issues as the Vroom and Yetton model.

When the strategic decisions made are consistent with the demands of the situation, teams will make more effective use of their resources. On the other hand, knowledge and energy can be squandered by poor matches between strategy and environment. No amount of impression management or charismatic aura will overcome the contingencies of the environment, as Hitler found out when he chose to fight a European war on two fronts. Social construction is an inadequate building platform in the face of competitive markets or hostile armies.

## SOME CONCLUSIONS ON THE FUNCTIONS OF LEADERSHIP

The classification and integration of theories on the basis of the leadership functions they address help to reconcile some of the apparent inconsistencies in the leadership literature. Within each facet (image management, relationship development, and resource utilization), the research and theory is in general agreement about what works best and why.

At the most positive level of each facet, the scientific evidence shares some communality with the popular literature. The zenith of image management is the impression of a highly competent individual driven by a compelling vision. Similarly, the essence of relationship development is the ability to motivate through an inspiring vision and concern for followers. Even in the area of resource utilization, the popular theories' emphasis on confidence is supported by considerable empirical research.

The discontinuity between contingency and one-best-way approaches can be resolved by examining the perspective of analysis and the function under study. When the dominant method for identifying an effective leader is through social perception, as is the case when interviews or surveys are used, cognitive biases like prototypes make it appear that all good leaders are similar. Two leaders with different environments might follow very different avenues for achieving a successful outcome. Yet, their success elicits a common stereotype of a successful leader.

Images and relationships are particularly susceptible to perceptual, constructionist effects, because they are based on subjective reactions. The perceptions of the leader and follower define the situation in which the interactions take place. When we look at the resource utilization function with its emphasis on objective performance outcomes, constructionist influences and cognitive biases become less important. The efficiency of a bomber crew on a target run, the amount of steel poured during an 8-hour shift, or the accuracy of a mission control team putting a satellite in orbit, are outcomes that have a basis in objective reality. Theories that attempt to predict such outcomes must also have an objective basis.

## AN INTEGRATIVE THEORY OF LEADERSHIP PROCESS

The three functional facets of effective leadership help to provide some common principles that can be integrated into a comprehensive theory of leadership. An additional perspective can be provided by examining the processes by which leadership is integrated at intrapersonal, interpersonal, and situational levels.

Leadership processes are complex enough that not all perspectives can be addressed simultaneously. The model to be presented here must accommodate that fact. The process is presented from the perspective of the leader who is treated as the central figure, although it is acknowledged that leadership is an interpersonal process in which followers play significant roles. The processes discussed in this integration are presented in a linear fashion with a static, slice-in-time perspective, even though leadership processes are truly multidimensional, reverberating, and dynamic systems.

The overall integrative process model is presented in Fig. 10.1. The model attempts to address individual, dyadic, group, and organizational interactions. The processes are divided into three zones. Each zone examines a predominant interface of persons and environment. Each zone is guided by a dominant causal principle, and each zone reflects a greater or lesser susceptibility of effects to objective or constructive forces. The theoretical principle that is consistent across all zones is the "match" concept, which states that the outcomes of leader and follower behavior are determined by the degree of fit between the behavior and the demands of the surrounding environment.

## Zone of Self-Deployment

The first zone depicts the interface of the leader and the environment. In this domain, the match between the leader's personal orientations and the demands posed by the environment are the central causal process. The box denoted by the numeral 1 represents the interaction of individual characteristics and relevant

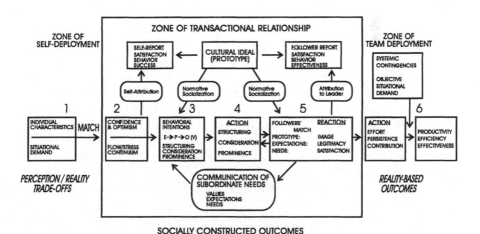

FIG. 10.1. Diagram of integrative process model of leadership.

situational demands. Individual characteristics or orientations refer to the leader's self-concept; values, needs, and goals; or habitual patterns of thought and behavior. The demands placed by the social and task environment may be more or less compatible with the leader's personal orientation resulting in either a good or poor fit. When the fit is good, the leader is said to be "in-match."

The concept of person–environment fit is common to many theories in social and organizational psychology. The empirical and theoretical background most relevant to the principle in the current case comes from the literature on the contingency model (Fiedler & Chemers, 1984), particularly the studies that indicate that in-match leaders experience greater positive affect, self-confidence, and task involvement (Chemers et al., 1993; Garcia, 1983; Nahavandi, 1983) and lower levels of stress and illness (Chemers et al., 1985).

Other research and theory reflects similar concepts based on a match of orientation and environment. Anderson (1987) studied the performance and satisfaction of nursing profession personnel whose gender might be considered to be either traditional or nontraditional for their roles. Female nurses and male administrators (traditional roles) were compared with male nurses and female administrators (nontraditional roles). Among the nontraditional role occupants, performance and satisfaction were related to the individual's ability to understand and respond to social expectations.

An extensive body of research on women leaders addresses issues of match in terms of the "congeniality" of the leadership environment (Eagly & Johnson, 1990). Women leaders perform more effectively and are more satisfied in environments that are congenial in terms of being traditionally feminine positions, having supportive subordinates (Rice, Bender, & Vitters, 1980), or encouraging positive expectations (Deaux & Farris, 1977; Eagly & Karau, 1991).

The mechanisms through which match affects positive cognitive and emotional states are suggested by a number of research literatures. In an experimental study of male and female leadership, Butler and Geis (1990) reported that women received less supportive nonverbal responses from subordinates than did male leaders. Ayman (1993) discussed the feelings of confusion and unease created by discontinuities between social roles for some nontraditional managers, such as women and minority group members. A comparable literature exists in intercultural studies (Brislin, 1981). Culture shock is the label given to feelings of disorientation and anxiety that result from a mismatch between a person's normative social expectations and those of others with whom the person interacts.

Deaux's (1984) analysis of gender effects on attributions for success and failure emphasized the role of performance expectations. On tasks or in situations in which people expect to perform well, causes of success are attributed internally and failure externally. That pattern of attribution results in heightened self-esteem, confidence, and aspiration level.

Leadership situations provide both an initial backdrop and subsequent feedback that can suggest to a leader that the situation is conducive to their personal orientation. Tasks on which the person has performed well in the past or that are compatible with the individual's perceptions of their abilities (e.g., mechanical, athletic, intellectual, interpersonal, etc.) will enhance confidence. The contingency model literature suggests that a sense of optimal levels of predictability and control may be a key feature of comfort and confidence in a situation.

Predictability and control are elements of both task and interpersonal environments. The Situational Control dimension acknowledges the role of both task and interpersonal features of certainty by including them in the specification of the construct. The particular individual characteristics or situational variables that are likely to be most salient or most relevant to creating a person–environment match will vary across individuals and organizational environments. However, the effects of that match have very important implications for the leadership process.

The zone of self-deployment is characterized by a trade-off between subjective and objective influences, between perception and reality. In an experimental examination of contingency model effects on mood and performance (Chemers et al., 1991) subjects' perceptions of Situational Control variables were a better predictor of performance and satisfaction than were more objective specifications. In real-world organizations, leaders may receive feedback from the environment that helps to make their perceptions more accurate. Nonetheless, environmental and personal aspects of situational fit are determined by perceptions rather than by an objective reality.

## Zone of Transactional Relationship

This zone of the model depicts the dynamic interaction of leader and followers. Of the three zones of the model, the relationship zone is the furthest removed from reality. Leaders and followers create their own understandings of their relationships. The results of these interactions determine the motivation, commitment, and satisfaction of each party.

*Confidence and Optimism: Leadership Mettle.* The arrow between the boxes denoted with numerals 1 and 2 indicates that the effects of person–environment match are manifested in the leader's affective and cognitive orientation. Box 2 is located within the zone of transactional relationship, because the effects of the leader's psychological states realize their impact in interactions with followers.

The sense of being "in-match" and of feeling that one is well suited to the challenges posed by the situation results in a set of thoughts and emotions that have been addressed in a number of theoretical areas. Mihalyi Csikszentmihalyi's (1982) concept of "flow" captures some of the sense of this state. Csikszentmihalyi described a phenomenological experience that occurs when an individual perceives that task-related capabilities are challenged, but are not exceeded by the demands of the environment. When skills exceed challenges, the experience is one of boredom or distraction. When challenges exceed one's ability, the result is stress and anxiety. But, when challenges and opportunities are matched to skill and ability, the person experiences a "dynamic state of consciousness" characterized by a positive mood and focused attention.

A number of other research constructs resemble flow. Research on topics such as self-esteem (Brockner, 1988), self-efficacy (Bandura, 1982; Bandura & Cervone, 1983), optimism (Scheier, Weintraub, & Carver, 1986), hope (Snyder et al., 1991), for example, view positive emotions and confident perceptions as providing an actor with a calm demeanor that aids information processing and analysis, with greater energy and enthusiasm affecting motivation, and with a resiliance to stressful events.

I use the term "mettle" to describe the confluence of these cognitive and emotional states as they are manifested in a leader's posture and attitude toward the situation. Webster's Dictionary (Soukhanov & Ellis, 1988) defines mettle as (1) inherent quality of character and temperament; and (2) fortitude and courage. Roget's Thesaurus (Dutch, 1962) interprets the phrase "on one's mettle" to mean "aroused to do one's best." Mettle captures the sense of a confident and optimistic leader whose perceptions, thoughts, and mood provide a reservoir of enthusiasm and energy for meeting the challenges presented by the leadership task.

The definitions of mettle also indirectly reflect the fact that the set of cognitive and affective characteristics that comprise mettle can be a manifestation of an enduring, dispositional, orientation of the individual or the product of a particular time and situation. Mettle may be the result of match or of an inherent quality of temperament.

*Self-Attributions and Self-Reports.*    The model depicts two influences on the leader's self-reports and causal attributions for success and failure. The arrow from Box 2 reflects the influence of mettle in determining the essentially positive or negative tone of these self-descriptions. The arrow representing the impact of cultural idealizations reflects the impact of implicit theories and prototypes on the content of those self-reports. Leaders, like other observers of leadership processes, are likely to be biased in the perception of the causes of behavior and might be especially susceptible to "romantic" explanations (Meindl, 1990). The leader's self descriptions and inferences will be influenced by commonly held assumptions.

*Behavioral Intentions.*    Proceeding horizontally across the diagram the model depicts a linkage between mettle and the leader's behavioral intentions. Leaders high in mettle feel in control, confident, and optimistic about the outcomes of their behavior. In the language of expectancy theory, confident leaders have high probability expectations that their efforts will lead to the performance they hope to attain (E - P), and are optimistic that performance will lead to outcomes (P - O) of high value or desirability (V). Leaders with such highly motivational expectations are likely to act decisively and to be seen as in control of and contributing to positive group outcomes. However, three general sets of influences determine the perceived utility of specific behaviors and the desirability of particular outcomes.

Three commonly observed categories of leader behavior are included here. Structuring refers to task-oriented behaviors intended to facilitate the group's movement toward a goal, that is, assigning tasks, giving directions, providing feedback. Consideration refers to behaviors oriented toward group morale and the promotion of positive interpersonal relations. The Prominence category acknowledges that leaders sometimes act simply to increase their own ego satisfaction by drawing attention to themselves and their contribution without true regard for goal attainment or other collective benefits.

The arrow descending from cultural ideals through the mechanism of normative expectations represents the role of long-term social influences on behavior. Leaders and followers learn from their cultures that certain prototypical behavior will be effective (Hofstede, 1980; Triandis, 1993). For example, leaders raised in cultures high in Power Distance might have more confidence in their ability to lead through directive and autocratic techniques and may have greater belief in the efficacy of such tactics for attaining a goal. Leaders from cultures high in Collectivism might place greater value and desirability on group activities that promote harmony and cohesiveness.

A second influence on intentions and behavior arises from the individual leader's habitual patterns of thought and action. Several theoretical orientations ackowledge that leaders may vary in values, motivational goals, favored decision-making strategies, that lead them to feel more comfortable with or to place greater confidence in one set of behaviors over another (Bass et al., 1985; Fiedler & Chemers, 1984; Vroom, 1959; Vroom & Jago, 1974).

The third influence on the leader's intentions comes from an analysis of the particular demands of the contemporary situation. The leader might analyze the nature of the task, deciding that a particular decision strategy will be easier to implement or more likely to yield a high quality or implementable solution. A leader might judge a subordinate's readiness for or responsiveness to a particular influence strategy, task assignment, or feedback style.

The arrow ascending to the behavioral intentions box from below completes a loop from followers to leader that reflects the importance of high quality communication between them. The leader's ability to elicit clear communication from followers and the capability to attend to subordinate communication and make accurate attributions concerning the implications of subordinate behavior and performance are related to the ultimate utility of the intended behaviors.

The language of expectancy theory, with its emphasis on perceived probabilities linking actions and outcomes, implies a strong cognitive and rational flavor to the leader's intentions. Such may not be the case. The leader's intentions and subsequent behavior may be under the influence of either controlled or automatic processes. A leader carefully analyzing task characteristics, follower maturity, and group goals, and avoiding defensiveness and bias, represents an ideal of controlled processing. However, leadership also involves stressful situations in which automatic, less rational processes predominate. The anxiety and defensiveness engendered by threats to self-evaluation arising from potential task or interpersonal failure may reduce the capacity for controlled processing and may throw the leader back on well-learned, self-protective thoughts and actions.

Fiedler (1993b) presented a recent analysis of leadership style that argues that leaders may have an almost "Jekyll and Hyde" transformation across situations. As stress increases, the leader's perspective narrows and goals become more personal and focused. A leader who can be calm and thoughtful under low stress conditions may turn autocratic and presumptuous when anxious and threatened.

*Action.* At Box 4, the leader's intentions are translated into behavior. The dual-directional arrows between Boxes 4 and 5 represent the fact that the interaction of leader and follower is a dynamic process in which each person's perceptions, intentions, and reactions are responsive to the other's. Some of the behaviors are guided by explicit intentions and some are relatively automatic reactions to the interplay of events. Many of these actions and reactions occur without conscious awareness. For example, a leader under the pressure to make a decision or accomplish a task may react emotionally to criticism without careful thought or analysis. These automatic, heavily affective aspects of the leadership dynamic have been almost completely ignored in leadership research and suggest a rich vein of important additions to current knowledge.

*Followers' Reactions.* Box 5 delineates the factors that determine follower reactions. The notion of match or fit between behavior, needs, and expectations is the causal process in these reactions. As reflected in the descending arrow from culture through normative socialization, many of the same forces that shape the leader's expectations are contributory for the followers'. Cultural expectations embodied in leadership prototypes and implicit theories, as well as personal values and motivations of a habitual or contemporary genesis, are included.

The match hypothesis suggests three levels of reaction of increasing intensity. When a leader's demeanor and behavior are consistent with the follower's image or prototype of a leader, the attribution is made that this is indeed a leader. When group outcomes, such as performance and goal attainment, are consistent with the follower's expectations, the leader's legitimacy is enhanced, and the leader is regarded as a "good leader." When the leader's activities lead to the satisfaction of the follower's personal needs leading to high levels of satisfaction, the leader elicits a highly positive emotional reaction from the follower.

The more intense the needs of the follower are, the more opportunity is provided for the leader to have a charismatic or transformational effect on the follower. Followers may bring intensely felt needs to the leadership situation because of contemporary situational factors, such as threats to physical or financial safety, or because of dispositional characteristics, such as self-esteem or intense ambition. Leaders may also arouse more powerful needs in followers, either by appeals to their basest natural tendencies of fear and hostility tapped by leaders like Hitler, or by appeals to their highest feelings of collective responsibility and moral purpose such as those encouraged by Martin Luther King, Jr.

When followers are asked to make attributions for the leader's effects, they are likely to fall back on the same causal schema, implicit theories, and cultural prototypes as the leader and other observers use. The information-processing literature on leadership (e.g., Lord & Maher, 1991) gives ample evidence that reports of leader behavior are strongly influenced by such mechanisms.

When leaders, acting with confidence and optimism, act and react to followers and situations in optimal ways, the group as a whole is mobilized for committed, highly motivated, effort. The resource that is represented by the group's commitment must be coordinated and applied to the group's task and organizational mission. That coordination takes us from the zone of transactional relationship into the zone of team deployment. We shift from the social constructions of leader–follower relations to the uncompromising reality-based venue of productivity and performance.

## Zone of Team Deployment

*Follower Actions.* Moving from Boxes 5 to 6, follower cognitive and affective reactions are translated into action. The actions of followers can be addressed from three perspectives. Motivated followers may demonstrate high levels of effort, working doggedly to accomplish the tasks assigned to them. Followers' goal-directed behavior may also reflect high levels of persistence. Motivated followers may give a sustained and steady level of attention and effort over time. A third way to conceptualize subordinate effort is in terms of contributions to problem solution and goal achievement. Here, the emphasis is on the followers adding something unique and personal to the group's resources.

The leader can harness the group's commitment and motivation and guide it in one of these three directions. Directive leadership with an emphasis on assigned tasks and specific behaviors is likely to result in large amounts of focused effort. Leadership that sets long-term goals and delegates responsibility for monitoring and adjustment to subordinates will usually result in greater self-regulation, attention, and perserverance. Highly participative, group-oriented leadership with extensive power sharing and support for subordinate development will provide a framework for followers to contribute to the definition and solution of group goals.

Contingency theories of leadership, as well as the organizational design literature (e.g., Lawrence & Lorsch, 1967) make it clear that ultimate utility of each of these patterns of coordination depends on the nature of systemic contingencies.

High levels of subordinate effort are likely to have the most positive effects on short-term tasks of a highly structured nature. When the situation provides the leader with clear guidelines for action, subordinate effort can be directed toward task accomplishment.

On difficult tasks, where situational vicissitudes make progress uncertain, perserverance should be associated with long-term performance. Groups that can maintain a high level of motivation and effort despite momentary ups and downs will have an advantage in long-term performance.

When either a fast-changing environment or a task that is not well understood causes high levels of unpredictability, subordinate contribution enhances the range and creativity of problem solving. Spontaneous goal-directed activity by a well-trained and highly informed team gives the organization flexibility in meeting challenges that cannot be anticipated or planned for in advance.

*Organizational Performance.*   When the coordination and direction of the activities of leaders and followers are appropriate to the demands of the situation, positive outcomes are realized. These outcomes can be conceptualized in terms of productivity (i.e., simple levels of output evaluated quantitatively), efficiency (i.e., the ratio of productivity to costs), or effectiveness (i.e., the extent to which group activities meet mission priorities).

## SOME IMPLICATIONS FOR THEORY AND RESEARCH

In the opening chapter of this book, the role of the leader was described as balancing the organization's need to maintain a reliable, internal orderliness with the requirement to adapt to the demands of a changing environment. The process model presented here describes the key elements in meeting that responsibility. Building a motivated team that recognizes the nature of its responsibility and that gives willing effort is the central feature of internal integration. Using appropriate strategies to accomplish the mission is the essence of external adaptation.

### For Theory

A number of questions and controversies were raised throughout this book. A few of the most general were raised again at the outset of this chapter. How are they addressed by an integrative theory?

The divergence of scientific and popular theories may now be a bit easier to understand. The approaches taken by popular theorists are heavily dependent on introspection; either by leaders or followers examining their own perceptions and memories or by observers (e.g., consultants) compiling their impressions. In either case, such approaches are particularly susceptible to subjective biases. In some respects, the conclusions of popular theories are surprisingly close to those of the more empirically based analyses. Good leaders do inspire their subordinates through vision and trustworthiness, and they are characterized by a strong confidence in themselves and in the people with whom they work.

Unfortunately, popular approaches can also be dangerous, both for what they fail to reveal and that what they reveal is not quite accurate. In the former category, the failure of popular theories to recognize the contingent nature of effective leaders tells an overly simplified story that can be quite problematic for practicing leaders who attempt to put the theories into action.

In the latter category, reifying innaccurate, stereotypic assumptions about dramatic leadership differences between men and women diverts attention from more productive ways of enhancing the effective utilization of managerial talent and diversity in organizations.

The question of contingency versus one-best-way explanations of leadership can probably be best answered by recognizing that the way in which productive leadership is accomplished may follow contingency principles, whereas the way in which it is perceived may be more absolute or universal. Both a task-oriented or a relationship-oriented leader can appear confident, in control, and sensitive to followers when the leader is in-match with the situation and draws on a wellspring of confidence and optimism. The effective leader will be described in terms that are consistent with the prototypes held by observers. If a prototype is shared, all effective leaders will be described similarly, giving rise to the impression that there is one best way to lead.

Contingency principles are applicable even to the charismatic leadership. The characteristics of transformational leaders will manifest themselves differently in different environments. House and Shamir (1993) made the point that even charisma is culture and context bound. What motivates an agrarian worker in a war-ravaged, starving populace will not be the same characteristics that energize the upwardly mobile, MBA in corporate America.

Finally, the knottiest question of all concerned the role of social construction in leadership. The proponents of subjectivity explanations make a strong case. People do evidence extensive bias in their perception of leaders, as they do in their perceptions of other social phenomena. Leadership is exaggerated, distorted, and overglamorized, but it is also a central fact of group life. Some aspects of the leadership phenomenon are heavily detached from an objective basis, but other aspects are more closely tied to an objective reality.

This does not mean that we should ignore the constructionist critiques of contemporary leadership theory. There is a place for both constructionist and positivist perspectives in the study of leadership. Perception is a critical feature of legitimacy, power, and influence. By incorporating the concepts the subjectivist theories present and the implications they reveal, leadership theory and practice can become more accurate, relevant, and effective. Constructionist approaches represent a useful addition to leadership theory, not a threat.

## For Research

The integrative perspective suggests a number of productive areas for new or continued research efforts. The area of affective influences on leadership processes is ripe for development. Anyone who has studied organizations, or has just worked in one, knows how emotional work relationships can be, especially those involving leadership.

It has long been an unspoken, but widely recognized fact among leadership researchers that leaders' descriptions of their own behavior or intentions bore only limited resemblance to any other basis of reality, that is, follower reports, observations, and so forth. Leadership researchers implicitly acknowledged that the leader was too ego involved to provide an accurate reflection of what was occurring. What we failed to recognize or follow up on was that the discrepancy between what leaders said and what might really be true was a potentially important area of study.

Emotion-driven, automatic, or habitual behavior (e.g., conflict avoidance in disagreeable interactions; stress-induced withdrawal; anxiety-aroused aggression) may control considerable variance in leadership interaction. Affectively caused behavior will bear little resemblance either to rationally constructed intentions or to self-serving post hoc explanations.

An area that is not new, but that bears increased attention concerns the role of culture in leadership. We may now be ready to move past the easier questions. It is a well-established finding that cultures differ somewhat in their prototypes of effective leadership and in their behavioral definitions of what constitutes good directive or considerate behavior. At the same time, cultures do not differ so much that leadership has grossly different functions in different cultures. Leaders in all organizations are important in motivating and coordinating the activities of subordinates to accomplish tasks. Those were some of the simpler issues to study.

Some more interesting questions concern the ways in which organizational environments and leadership processes are construed in different cultural milieus. For example, how are disparate cultural traditions, such as those of Japan and the United States, able to achieve comparable results in similar markets with such dramatically different leadership styles and subordinate values and expectations? How do different cultures redefine the nature of their tasks to suit their inherent proclivities? How does culture affect the nature of contingency variables? Do cultures, as Triandis (1993) suggested, provide differential frames of reference for what constitutes a structured task or a powerful position?

In a related vein, it may be time to move past cultural explanations where we have found they do not apply, as in the case of women leaders. By emphasizing differences that are not important, we may obscure other more important implications of social category effects on group dynamics. More interesting theoretical and more pragmatically important questions present themselves. For example, what factors facilitate the management of intergroup relations? What are the most effective ways of leading groups so that differing points of view can result in creative problem solving?

A third area of research made more salient by an integrative approach is the interface of small group, organizational, and environmental variables. Finding a way to communicate from the micro-oriented language of motivation and interaction to the macro-oriented world of strategy and organizational design represents a promising direction. For example, Nahavandi and Malekzadeh (1993) integrated ideas from leadership theory, cross-cultural psychology, and strategic management studies to analyze corporate mergers and acquisitions. Building theories that bridge across levels of analysis is difficult, but may ultimately prove to be very productive.

## A SUMMARY AND FINAL CONCLUSION

Effective leaders must accomplish three functions:

- Leaders must project an image of competence and trustworthiness. They accomplish that projection by matching their behavior to commonly held prototypes.

- Leaders must establish a relationship with followers that guides, develops, and inspires them to make meaningful contributions to group goals and the organizational mission. Such relationships must match the needs and expectations of followers, which leaders discern through nondefensive judgments.
- Leaders must mobilize and deploy the collective resources of self and team to the organizational mission by matching operational strategy to the characteristics of the environment.

A final conclusion is that in terms of a coherent theoretical literature, an exciting area of research, and a meaningful knowledge base for application, leadership study is alive and well. Integration across perspectives may allow us to construct a base from what we know that can provide a stepping stone for moving to the next level of study. Given the importance of leadership to organizational and societal success, the challenge is worth taking.

# References

Adams, J. S. (1963). Toward an understanding of inequity. *Journal of Abnormal and Social Psychology*, *67*, 422–436.

Anderson, L. R. (1987). Self-monitoring and performance in non-traditional occupations. *Basic and Applied Social Psychology, 8*, 85–96.

Ansari, A. A., & Kapoor, A. (1987). Organizational context and upward influence tactics. *Organizational Behavior and Human Decision Processes*, *40*, 39–49.

Ashour, A. S. (1973). The contingency model of leadership effectiveness: An evaluation. *Organizational Behavior and Human Performance*, *9*, 339–355.

Avolio, B. J., & Howell, J. M. (1990, July). *The effects of leader–follower personality congruence: Predicting follower satisfaction and business unit performance*. Paper presented at the 1990 International Congress of Applied Psychology, Kyoto, Japan.

Ayman, R. (1993). Leadership perception: The role of culture and gender. In M. M. Chemers & R. Ayman (Eds.), *Leadership theory and research: Perspectives and directions* (pp. 137–166). San Diego: Academic Press.

Ayman, R. & Chemers, M. M. (1983). The relationship of supervisory behavior ratings to work group effectiveness and subordinate satisfaction among Iranian managers. *Journal of Applied Psychology*, *68*, 338–341.

Ayman, R., & Chemers, M. M. (1991). The effect of leadership match on subordinate satisfaction in Mexican organizations: Some moderating influences of self-monitoring. *International Review of Applied Psychology*, *40*, 299–331

Bakan, D. (1966). *The duality of human existence: An essay on psychology and religion*. Chicago: Rand McNally.

Bales, R. F. (1950). *Interaction process analysis*. Reading, MA: Addison-Wesley.

Bales, R. F., & Slater, P. E. (1955). Role differentiation in small decision-making groups. In T. Parsons, (Eds.), *Family, socialization, and interaction processes*. Glencoe, IL: Free Press.

Bales, R. F., & Strodtbeck, F. L. (1951). Phases in group problem solving. *Journal of Abnormal and Social Psychology*, *46*, 485–495.

Bandura, A. (1969). *Principles of behavior modification*. New York: Holt, Rinehart, & Winston.

Bandura, A. (1982). Self-efficacy mechanism in human agency. *American Psychologist, 37*, 122–147.

Bandura, A. (1986). *Social foundations of thought and action: A social-cognitive theory*. Englewood Cliffs, NJ: Prentice-Hall.

Bandura, A., & Cervone, D. (1983). Self-evaluative and self-efficacy mechanisms governing motivational effects of goal systems. *Journal of Personality and Social Psychology, 45*, 1017–1028.

Barnard, C. I. (1938). *The functions of the executive*. Cambridge, MA: Harvard University Press.

Bartol, K. M. (1974). Male vs. female leaders: The effect of leader need for dominance on follower satisfaction. *Academy of Management Journal, 17*, 225–233.

Bartol, K. M. (1976). Relationship of sex and professional training area to job orientation. *Journal of Applied Psychology, 61*, 368–370.

Bartol, K. M., & Butterfield, D. A. (1976). Sex effects in evaluating leaders. *Journal of Applied Psychology, 61,* 446–454.

Bass, B. M. (1981). *Stogdill's handbook of leadership* (2nd ed.). New York: Free Press.

Bass, B. M. (1985). *Leadership and performance beyond expectations.* New York: Free Press.

Bass, B. M. (1988). Evolving perspectives on charismatic leadership. In J. Conger & R. N. Kanungo (Eds.), *Charismatic leadership: The elusive factor in organizational effectiveness.* San Francisco: Jossey-Bass.

Bass, B. M. (1990). *Bass and Stogdill's handbook of leadership* (3rd ed.). New York: Free Press.

Bass, B. M., & Avolio, B. J. (1990a). *Manual for the multifactor leadership questionnaire.* Palo Alto, CA: Consulting Psychologist Press.

Bass, B. M., & Avolio, B. J. (1990b). The implications of transactional and transformational leadership for individual, team, and organizational development. In R. W. Woodman & W. A. Passmore (Eds.), *Research in organizational change and development.* Greenwich, CT: JAI Press.

Bass, B. M., & Avolio, B. J. (1993). Transformational leadership: A response to critiques. In M. M. Chemers & R. Ayman (Eds.), *Leadership theory and research: Perspectives and directions* (pp. 49–80). San Diego: Academic Press.

Bass, B. M., Klubeck, S., & Wurster, C. R. (1953). Factors influencing the reliability and validity of leaderless group discussion assessment. *Journal of Applied Psychology, 37,* 26–30.

Bass, B. M., Krusell, J., & Alexander, R. A. (1971). Male managers' attitudes toward working women. *American Behavioral Scientist, 15,* 221–236.

Bass, B. M., & Valenzi, E. R. (1974). Contingency aspects of effective management styles. In J. G. Hunt & L. L. Larsen (Eds.), *Contingency approaches to leadership.* Carbondale, IL: Southern Illinois University Press.

Bass, B. M., Valenzi, E. R., Farrow, D. L., & Solomon, R. J. (1975). Management style associated with organizational, task, personal, and interpersonal contingencies. *Journal of Applied Psychology, 60,* 720–729.

Bass, B. M. & Yokochi, N. (1991, Winter/Spring). Charisma among senior executives and the special case of Japanese CEO's. *Consulting Psychology Bulletin, 1,* 31–38.

Bavelas, A., Hastorf, A. H., Gross, A. E., & Kite, W. R. (1965). Experiments on the alteration of group structure. *Journal of Experimental Social Psychology, 1,* 55–70.

Bell, L.G., Wicklund, R. A., Manko, G., & Larkin, C. (1976). When unexpected behavior is attributed to the environment. *Journal of Research in Personality, 10,* 316–327.

Bem, S. L. (1974). The measurement of psychological androgyny. *Journal of Consulting and Clinical Psychology, 42,* 155–162.

Bem, S. L. (1977). On the utility of alternative procedures for measuring psychological androgyny. *Journal of Consulting and Clinical Psychology, 45,* 196–205.

Bennis, W., & Nanus, B. (1985). *Leaders: The strategies for taking charge.* New York: Harper & Row.

Berger, J., Conner, B. P., & Zelditch, M. (1972). Status characteristics and social interaction. *American Sociological Review, 37,* 241–255.

Binet, A. & Simon, T. (1908). Le development de l'intelligence chez les infants [The development of children's intelligence]. *Année Psychologique, 14,* 245–366.

Blades, J. W., & Fiedler, F. E. (1973). *The influence of intelligence, task ability, and motivation on group performance.* (Organizational Research Tech. Rep. 76-78). Seattle: University of Washington.

Bons, P. M., & Fiedler, F. E. (1976). The effects of changes in command environment on the behavior of relationship- and task-motivated leaders. *Administrative Science Quarterly, 21,* 453–473.

Bowman, G. W., Worthy, N. B., & Greyser, S. A. (1965). Are women executives people? *Harvard Business Review, 43,* 14–28.

Brief, A. P., & Aldag, R. J. (1975). Male–female differences in occupational values within majority groups. *Journal of Vocational Behavior, 6,* 305–314.

Brief, A. P., & Oliver, R. L. (1976). Male–female differences in work attitudes among retail sales managers. *Journal of Applied Psychology, 61,* 526–528.

Brislin, R. W. (1981). *Cross-cultural encounters.* New York: Pergamon Press.

Brockner, J. (1988). *Self-esteem at work: Research, theory and practice*. Lexington, MA: D. C. Heath and Company.

Broverman, I. K., Vogel, S. R., Broverman, D. M., Clarkson, F. E., & Rosenkrantz, P. S. (1972). Sex-role stereotypes: A current appraisal. *Journal of Social Issues, 28*, 59–78.

Brown, K. A. (1984). Explaining group poor performance: An attributional analysis. *Academy of Management Review, 9*, 54–63.

Burns, J. M. (1978). *Leadership*. New York: Harper & Row.

Burns, T., & Stalker, G. (1961). *The management of innovation*. London: Tavistock Publications.

Butler, D., & Geis, F. L. (1990). Nonverbal affect responses to male and female leaders: Implications for leadership evaluation. *Journal of Personality and Social Psychology, 58*, 48–59.

Butterfield, D. A., & Powell, G. N. (1981). Effect of group performance, leader sex, and rater sex on ratings of leader behavior. *Organizational Behavior and Human Performance, 28*, 129–141.

Calder, B. J. (1977). An attribution theory of leadership. In B. M. Staw & G. R. Salancik (Eds.), *New directions in organizational behavior*. Chicago: St Clair Press.

Cantor, N., & Mischel, W. (1979). Prototypes in person perception. In L. Berkowitz (Ed.), *Advances in experimental social psychology* (Vol. 12). New York: Academic Press.

Carlyle, T. (1907). *Heroes and hero worship*. Boston: Adams. (Original work published 1841).

Carter, L. F. (1953). Leadership and small group behavior. In M. Sherif & M. O. Wilson (Eds.), *Group relations at the crossroads*. New York: Harper.

Cartwright, D., & Zander, A. (Eds.). (1968). *Group dynamics* (3rd ed.). New York: Harper & Row.

Chemers, M. M. (1969). Cross-cultural training as a means for improving situational favorableness. *Human Relations, 22*, 531–546.

Chemers, M. M. (1991, August). *The cultural universality of contingency approaches to leadership*. Presented at Academy of Management meetings, Miami Beach, FL.

Chemers, M. M. (1993). An integrative theory of leadership. In M. M. Chemers & R. Ayman (Eds.), *Leadership theory and research* (pp. 293–320). San Diego: Academic Press.

Chemers, M. M., & Ayman, R. (1985). Leadership orientation as a moderator of the relationship between performance and satisfaction of Mexican managers. *Personality and Social Psychology Bulletin, 11*, 359–367.

Chemers, M. M., Ayman, R., Sorod, B., & Akimoto, S. (1991, July). *Self-monitoring as a moderator of leader–follower relationships*. Presented at the International Congress of Psychology, Brussels.

Chemers, M. M., & Cunningham, J. M. (1989, April). *The centrality of leader feedback to worker satisfaction*. Presented at the meetings of the Western Psychological Association, San Francisco, CA.

Chemers, M. M., Watson, C. B., & May, S. (1996, June). *Heavy mettle: Confidence and optimism in leadership effectiveness*. Presented at the meetings of the American Psychological Society, San Francisco.

Chemers, M. M., Hays, R., Rhodewalt, F., & Wysocki, J. (1985). A person–environment analysis of job stress: A contingency model explanation. *Journal of Personality and Social Psychology, 49*, 628–635.

Chemers, M. M., Hill, C., & Sorod, B. (1986, August). *Personality-environment match and health: Support for the contingency model*. Paper presented at the meetings of the American Psychological Association, Chicago, IL.

Chemers, M. M., & Murphy, S. E. (1995). Leadership for diversity in groups and organizations. In M. M. Chemers, S. Oskamp, & M. A. Costanzo (Eds.), *Diversity in organizations: Perspectives on a changing workplace* (pp. 157–188). Newbury Park, CA: Sage.

Chemers, M. M., Oskamp, S. & Costanzo. M. A. (Eds.) (1995). *Diversity in organizations: Perspectives on a changing workplace*. Newbury Park, CA: Sage.

Chemers, M. M., & Skrzypek, G. J. (1972). Experimental test of the contingency model of leadership effectiveness. *Journal of Personality and Social Psychology, 24*, 172–177.

Chi, M. T. H., Glaser, R., & Farr, M. J. (1988). *The nature of expertise*. Hillsdale, NJ: Lawrence Erlbaum Associates.

Cleven, W. A., & Fiedler, F. E. (1956). Interpersonal perceptions of open-hearth foremen and steel production. *Journal of Applied Psychology, 40*, 312–314.

Cohen, S. L., Bunker, K. A., Burton, A. L., & McManus, P. D. (1978). Reactions of male subordinates to sex-role congruency of immediate supervision. *Sex Roles, 4,* 297–311.

Conger, J. A. (Ed.). (1989). The dark side of the charismatic leader. In J. A. Conger (Ed.), *The charismatic leader.* San Francisco: Jossey-Bass.

Conger, J. A., & Kanungo, R. A. (1987). Towards a behavioral theory of charismatic leadership in organizational settings. *Academy of Management Review, 12,* 637–647.

Couch, A., & Carter, L. F. (1952). A factorial study of the related behavior of group members. *American Psychologist, 8,* 333.

Csikszentmihalyi, M., & Rasthunde, K. (1992). The measurement of flow in everyday life: Toward a theory of emergent motivation. In J. E. Jacobs (Ed.), *Nebraska symposium on motivation* (Vol. 40, pp. 57–97). Lincoln: University of Nebraska Press.

Dachler, H. P. (1984). On refocusing leadership from a social systems perspective. In J. G. Hunt, D. M. Hosking, C. A. Schriesheim, & R. Stewart (Eds.), *Leaders and managers: International perspectives on managerial behavior and leadership* (pp. 100–108). New York: Pergamon Press.

Dachler, H. P. (1988). Constraints on the emergence of new vistas in leadership and management research: An epistemological overview. In J. G. Hunt, B. R. Baliga, H. P. Dachler, & C. A. Schriesheim (Eds.), *Emerging leadership vistas.* Lexington, MA: Lexington.

Dansereau, F., Graen, G., & Haga, W. J. (1975). A vertical dyad linkage approach to leadership within formal organizations. *Organizational Behavior and Human Performance, 13,* 46–78.

Darley, J. M., & Fazio, R. H. (1980). Expectancy confirmation processes arising in the social interaction sequence. *American Psychologist, 35,* 867–881.

Day, D. R., & Stogdill, R. M. (1972). Leader behavior of male and female supervisors: A comparative study. *Personnel Psychology, 25,* 353–360.

Day, D. V., & Lord, R. G. (1988). Executive leadership and organizational performance: Suggestions for a new theory and methodology. *Journal of Management, 14,* 111–122.

Deaux, K. (1984). From individual differences to social categories. *American Psychologist, 39,* 105–116.

Deaux, K., & Farris, E. (1974). *Attributing causes for one's own performance: The effects of sex, norms, and outcomes.* Unpublished manuscript, Purdue University.

Deaux, K., & Farris, E. (1977). Attributing causes for one's own performance: The effects of sex, norms, and outcome. *Journal of Research in Personality, 11,* 59–72.

Deaux, K., White, L., & Farris, E. (1975). Skill versus luck: Field and laboratory studies of male and female preferences. *Journal of Personality and Social Psychology, 32,* 629–636.

Deci, E. L., & Ryan, R. (1980). The empirical exploration of intrinsic motivational processes. In L. Berkowitz (Ed.), *Advances in experimental social psychology* (Vol. 13, pp. 39–80). New York: Academic Press.

Deluga, R. J. (1990). The effects of transformational, transactional, and laissez-faire leadership characteristics on subordinate influencing behavior. *Basic and Applied Social Psychology, 11,* 191–203.

Dessler, G., & Valenzi, E. R. (1977). Initiation of structure and subordinate satisfaction: A path analysis test of path–goal theory. *Academy of Management Journal, 20,* 251–259.

Diamond, S. (1969). *In search of the primitive.* New Brunswick, NJ: Transaction Books.

Dobbins, G. H., & Platz, S. J. (1986). Sex differences in leadership: How real are they? *Academy of Management Review, 11,* 118–127.

Downey, H. K., Sheridan, J. E., & Slocum, J. W., Jr. (1975). Analysis of relationships among leader behavior, subordinate job performance, and satisfaction: A path–goal approach. *Academy of Management Journal, 18,* 253–262.

Downey, H. K., Sheridan, J. E., & Slocum, J. W., Jr. (1976). The path–goal theory of leadership: A longitudinal analysis. *Organizational Behavior and Human Performance, 16,* 156–176.

Downey, J. K., Chacko, T. I., & McElroy, J. C. (1979). Attributions of "causes" of performance: A constructive quasi-longitudinal replication of the Staw (1975) study. *Organizational Behavior and Human Performance, 24,* 287–289.

Drucker, P. (1954). *The practice of management*. New York: Harper & Row.

Dutch, R. A. (1962). *Roget's thesaurus*. New York: St. Martin's.

Dweck, C. S., & Repucci, N. D. (1973). Learned helplessness and reinforcement responsibility in children. *Journal of Personality and Social Psychology, 25*, 109–116.

Eagly, A. H. (1987). *Sex differences in social behavior: A social-role interpretation*. Hillsdale, NJ: Lawrence Erlbaum Associates.

Eagly, A. H., & Carli, L. L. (1981). Sex of researchers and sex-typed communications as determinants of sex differences in influenceability: A meta-analysis of social influence studies. *Psychological Bulletin, 90*, 1–20.

Eagly, A. H., & Johnson, B. T. (1990). Gender and leadership style: A meta-analysis. *Psychological Bulletin, 108*, 233–256.

Eagly, A. H., & Karau, S. J. (1991). Gender and the emergence of leaders: A meta-analysis. *Journal of Personality and Social Psychology, 60*, 685–710.

Eagly, A. H., Makhijani, M. G., & Klonsky, B. G. (1992). Gender and the evaluation of leaders: A meta-analysis. *Psychological Bulletin, 111*, 3–22.

Eden, D., & Leviatan, U. (1975). Implicit leadership theory as a determinant of the factor structure underlying supervisory behavior scales. *Journal of Applied Psychology, 60*, 736–741.

England, G. W. (1976). *The manager and his values: An international perspective from the United States, Japan, Korea, India, and Australia*. Cambridge, MA: Ballinger.

England, G. W., & Lee, R. (1971). The relationship between managerial values and managerial success in the United States, Japan, India, and Australia. *Journal of Applied Psychology, 59*, 411–419.

England, G. W., & Lee, R. (1974). Organizational goals and expected behaviors among American, Japanese, and Korean managers: A comparative study. *Academy of Management Journal, 14*, 425–438.

Erez, M., & Rim, Y. (1982). The relationship between goals, influence tactics, and personal and organizational variables. *Human Relations, 35*, 871–878.

Etzioni, A. (1975). *A comparative analysis of complex organizations*. New York: Free Press.

Evans, M. G. (1970). The effects of supervisory behavior on the path–goal relationship. *Organizational Behavior and Human Performance, 5*, 277–298.

Ferris, G. R. (1985). Role of leadership in the employee withdrawal process: A constructive replication. *Journal of Applied Psychology, 70*, 777–781.

Festinger, L., & Carlsmith, J. M. (1959). Cognitive consequences of forced compliance. *Journal of Abnormal and Social Psychology, 58*, 203–210.

Fiedler, F. E. (1951). A method of objective quantification of certain countertransference attitudes. *Journal of Clinical Psychology, 7*, 101–107.

Fiedler, F. E. (1953). *Assumed similarity measures as predictors of team effectiveness in surveying*. Bureau of Research Services, Technical Report No. 6. Urbana: University of Illinois.

Fiedler, F. E. (1954). Assumed similarity measures and predictors of team effectiveness. *Journal of Abnormal and Social Psychology, 49*, 381–388.

Fiedler, F. E. (1955). The influence of leader–keyman relations on combat crew effectiveness. *Journal of Abnormal and Social Psychology, 51*, 227–235.

Fiedler, F. E. (1958). *Leader attitudes and group effectiveness*. New York: McGraw-Hill.

Fiedler, F. E. (1964). A contingency model of leadership effectiveness. In L. Berkowitz (Ed.), *Advances in experimental social psychology* (Vol. 1, pp. 149–190). New York: Academic Press.

Fiedler, F. E. (1966). The effect of leadership and cultural heterogeneity on group performance: A test of the contingency model. *Journal of Experimental Social Psychology, 2*, 237–264.

Fiedler, F. E. (1967). *A theory of leadership effectiveness*. New York: McGraw-Hill.

Fiedler, F. E. (1970). Leadership experience and leader performance—Another hypothesis shot to hell. *Organizational Behavior and Human Performance, 5*, 1–14.

Fiedler, F. E. (1971). Validation and extension of the contingency model of leadership effectiveness: A review of empirical findings. *Psychological Bulletin, 76*, 128–148.

Fiedler, F. E. (1972). Personality, motivational systems, and the behavior of high and low LPC persons. *Human Relations, 25,* 391–412.

Fiedler, F. E. (1978). The contingency model and the dynamics of the leadership process. In L. Berkowitz (Ed.), *Advances in experimental social psychology* (Vol. 11, pp. 59–112). New York: Academic Press.

Fiedler, F. E. (1993a). *Leadership experience and leadership performance.* Alexandria, VA: U.S. Army Research Institute.

Fiedler, F. E. (1993b). The leadership situation and the Black Box in contingency theories. In M. M. Chemers & R. Ayman (Eds.), *Leadership theory and research: Perspectives and directions* (pp. 1–28). San Diego: Academic Press.

Fiedler, F. E., & Chemers, M. M. (1968). *Group performance under experienced and inexperienced leaders: A validation experiment.* Urbana: University of Illinois, Group Effectiveness Research Laboratory.

Fiedler, F. E., & Chemers, M. M. (1974). *Leadership and effective management.* Glenview, IL: Scott, Foresman.

Fiedler, F. E., & Chemers, M. M. (1984). *Improving leadership effectiveness: The leader match concept* (2nd ed.). New York: Wiley.

Fiedler, F. E., Chemers, M. M., & Mahar, L. (1976). *Improving leadership effectiveness: The leader match concept.* New York: Wiley.

Fiedler, F. E., & Garcia, J. E. (1987). *New approaches to effective leadership: Cognitive resources and organizational performance.* New York: Wiley.

Fiedler, F. E., & Leister, A. F. (1977). Leader intelligence and task performance: A test of the multiple screen model. *Organizational Behavior and Human Performance, 20,* 1–14.

Fiedler, F. E., Meuwese, W. A. T., & Oonk, S. (1960). An exploratory study of group creativity in laboratory tasks. *Acta Psychologica, 18,* 100–119.

Fiedler, F. E., Nealey, S. M., & Wood, M. T. (1968). *The effects of training on the performance of post office supervisors.* Unpublished manuscript: University of Illinois at Urbana, Group Effectiveness Research Laboratory.

Fiedler, F. E., O'Brien, G. E., & Ilgen, D. R. (1969). The effect of leadership style upon the performance and adjustment of volunteer teams operating in a stressful foreign environment. *Human Relations, 22,* 503–514.

Fiedler, F. E., Potter, E. H., Zais, M. M., & Knowlton, W. A., Jr. (1979). Organizational stress and the use and misuse of managerial intelligence and experience. *Journal of Applied Psychology, 64,* 635–647.

Fiedler, F. E., Warrington, W. G., & Blaisdell, F. J. (1952). Unconscious attitudes as correlates of sociometric choice in social groups. *Journal of Abnormal and Social Psychology, 47,* 790–796.

Field, R. H. G., & House, R. J. (1990). A test of the Vroom–Yetton model using manager and subordinate reports. *Journal of Applied Psychology, 75,* 362–366.

Filley, A. C., & House, R. J. (1969). *Managerial process and organizational behavior.* Glenview, IL: Scott, Foresman.

Fishbein, M., Landy, E., & Hatch, G. (1969). A consideration of two assumptions underlying Fiedler's Contingency Model for prediction of leadership effectiveness. *American Journal of Psychology, 82,* 457–473.

Fiske, A. P. (1991). *Structures of social life: The four elementary forms of human relations.* New York: Free Press.

Fleishman, E. A., & Harris, E. F. (1962). Patterns of leadership behavior related to employee greivances and turnover. *Personnel Psychology, 15,* 43–54.

Foa, U. G., Mitchell, T. R., & Fiedler, F. E. (1971). Differential matching. *Behavioral Science, 16,* 130–142.

Frankfort, H., Frankfort, H. A., Wilson, J. A., & Jacobsen, T. (1949). *Before philosophy.* Baltimore: Penguin Books.

French, J. R. P., & Raven, B. H. (1959). The bases of social power. In D. Cartwright (Ed.), *Studies in social power* (pp. 150–167). Ann Arbor: University of Michigan Institute of Social Research.

Frieze, I. H., Parsons, J. E., Johnson, P. B., Ruble, D. N., & Zellman, G. L. (1978). *Women and sex roles: A social psychological perspective.* New York: Norton.

Galambos, J. A., Abelson, R. P., & Black, J. B. (1986). *Knowledge structures.* Hillsdale, NJ: Lawrence Erlbaum Associates.

Garcia, J. E. (1983). *An investigation of a person–situation match interpretation of the esteem for the least preferred co-worker scale (LPC).* Unpublished doctoral dissertation, University of Utah, Salt Lake City.

Garland, H., & Price, K. H. (1977). Attitudes toward women in management and attributions for their success and failure in a managerial position. *Journal of Applied Psychology, 62,* 29– 33.

Georgopoulos, B. S., Mahoney, G. M., & Jones, N. W. (1957). A path–goal approach to productivity. *Journal of Applied Psychology, 41,* 345–353.

Gilbert, D. T., Krull, D. S., & Pelham, B. W. (1988). Of thoughts unspoken: Social inference and the self-regulation of behavior. *Journal of Personality and Social Psychology, 55,* 685–694.

Gilbert, D. T., Pelham, B. W., & Krull, D. S. (1988). On cognitive busyness: When person perceivers meet persons perceived. *Journal of Personality and Social Psychology, 54,* 733– 740.

Godfrey, E. B., Fiedler, F. E., & Hall, D. M. (1959). *Boards, management, and company success.* Danville, IL: Interstate.

Gordon, L. V. (1975). *The measurement of interpersonal values.* Chicago: Science Research Associates.

Gordon, L. V. (1976). *Survery of interpersonal values—revised manual.* Chicago: Science Research Associates.

Graen, G. (1976). Role making processes within complex organizations. In M. D. Dunnette (Ed.), *Handbook of industrial and organizational psychology* (pp.1202–1245). Chicago: Rand McNally.

Graen, G., Alvarez, K., Orris, J. B., & Martella, S. A. (1970). Contingency model of leadership effectiveness: Antecedent and evidential results. *Psychological Bulletin, 74,* 285–296.

Graen, G., & Cashman, J. (1975). A role-making model of leadership in formal organizations: A developmental approach. In J. G. Hunt & L. L. Larson (Eds.), *Leadership frontiers.* Kent, OH: Kent State University Press.

Graen, G., Cashman, J. F., Ginsburgh, S., & Schiemann, W. (1978). Effects of linking-pin quality on the quality of working life of lower participants: A longitudinal investigation of the managerial understructure. *Administrative Science Quarterly, 22,* 491–504.

Graen, G., & Ginsburgh, S. (1977). Job resignation as a function of role orientation and leader acceptance: A longitudinal investigation of organizational assimilation. *Organizational Behavior and Human Performance, 19,* 1–17.

Graen, G., Liden, R., & Hoel, W. (1982). The role of leadership in the employee withdrawal process. *Journal of Applied Psychology, 67,* 868–872.

Graen, G., Novak, M., & Sommerkamp, P. (1982). The effects of leader–member exchange and job design on productivity and job satisfaction: Testing a dual attachment model. *Organizational Behavior and Human Performance, 30,* 109–131.

Graen, G., Orris, D., & Johnson, T. (1973). Role assimilation processes in a complex organization. *Journal of Vocational Behavior, 3,* 395–420.

Graen, G., & Scandura, T. A. (1987). Toward a psychology of dyadic organizing. *Research in Organizational Behavior, 9,* 175–208.

Green, S. G., & Mitchell, T. R. (1979). Attributional processes of leaders in leader–member interactions. *Organizational Behavior and Human Performance, 23,* 429–458.

Griffin, R. N. (1981). Relationships among individual, task design, and leader behavior variables. *Academy of Management Journal, 23,* 665–683.

Gruenfeld, L. W., Rance, D. E., & Weissenberg, P. (1969). The behavior of task-oriented (low LPC) and socially oriented (high LPC) leaders under several conditions of social support. *Journal of Social Psychology, 79,* 99–107.

Guttman, L. (1968). A general nonmetric technique for finding the smallest coordinate space for a configuration of points. *Psychometrika, 33,* 461–469.

Haccoun, D. M., Haccoun, R. R., & Sallay, G. (1978). Sex differences in the appropriateness of supervisory style: A nonmanagement view. *Journal of Applied Psychology, 63,* 124–127.

Hackman, J. R., & Oldham, G. R. (1976). Motivation through the design of work: Test of a theory. *Organizational Behavior and Human Performance, 16,* 250–279.

Haire, M., Ghiselli, E. E., & Porter, L. W. (1966). *Managerial thinking.* New York: Wiley.

Halpin, A. W., & Winer, B. J. (1957). A factorial study of the leader behavior descriptions. In R. M. Stogdill & A. E. Coons (Eds.), *Leader behavior: Its description and measurement.* Columbus: Ohio State University Bureau of Business Research.

Hamberg, C. (1989). *The effect of attributions on leadership actions.* Unpublished Bachelor's thesis, Claremont McKenna, Claremont, CA.

Hastorf, A. H., Schneider, D., & Polefka, J. (1970). *Person perception.* Reading, MA: Addison-Wesley.

Hater, J. J., & Bass, B. M. (1988). Supervisor's evaluations and subordinate's perceptions of transformational leadership. *Journal of Applied Psychology, 73,* 695–702.

Haythorn, W. W., Couch, A., Haefner, D., Langham, P., & Carter, L. F. (1956). The effects of varying combinations of authoritarian and equalitarian leaders and followers. *Journal of Abnormal and Social Psychology, 53,* 210–219.

Heider, F. (1944). Social perception and phenomenal causality. *Psychological Review, 51,* 358–374.

Heider, F. (1958). *The psychology of interpersonal relations.* New York: Wiley.

Heilman, M. E., Block, C. J., Martell, R. F., & Simon, M. C. (1989). Has anything changed? Current characterizations of men, women, and managers. *Journal of Applied Psychology, 74,* 935–942.

Heilman, M. E., Hornstein, H. A., Cage, J. H., & Herschlag, J. K. (1984). Reactions to prescribed leader behavior as a function of role perspective: The case of the Vroom–Yetton model. *Journal of Applied Psychology, 69,* 50–60.

Heilman, M. E., Martell, R. F., & Simon, M. C. (1988). The vagaries of sex bias: Conditions regulating the undervaluation, equivaluation, and overvaluation of female job applicants. *Organizational Behavior and Human Decision Processes, 41,* 98–110.

Helson, H. (1964). *Adaptation-level theory.* New York: Harper & Row.

Hemphill, J. K. (1949). *Situational factors in leadership.* Columbus: Ohio State University, Bureau of Educational Research.

Hemphill, J. K. (1950). *Leader behavior description.* Columbus: Ohio State University Personnel Research Board.

Hennig, M., & Jardim, A. (1977). *The managerial woman.* New York: Anchor Press.

Hersey, P., & Blanchard, K. H. (1969). Life cycle theory of leadership. *Training and Development Journal.*

Hersey, P., & Blanchard, K. H. (1977). *Management of organizational behavior.* Englewood Cliffs, NJ: Prentice-Hall.

Hersey, P., Blanchard, K. H., & Hambleton, R. K. (1980). Contracting for leadership style: A process and instrumentation for building effective work relationships. In P. Hersey & J. Stinson (Eds.), *Perspectives in leader effectiveness* (pp. 95–120). Athens, OH: The Center for Leadership Studies.

Hill, P. E., & Schmitt, N. (1977). Individual differences in leadership decision making. *Organizational Behavior and Human Performance, 19,* 353–367.

Hofstede, G. (1980). *Culture's consequences: International differences in work-related values.* Beverly Hills, CA: Sage.

Hofstede, G. (1983). Motivation, leadership, and organization: Do American theories apply abroad? *Organizational Dynamics, 9,* 42–63.

Hofstede, G. (1984). *Culture's consequences: International differences in work-related values* (Abridged ed.). Beverly Hills, CA: Sage.

Hofstede, G. (1993). Cultural constraints in management theories. *Academy of Management Executive, 7,* 81–94.

Hofstede, G., & Bond, M. H. (1988, Spring). The Confucius connection: From cultural roots to economic growth. *Organizational Dynamics, 14,* 5–39.

Hollander, E. P. (1958). Conformity, status, and idiosyncrasy credit. *Psychological Review, 65,* 117–127.

Hollander, E. P. (1960). Competence and conformity in the acceptance of influence. *Journal of Abnormal and Social Psychology, 61*, 365–369.

Hollander, E. P. (1961). Some effects of perceived status on responses to innovative behavior. *Journal of Abnormal and Social Psychology, 63*, 247–250.

Hollander, E. P. (1964). *Leaders, groups, and influence*. New York: Oxford University Press.

Hollander, E. P. (1978). *Leadership dynamics: A practical guide to effective relationships*. New York: Free Press.

Hollander, E. P. (1993). Legitimacy, power, and influence: A perspective on relational features of leadership. In M. M. Chemers & R. Ayman (Eds.), *Leadership theory and research: Perspectives and directions* (pp. 29–48). San Diego: Academic Press.

Hollander, E. P., & Julian, J. W. (1970). Studies in leader legitimacy, influence, and innovation. In L. Berkowitz (Ed.), *Advances in experimental social psychology* (Vol. 5, pp. 33–69). New York: Academic Press.

Homans, G. C. (1958). Social behavior as exchange. *American Journal of Sociology, 63,* 597–606.

Homans, G. C. (1961). *Social behavior: Its elementary forms*. New York: Harcourt Brace.

Homans, G. C. (1974). *Social behavior: Its elementary forms* (2nd ed.). New York: Harcourt Brace.

House, J. (1981). Social structure and personality. In M. Rosenberg & R. Turner (Eds.), *Social psychology: Sociological perspectives* (pp. 525–561). New York: Basic Books.

House, R. J. (1971). A path–goal theory of leadership. *Administrative Science Quarterly, 16*, 321–338.

House, R. J. (1977). A 1976 theory of charismatic leadership. In J. G. Hunt & L. L. Larson (Eds.), *Leadership: The cutting edge*. Carbondale, IL: Southern Illinois University Press.

House, R. J., & Baetz, M. L. (1979). Leadership: Some generalizations and new research directions. B. Staw (Ed.), *Research in organizational behavior*. Greenwich, CN: JAI Press.

House, R. J., & Dessler, G. (1974). The path–goal theory of leadership: Some post hoc and a priori tests. In J. G. Hunt & L. L. Larson (Eds.), *Contingency approaches to leadership*. Carbondale, IL: Southern Illinois University Press.

House, R. J., & Mitchell, T. R. (1974). Path–goal theory of leadership. *Journal of Contemporary Business, 3*, 81–98.

House, R. J., & Shamir, B. (1993). In M. M. Chemers & R. Ayman (Eds.), *Leadership theory and research: Perspectives and directions* (pp. 81–108). San Diego: Academic Press.

Howells, L. T., & Becker, S. W. (1962). Seating arrangement and leadership emergence. *Journal of Abnormal and Social Psychology, 64*, 148–150.

Hunt, J. G. (1967). Fiedler's contingency model: An empirical test of three organizations. *Organizational Behavior and Human Performance, 2*, 290–308.

Hunt, J. G. (1983). Organizational leadership: The contingency paradigm and its challenges. In B. Kellerman (Ed.), *Leadership: Multiple perspectives*. Englewood Cliffs, NJ: Prentice-Hall.

Hunt, J. G., & Osborn, R. N. (1980). A multiple-influence approach to leadership for managers. In P. Hersey & J. Stinson (Eds.), *Perspectives in leader effectiveness* (pp. 47–62). Athens, OH: The Center for Leadership Studies.

Hunt, J. G., & Osborn, R. N. (1982). Toward a macro-oriented model of leadership: An odyssey. In J. G. Hunt, U. Sekaran, & C. Schriesheim (Eds.), *Leadership: Beyond establishment views*. Carbondale, IL: Southern Illinois University Press.

Hunt, J. G., Osborn, R. N., & Martin, H. (1983). *A multiple influence model of leadership*. Alexandria, VA: Army Research Institute for the Behavioral and Social Sciences.

Hunt, J. G., & Schuler, R. S. (1976). *Leader reward and sanctions behavior in a public utility: What difference does it make?* Working paper, Southern Illinois University, Carbondale.

Hurwitz, J. I., Zander, A. F., & Hymovitch, B. (1953). Some effects of power on the relations among group members. in D. Cartwright & A. Zander (Eds.), *Group dynamics*. Evanston, IL: Row, Peterson.

Ilgen, D. R., & Fujii, D. S. (1976). An investigation of the validity of leader behavior descriptions obtained from subordinates. *Journal of Applied Psychology, 61*, 642–651.

Indvik, J. (1986). Path–goal theory of leadership: A meta-analysis. *Proceedings of the 46th Annual Meeting of the Academy of Management*, 189–192.

Jacobs, T. O. (1970). *Leadership and exchange in formal organizations*. Alexandria, VA: Human Resources Research Organization.

Johnson, P. (1976). Women and power: Toward a theory of effectiveness. *Journal of Social Issues, 32,* 99–110.

Jones, E. E., & Davis, K. E. (1965). From acts to dispositions: The attribution process in person perception. In L. Berkowitz (Ed.), *Advances in experimental social psychology* (Vol. 2, 219–226). New York: Academic Press.

Jones, E. E., & Nisbett, R. E. (1971). *The actor and the observer: Divergent perceptions of the causes of behavior*. Morristown, NJ: General Learning Press.

Kahn, R. L. (1951). An analysis of supervisory practices and components of morale. In H. Guetzkow (Ed.), *Groups, leadership, and men*. Pittsburgh: Carnegie Press.

Kanter, R. M. (1977). *Men and women of the corporation*. New York: Basic Books.

Katz, D., & Kahn, R. L. (1951). Human organization and worker motivation. In L. R. Tripp (Ed.), *Industrial productivity*. Madison, WI: Industrial Relations Research Association.

Katz, D., & Kahn, R. L. (1966). *The social psychology of organizations*. New York: Wiley.

Kelley, H. H. (1967). Attribution theory in social psychology. In D. Levine (Ed.), *Nebraska symposium on motivation*. Lincoln: University of Nebraska Press.

Kelley, H. H. (1973). The process of causal attribution. *American Psychologist, 28,* 107–128.

Kelley, H. H. & Thibaut, J. W. (1978). *Interpersonal relations: A theory of interdependence*. New York: Wiley.

Kelly, G. A. (1955). *The psychology of personal constructs*. New York: Norton.

Kennedy, J. K. (1982). Middle LPC leaders and the contingency model of leadership effectiveness. *Organizational Behavior and Human Performance, 30,* 1–14.

Kenny, D. A., & Zaccaro, S. J. (1983). An estimate of variance due to traits in leadership. *Journal of Applied Psychology, 68,* 678–685.

Kerr, S., & Jermier, J. M. (1978). Substitutes for leadership: Their meaning and measurement. *Organizational Behavior and Human Performance, 22,* 375–403.

Kiesler, S. B. (1975). Actuarial prejudice toward women and its implications. *Journal of Applied Social Psychology, 5,* 201–216.

Kipnis, D. M. (1957). Interaction between members of bomber crews as a determinant of sociometric choice. *Human Relations, 10,* 263–270.

Kipnis, D. M., Castell, P. J., Gergen, M., & Mauch, D. (1976). Metamorphic effects of power. *Journal of Applied Psychology, 61,* 127–135.

Kipnis, D. M., & Cosentino, J. (1969). Use of leadership powers in industry. *Journal of Applied Psychology, 53,* 460–466.

Kipnis, D. M., & Schmidt, S. M. (1982). *Profiles of organizational influence strategies [Form M]*. San Diego: University Associates.

Kipnis, D. M., Schmidt, S. M., Price, K., & Stitt, C. (1981). Why do I like thee: Is it your performance or my orders? *Journal of Applied Psychology, 66,* 324–328.

Kipnis, D. M., Schmidt, S. M., Swaffin-Smith, C., & Wilkinson, I. (1984). Patterns of managerial influence: Shotgun managers, tacticians, and bystanders. *Organizational Dynamics, 13,* 58–67.

Kipnis, D. M., Schmidt, S. M., & Wilkinson, I. (1980). Intraorganizational influence tactics: Explorations in getting one's way. *Journal of Applied Psychology, 65,* 440–452.

Kipnis, D. M., & Vandeveer, R. (1971). Ingratiation and the use of power. *Journal of Personality and Social Psychology, 17,* 280–286.

Knowlton, W. A., Jr., & Mitchell, T. R. (1980). The effects of causal attributions on supervisors' evaluations of subordinate performance. *Journal of Applied Psychology, 65,* 459–466.

Koh, W. L. (1990). *An empirical validation of the theory of transformational leadership in secondary schools in Singapore*. Unpublished doctoral dissertation, University of Oregon, Eugene.

Komaki, J. (1986). Toward effective supervision. *Journal of Applied Psychology, 71,* 270–279.

Komaki, J., & Desselles, M. L. (1990). *Supervision reexamined: The role of monitors and consequences*. Boston: Allyn & Unwin.

Komaki, J., Desselles, M. L., & Bowman, E. D. (1989). Definitely not a breeze: Extending an operant model of effective supervision to teams. *Journal of Applied Psychology, 74*, 522– 529.

Komaki, J. L., Zlotnick, S., & Jensen, M. (1986). Development of an operant-based taxonomy and observational index of supervisory behavior. *Journal of Applied Psychology, 71*, 260–269.

Korman, A. K. (1966). "Consideration,""Initiating Structure," and organizational criteria. *Personnel Psychology, 18*, 349–360.

Kotter, J. P. (1982). *The general managers.* New York: Free Press.

Kouzes, J. M., & Posner, B. Z. (1987). *The leadership challenge: How to get extraordinary things done in organizations.* San Francisco: Jossey-Bass.

Latham, G. P., & Yukl, G. A. (1975). A review of research on the application of goal setting in organizations. *Academy of Management Journal, 18*, 824–845.

Lawrence, P. R., & Lorsch, J. W. (1967). *Organization and environment.* Cambridge, MA: Harvard Universtiy Press.

Leavitt, H. J. (1951). Some effects of certain communication patterns on group performance. *Journal of Abnormal and Social Psychology, 46*, 38–50.

Lee, D. M., & Alvares, K. M. (1977). Effects of sex on descriptions and evaluations of supervisory behavior in a simulated industrial setting. *Journal of Applied Psychology, 62*, 405–410.

Levinson, R. M. (1975). Sex discrimination and employment practices: An experiment with unconventional job inquiries. *Social Problems, 22*, 533–543.

Lewin, K., Lippitt, R., & White, R. K. (1939). Patterns of aggressive behavior in experimentally created social climates. *Journal of Social Psychology, 10*, 271–301.

Liden, R., & Graen, G. (1980). Generalizability of the vertical dyad linkage model of leadership. *Academy of Management Journal, 23*, 451–465.

Liden, R., Wayne, S., & Stilwell, D. (1993). A longitudinal study of the early development of leader–member exchanges. *Journal of Applied Psychology, 78*, 662–674.

Likert, R. (1961). The principles of supportive relationships. In J. M. Shafritz & P. H. Whitbeck (Eds.), *Classics of organization theory.* Oak Park, IL: Moore.

Lipman-Blumen, J., Handley-Isaksen, A., & Leavitt, H. J. (1983). Achieving styles in men and women: A model, an instrument, and some findings. In J. T. Spence (Ed.), *Achievement and achievement motives: Psychological and sociological approaches.* San Francisco: Freeman.

Lippitt, R., & White, R. K. (1943). The social climate of children's groups. In R. G. Baker, J. S. Kounin, & H. F. Wright (Eds.), *Child behavior and development.* New York: McGraw-Hill.

Locke, E. A. (1968). Toward a theory of task motivation and incentives. *Organizational Behavior and Human Performance, 3*, 157–189.

Locke, E. A., & Latham, G. P. (1990a). *A theory of goal setting and task performance.* Englewood Cliffs, NJ: Prentice-Hall.

Locke, E. A., & Latham, G. P. (1990b). Work motivation and satisfaction: Light at the end of the tunnel. *Psychological Science, 1*, 240–246.

Locksley, A., Borgida, E., Brekke, N., & Hepburn, C. (1980). Sex stereotypes and social judgment. *Journal of Personality and Social Psychology, 39*, 821–831.

Loden, M. (1985). *Feminine leadership or how to succeed in business without being one of the boys.* New York: Times Books.

Lord, R. G. (1985). An information processing approach to social perceptions, leadership, and behavioral measurement in organizations. In B. M. Staw & L. L. Cummings (Eds.), *Research in organizational behavior* (Vol. 7). Greenwich, CT: JAI Press.

Lord, R. G., Binning, J. F., Rush, M. C., & Thomas, J. C. (1978). The effect of performance cues and leader behavior on questionnaire ratings of leadership behavior. *Organizational Behavior and Human Performance, 21*, 27–39.

Lord, R. G., Foti, R. J., & De Vader, C. (1984). A test of leadership categorization theory: Internal structure, information processing, and leadership perceptions. *Organizational Behavior and Human Performance, 34*, 343–378.

Lord, R. G., Foti, R. J., & Phillips, J. S. (1982). A theory of leadership categorization. In J. G. Hunt, U. Sekaran, & C. Schriesheim (Eds.), *Leadership: Beyond establishment views*. Carbondale, IL: Southern Illinois University Press.

Lord, R. G., & Maher, K. J. (1990). Alternative information processing models and their implications for theory, research, and practice. *Academy of Management Review*, *15*, 9–28.

Lord, R. G., & Maher, K. J. (1991). *Leadership and information processing: Linking perceptions and performance*. Boston: Unwin-Hyman.

Lord, R. G., Phillips, J. S., & Rush, M. C. (1980). Effects of sex and personality on perception of emergent leadership, influence, and social power. *Journal of Applied Psychology*, *65*, 176–182.

Lord, R. G., & Smith, J. E. (1983). Theoretical, information processing, and situational factors affecting attribution theory models of organizational behavior. *Academy of Management Review*, *8*, 50–60.

Luthans, F., & Kreitner, R. (1975). *Organizational behavior modification*. Glenview, IL: Scott, Foresman.

Maccoby, E. E., & Jacklin, C. N. (1974). *The psychology of sex differences*. Stanford, CA: Stanford University Press.

Maier, N. R. F. (1963). *Problem solving discussion and conferences: Leadership methods and skills*. New York: McGraw-Hill.

Mann, R. D. (1959). A review of the relationship between personality and performance in small groups. *Psychological Bulletin*, *56*, 241–270.

Manz, C. C., & Sims, H. P. Jr. (1980). Self-management as a substitute for leadership: A social learning theory perspective. *Academy of Management Review*, *5*, 361–367.

March, J. G., & Simon, H. A. (1958). *Organizations*. New York: Wiley.

Margerison, C., & Glube, R. (1979). Leadership decision making: An empirical test of the Vroom and Yetton model. *Journal of Management Studies*, *16*, 45–55.

Markus, H. R., & Kitayama, S. (1991). Culture and the self: Implications for cognition, emotion, and motivation. *Psychological Bulletin*, *98*, 224–253.

Maslow, A. H. (1954). *Motivation and personality*. New York: Harper & Row.

Massengill, D., & DiMarco, N. (1979). Sex-role stereotypes and requisite management characteristics: A current replication. *Sex Roles*, *5*, 561–576.

Matsui, T., & Ohtsuka, Y. (1978). Within–person expectancy theory predictions of supervisory consideration and structure behavior. *Journal of Applied Psychology*, *63*, 128–131.

May, S. M. (1993). *Heavy mettle: The role of confidence and optimism in leadership performance*. Unpublished bachelors thesis, Claremont McKenna College, Claremont, CA.

Mayo, M., Pastor, J. C., & Meindl, J. R. (1992). *The effects of arousal on attributions of charisma*. Unpublished manuscript.

McArthur, L. Z. (1972). The how and what of why: Some determinants and consequences of causal attribution. *Journal of Personality and Social Psychology*, *22*, 171–193.

McCall, M. W., Jr., & Lombardo, M. (Eds.). (1978). *Leadership: Where else can we go?* Durham, NC: Duke University Press.

McClelland, D. C. & Boyatzis, R. E. (1982). Leadership motive pattern and long-term success in management. *Journal of Applied Psychology*, *67*, 737–743.

McGrath, J. E. (1976). Stress and behavior in organizations. In M. D. Dunnette (Ed.), *Handbook of industrial and organizational psychology*. Chicago: Rand McNally.

McGrath, J. E., & Altman, I. (1966). *Small group research: A synthesis and critique*. New York: Holt, Rinehart & Winston.

McMahon, J. T. (1972). The contingency theory: Logical method revisited. *Personnel Psychology*, *25*, 697–710.

Meindl, J. R. (1988). *On the romanticized perception of charisma*. Unpublished manuscript, School of Management, State University of New York at Buffalo.

Meindl, J. R. (1990). On leadership: An alternative to the conventional wisdom. In B. A. Staw (Ed.), *Research in organizational behavior* (Vol. 12, pp. 159–203). New York: JAI Press.

Meindl, J. R., & Ehrlich, S. B. (1987). The romance of leadership and the evaluation of organizational performance. *Academy of Management Journal, 30,* 91–109.

Meindl, J. R., & Ehrlich, S. B. (1988). Developing a "romance of leadership" scale. *Proceedings of the Eastern Academy of Management, 47,* 133–135.

Meindl, J. R., Ehrlich, S. B., & Dukerich, J. M. (1985). The romance of leadership. *Administrative Science Quarterly, 30,* 91–109.

Meindl, J. R., & Lerner, M. J. (1983). The heroic motive: Some experimental demonstrations. *Journal of Experimental Social Psychology, 19,* 1–20.

Melcher, A. J. (1979). Leadership models and research approaches. In J. G. Hunt & L. L. Larsen (Eds.), *Leadership: The cutting edge* (pp. 94–108). Carbondale: Southern Illinois University Press.

Meuwese, W. A. T., & Fiedler, F. E. (1964). *Leadership and group creativity under varying conditions of stress.* (Tech. Rep.). Urbana: University of Illinois, Group Effectiveness Research Laboratory.

Miles, R. R., & Petty, M. M. (1977). Leader effectiveness in small bureaucracies. *Academy of Management Journal, 20,* 238–250.

Misumi, J. (1984). *The behavioral science of leadership* (2nd ed.). Tokyo: Yuhikaku Publishing.

Misumi, J., & Peterson, M. F. (1985). The Performance-Maintenance (PM) theory of leadership: Review of a Japanese research program. *Administrative Science Quarterly, 30,* 198–223.

Misumi, J., & Shirakashi, S. (1966). An experimental study of supervisory behavior on productivity and morale in a hierarchical organization. *Human Relations, 19,* 297–307.

Misumi, J., & Tasaki, J. (1965). A study on the effectiveness of supervisory patterns in a Japanese hierarchical organization. *Japanese Psychological Research, 7,* 151–162.

Mitchell, T. R. (1970). Leader complexity and leadership style. *Journal of Personality and Social Psychology, 16,* 166–174.

Mitchell, T. R., & Kalb, L. S. (1982). Effects of job experience on supervisor attributions for a subordinate's poor performance. *Journal of Applied Psychology, 67,* 181–188.

Mitchell, T. R., Larson, J. R., & Green, S. G. (1977). Leader behavior situational moderators in group performance: An attributional analysis. *Organizational Behavior and Human Performance, 18,* 254–268.

Mitchell, T. R., & Wood, R. E. (1980). Supervisor's responses to subordinate poor performance: A test of an attribution model. *Organizational Behavior and Human Performance, 25,* 123–138.

Morris, C. G. (1966). Effects of task characteristics on group process, Doctoral dissertation, *Dissertation Abstracts, 26,* 7477, University of Illinois.

Morris, C. G. & Hackman, J. R. (1969). Behavioral correlates of perceived leadership. *Journal of Personality and Social Psychology, 13,* 350–361.

Morse, J. H., & Lorsch, J. W. (1970). Beyond theory y. *Harvard Business Review, 48,* 61–68.

Myers, D. (1987). *Social psychology* (2nd ed.). New York: McGraw-Hill.

Nahavandi, A. (1983). *The effects of personal and situational factors on satisfaction with leadership.* Unpublished doctoral dissertation, University of Utah, Salt Lake City.

Nahavandi, A., & Malekzadeh, A. R. (1993). *Organizational culture in the management of mergers.* Westport, CT: Quorum Books.

Nebeker, D. M., & Mitchell, T. R. (1974). Leader behavior: An expectancy theory approach. *Organizational Behavior and Human Performance, 11,* 355–367.

Ng, S. H., Hossain, A. B. M., Ball, P., Bond, M. H., Hayashi, K., Lim, S. P., O'Driscoll, M. P., Sinha, D., & Yang, K. S. (1982). Human values in nine countries. In R. Rath, H. S. Asthana, D. Sinha, & J. B. H. Sinha (Eds.), *Diversity and unity in cross-cultural psychology.* Lisse, Netherlands: Swets and Zeitlinger.

Nieva, V. F., & Gutek, B. A. (1980). Sex effects on evaluation. *Academy of Management Review, 5,* 267–276.

Nieva, V. F., & Gutek, B. A. (1981). *Women and work: A psychological perspective.* New York: Praeger.

Nisbett, R. E., & Borgida, E. (1975). Attribution and the psychology of prediction. *Journal of Personality and Social Psychology, 32,* 932–943.

Oberg, W. (1972). Charisma, commitment, and contemporary organization theory. *Business Topics, 20*, 18–32.

Odiorne, G. S. (1965). *Management by objectives: A system of managerial leadership.* New York: Pitman Publishing Corporation.

O'Leary, V. E. (1974). Some attitudinal barriers to occupational aspirations in women. *Psychological Bulletin, 81*, 809–826.

Osborn, R. N., & Vicars, W. M. (1976). Sex stereotypes: An artifact in leader behavior and subordinate satisfaction analysis? *Academy of Management Journal, 19*, 439–449.

Osgood, C. E. (1952). The nature and measurement of meaning. *Psychological Bulletin, 49*, 251–262.

Paul, R. J., & Ebadi, Y. M. (1989). Leadership decision making in a service organization: A field test of the Vroom–Yetton model. *Journal of Occupational Psychology, 62*, 201–211.

Pelto, P. J. (1968). The differences between "tight" and "loose" societies. *Transaction, 5*, 37–40.

Pelz, D. C. (1952). Influence: A key to effective leadership. *Personnel, 29*, 209–217.

Peters, L. H., Hartke, D. D., & Pohlmann, J. T. (1983). Fiedler's contingency theory of leadership: An application of the meta-analysis procedure of Schmidt and Hunter. *Psychological Bulletin, 97*, 274–285.

Petty, M. M., & Lee, G. K. (1975). Moderating effects of sex of supervisor and subordinate on the relationship between supervisory behavior and subordinate satisfaction. *Journal of Applied Psychology, 60*, 624–628.

Petty, M. M., & Miles, R. H. (1976). Leader sex-role stereotyping in a female dominant work culture. *Personnel Psychology, 29*, 393–404.

Pfeffer, J. (1981). *Power in organizations.* Boston: Pitman Publishing.

Phillips, J. S., & Lord, R. G. (1981). Causal attributions and perceptions of leadership. *Organizational Behavior and Human Performance, 28*, 143–163.

Podsakoff, P. M., Niehoff, B. P., MacKenzie, S. B., & Williams, M. L. (1993). Do substitutes for leadership really substitute for leadership? An empirical examination of Kerr and Jermier's situational leadership model. *Organizational Behavior and Human Decision Processes, 54*, 1–44.

Podsakoff, P. M., & Schriesheim, C. A. (1985). Field studies of French and Raven's bases of power: Critique, reanalysis, and suggestions for future research. *Psychological Bulletin, 97*, 387–411.

Podsakoff, P. M., Todor, W. D., & Skov, R. (1982). Effects of leader contingent and noncontingent reward and punishment on subordinate performance and satisfaction. *Academy of Management Journal, 25*, 810–821.

Posthuma, A. B. (1970). *Normative data on the least preferred coworker scale (LPC) and the group atmosphere questionnaire (GA)* (Organizational Research, Tech. Rep. No. 70-8). Seattle: University of Washington.

Powell, G. N., & Butterfield, D. A. (1979). The "good manager": Masculine or androgynous. *Academy of Management Journal, 22*, 395–403.

Punnett, B. J. & Ronen, S. (1984, August). *Operationalizing cross-cultural variables.* Paper delivered at the forty-fourth annual meeting of the Academy of Management, Boston, MA.

Quinn, (1984, May–June). Manging innovation: Controlled chaos. *Harvard Business Review*, 73–84.

Ragins, B. R. (1989). Power and gender congruency effects in evaluations of male and female managers. *Journal of Management, 15*, 65–76.

Ragins, B. R. (1991). Gender effects in subordinate evaluations of leaders: Real or artifact? *Journal of Organizational Behavior, 12*, 258–268.

Ragins, B. R., & Sundstrom, E. (1989). Gender and power in organizations: A longitudinal perspective. *Psychological Bulletin, 105*, 51–88.

Ragins, B. R., & Sundstrom, E. (1990). Gender and perceived power in manager–subordinate relations. *Journal of Occupational Psychology, 63*, 273–287.

Read, W. H. (1962). Upward communication in industrial hierarchies. *Human Relations, 15*, 3–15.

Rice, R. W. (1978). Construct validity of the least preferred coworker. *Psychological Bulletin, 85*, 1199–1237.

Rice, R. W., Bender, L. R., & Vitters, A. G. (1980). Leader sex, follower attitudes toward women, and leadership effectiveness: A laboratory experiment. *Organizational Behavior and Human Performance, 25,* 46–78.

Rice, R. W., Instone, D., & Adams, J. (1984). Leader sex, leader success, and leadership process: Two field studies. *Journal of Applied Psychology, 69,* 12–32.

Rice, R. W., Marwick, N. J., Chemers, M. M., & Bentley, J. C. (1982). Task performance and satisfaction: Least preferred coworker (LPC) as a moderator. *Personality and Social Psychology Bulletin, 8,* 534–541.

Rokeach, J. (1973). *The nature of human values.* New York: Free Press.

Ronen, S., & Kraut, A. I. (1977). Similarities among countries based on work values and attitudes. *Columbia Journal of World Business, 12,* 89–96.

Ronen, S., & Shenkar, O. (1985). Clustering countries on attitudinal dimensions: A review and synthesis. *Academy of Management Review, 10,* 435–454.

Rosch, E. (1978). Principles of categorization. In E. Rosch & B. B. Lloyd (Eds.), *Cognition and categorization.* Hillsdale, NJ: Lawrence Erlbaum Associates.

Rosen, B., & Jerdee, T. H. (1973). The influence of sex-role stereotypes on evaluations of male and female supervisory behavior. *Journal of Applied Psychology, 57,* 44–48.

Rosen, D. M. (1983). Leadership in world cultures. In B. Kellerman (Ed.), *Leadership: Multidisciplinary perspectives.* Englewood Cliffs, NJ: Prentice-Hall.

Ross, L. (1978). The intuitive psychologist and his shortcomings. In L. Berkowitz (Ed.), *Cognitive theories in social psychology.* New York: Academic Press.

Rush, M. C., Phillips, J. S., & Lord, R. G. (1981). Effects of temporal delay in rating on leader behavior descriptions: A laboratory investigation. *Journal of Applied Psychology, 66,* 442–450.

Rush, M. C., Thomas, J. C., & Lord, R. G. (1977). Implicit leadership theory: A potential threat to the internal validity of leader behavior questionnaires. *Organizational Behavior and Human Performance, 20,* 93–110.

Sahlins, M. (1958). *Social stratification in Polynesia.* Seattle: University of Washington Press.

Sahlins, M. (1972). *Stone age economics.* Chicago: Aldine Publishing Company.

Salancik, G. R., & Pfeffer, J. (1978). A social information processing approach to job attitudes in task design. *Administrative Science Quarterly, 23,* 224–253.

Sarachek, B. (1968). Greek concepts of leadership. *Academy of Management Journal, 11,* 39–48.

Sargent, A. G. (1981). *The androgynous manager.* New York: Amacom.

Sashkin, M. (1988). The visionary leaders. In J. A. Conger & R. A. Kanungo (Eds.), *Charismatic leadership: The elusive actor in organizational effectiveness.* San Francisco: Jossey-Bass.

Scandura, T. A., Graen, G., & Novak, M. A. (1986). When managers decide not to decide autocratically: An investigation of leader-member exchange and decision influence. *Journal of Applied Psychology, 71,* 579–584.

Schacter, S. (1964). The interaction of cognitive and physiological determinants of emotional state. In L. Berkowitz (Ed.), *Advances in experimental social psychology* (Vol. 1, pp. 49–80). New York: Academic Press.

Scheier, M. F., & Carver, C. S. (1985). Optimism, coping, and health: Assessment and implications of generalized outcome expectancies. *Health Psychology, 4,* 219–247.

Scheier, M. F., Weintraub, J. G., & Carver, C. S. (1986). Coping with stress: Divergent strategies of optimists and pessimists. *Journal of Personality and Social Psychology, 51,* 1257–1264.

Schein, V. E. (1973). The relationship of sex role stereotypes and requisite management characteristics. *Journal of Applied Psychology, 57,* 95–100.

Schein, V. E. (1975). The relationship of sex role stereotypes and requisite management characteristics among female managers. *Journal of Applied Psychology, 60,* 340–344.

Schiemann, W., & Graen, G. (1978). Leader–member agreement: A vertical dyad linkage approach. *Journal of Applied Psychology, 63,* 206–212.

Schmidt, S. M., & Yeh, R. S. (1992). The structure of leadership influence: A cross-national comparison. *Journal of Cross-Cultural Psychology, 23,* 251–264.

Schriesheim, C. A., & DeNisi, A. S. (1981). Task dimensions as moderators of the effects of intrumental leadership: A two sample replicated test of Path–Goal leadership theory. *Journal of Applied Psychology, 66,* 589–597.

Schriesheim, C. A. & Kerr, S. (1977). Theories and measures of leadership: A critical appraisal of present and future directions. In J. G. Hunt & L. L. Larson (Eds.), *Leadership: The cutting edge.* Carbondale: Southern Illinois University Press.

Schriesheim, C. A., Kinicki, H. A., & Schriesheim, J. F. (1979). The effect of leniency on leadership behavior descriptions. *Organizational Behavior and Human Performance, 23,* 1–29.

Schriesheim, C. A. & Murphy, C. J. (1976). Relationships between leader behavior and subordinate satisfaction and performance: A test of some situational moderators. *Journal of Applied Psychology, 61,* 634–641.

Schuler, R. S. (1980). Definition and conceptualization of stress in organizations. *Organizational Behavior and Human Performance, 25,* 184–215.

Seligman, M. E. P. (1991). *Learned optimism.* New York: Knopf.

Shapira, Z. (1976). A facet analysis of leadership styles. *Journal of Applied Psychology, 61,* 136– 139.

Shartle, C. L. (1950). Studies of leadership by interdisciplinary methods. In A. G. Grace (Ed.), *Leadership in American education.* Chicago: University of Chicago Press.

Shartle, C. L. (1951). Studies in naval leadership. In H. Guetzkow (Ed.), *Groups, leadership, and men.* Pittsburgh: Carnegie Press.

Shaw, M. (1963). *Scaling group tasks: A method for dimensional analysis* (Tech. Rep. No. 1). Gainesville: University of Florida.

Shaw, M. (1973). Scaling group tasks: A method for dimensional analysis. *JSAS Catalog of Selected Documents in Psychology, 3,* 8.

Shaw, M., & Costanzo, P. R. (1982). *Theories of social psychology,* (2nd edition). New York: McGraw–Hill.

Sherif, M., & Sherif, C. W. (1969). *Social psychology.* New York: Harper & Row.

Shiffrin, R. M., & Schneider, W. (1977). Controlled and automatic human information processing: Perceptual learning, automatic attending, and a general theory. *Psychological Review, 84,* 127–190.

Shirakashi, S. (1991). Job stress of managers: A contingency model analysis. *Organizational Science, 25,* 42–51.

Simon, H. A. (1957). *Administrative behavior* (2nd ed.). New York: MacMillan.

Sims, H. P., Jr. (1977). The leader as a manager of reinforcement contingencies: An empirical example and a model. In J. G. Hunt & L. L. Larson (Eds.), *Leadership: The cutting edge.* Carbondale, IL: Southern Illinois University Press.

Sims, H. P., Jr., & Lorenzi, P. (1992). *The new leadership paradigm: Social learning and cognition in organizations.* Newbury Park, CA: Sage.

Sims, H. P., Jr., & Szilagyi, A. D. (1975a). Leader structure and subordinate satisfaction for two hospital administrative levels: A path analysis approach. *Journal of Applied Psychology, 60,* 194–197.

Sims, H. P., Jr., & Szilagyi, A. D. (1975b). Leader reward behavior and subordinate satisfaction and performance. *Organizational Behavior and Human Performance, 14,* 426–438.

Sinha, J. B. P. (1990, July). The nurturant task style of leadership. In R. Ayman (Chair), *Establishing a global view of leadership: East meets west.* Symposium conducted at the International Congress of Applied Psychology, Kyoto, Japan.

Smith, P. B., Misumi, J., Tayeb, M., Peterson, M., & Bond, M. (1989). On the generality of leadership style measures across cultures. *Journal of Occupational Psychology, 62,* 97–109.

Smith, P. C., Kendall, L. M., & Hulin, C. A. (1969). *The measurement of satisfaction in work and retirement.* Chicago: Rand McNally.

Snyder, C. R., Harris, C., Anderson, J. R., Holleran, S. A., Irving, L. M., Sigmon, S. T., Yoshinobu, L., Gibb, J., Langelle, C., & Harney, P. (1991). The will and the way: Development and validation of an individual-differences measure of hope. *Journal of Personality and Social Psychology, 60,* 570–585.

Snyder, M. (1974). Self-monitoring of expressive behavior. *Journal of Personality and Social Psychology, 30,* 526–537.

Sommer, R. (1961). Leadership and group geography. *Sociometry, 24*, 99–110.

Soukhanov, A. H., & Ellis, K. (1988). *Webster's II new riverside dictionary*. Boston: Houghton Mifflin.

Spence, J. T., & Helmreich, R. L. (1978). *Masculinity & femininity: Their psychological dimensions, correlates, and antecedents*. Austin: University of Texas Press.

Spence, J. T., Helmreich, R. L., & Stapp, J. (1974). The Personal Attributes Questionnaire: A measure of sex role stereotypes and masculinity-femininity (Ms. No. 617). *JSAS Catalog of Selected Documents in Psychology, 4*, 43.

Staw, B. M. (1975). Attribution of the "causes" of performance: A general alternative interpretation of cross-sectional research on organizations. *Organizational Behavior and Human Performance, 13*, 414–432.

Staw, B. M., & Barsade, S. G. (1992). Affect and managerial performance: A test of the sadder-but-wiser vs. happier-and-smarter hypothesis. *Administrative Science Quarterly, 38*, 304–331.

Steele, C. M. (1988). The psychology of self-affirmation: Sustaining the integrity of the self. In L. Berkowitz (Ed.), *Advances in experimental social psychology* (Vol. 21, pp. 181–227). San Diego, CA: Academic Press.

Steinzor, B. (1950). The spatial factor in face to face discussion groups. *Journal of Abnormal and Social Psychology, 45*, 552–555.

Stevens, L., & Jones, E. E. (1976). Defense attributions and the Kelley cube. *Journal of Personality and Social Psychology, 25*, 809–820.

Stewart, R. (1982a). *Choices for the manager*. Englewood Cliffs, NJ: Prentice-Hall.

Stewart, R. (1982b). The relevance of some studies of managerial work and behavior to leadership research. In J. G. Hunt, U. Sekaran, & C. A. Schriesheim (Eds.), *Leadership: Beyond establishment views*. Carbondale, IL: Southern Illinois University Press.

Stinson, J. E., & Johnson, T. W. (1975). The path–goal theory of leadership: A partial test and suggested refinement. *Academy of Management Journal, 18*, 242–252.

Stogdill, R. M. (1948). Personal factors associated with leadership: A survey of the literature. *Journal of Psychology, 25*, 35–71.

Stogdill, R. M. (1974). *Handbook of leadership: A survey of theory and research*. New York: Free Press.

Stogdill, R. M., & Coons, A. E. (1957). *Leader behavior: Its description and measurement*. Columbus, OH: Bureau of Business Research, Ohio State University.

Strube, M. J., & Garcia, J. E. (1981). A meta-analytical investigation of Fiedler's Contingency Model of leadership effectiveness. *Psychological Bulletin, 90*, 307–321.

Tasaki, T., & Misumi, J. (1976). A study of the effect of leadership behavior on group norms in the job situation of an industrial organization. *Japanese Journal of Experimental Social Psychology, 16*, 1–7.

Terborg, J. R. (1977). Women in management: A research review. *Journal of Applied Psychology, 62*, 647–664.

Terborg, J. R., & Ilgen, D. R. (1975). A theoretical approach to sex discrimination in traditionally masculine occupations. *Organizational Behavior and Human Performance, 13*, 352–376.

Thibaut, J. W., & Kelley, H. H. (1959). *The social psychology of groups*. New York: Wiley.

Thompson, J. (1967). *Organizations in action*. New York: McGraw-Hill.

Thompson, K. J., & Chemers, M. M. (1993, May). *Gender consciousness and leader behavior expectancies*. Presented at the meetings of the Society for Industrial and Organizational Psychology, San Francisco.

Tichy, N. M., & Devanna, M. A. (1986). *The transformational leader*. New York: Wiley.

Tosi, H. (1982). Toward a paradigm shift in the study of leadership. In J. G. Hunt, U. Sekaran, & C. A. Schriesheim (Eds.), *Leadership: Beyond establishment views*. Carbondale, IL: Southern Illinois University Press.

Trahey, J. (1977). *Women and power*. New York: Avon Books.

Trempe, J., Rigny, A., & Haccoun, R. (1985). Subordinate satisfaction with male and female managers: Role of perceived supervisory influence. *Journal of Applied Psychology, 70*, 44–47.

Triandis, H. C. (1972). *The analysis of subjective culture*. New York: Wiley.

Triandis, H. C. (1978). Some universals of social behavior. *Personality and Social Psychology Bulletin*, *4*, 1–16.

Triandis, H. C. (1990). Cross-cultural studies of individualism and collectivism. In J. Berman (Ed.), *Nebraska symposium on motivation, 1989* (pp. 41–133). Lincoln: University of Nebraska Press.

Triandis, H. C. (1993). The contingency model in cross-cultural perspective. In M. M. Chemers & R. Ayman (Eds.), *Leadership theory and research: Perspectives and directions* (pp. 167–188). San Diego: Academic Press.

Triandis, H. C., & Brislin, R. W. (1980). *Handbook of cross-cultural psychology: Social psychology*. Boston: Allyn & Bacon.

Triandis, H. C., Kurowski, L. L., & Gelfand, M. J. (1990). Workplace diversity. In M. D. Dunnette & L. M. Hough (Eds.), *Handbook of industrial & organizational psycholgy* (2nd ed., Vol. 1.). Palo Alto, CA: Consulting Psychologists Press.

Valenzi, E. R., & Dessler, G. (1978). Relationships of leader behavior, subordinate role ambiguity, and subordinate satisfaction. *Academy of Management Journal*, *21*, 671–678.

Vecchio, R. P. (1977). Empirical examination of the validity of Fiedler's model of leadership effectiveness. *Organizational Behavior and Human Performance*, *19*, 180–206.

Vecchio, R. P. (1987). Situational leadership theory: An examination of a prescriptive theory. *Journal of Applied Psychology*, *72*, 444–451.

Vroom, V. H. (1959). *Some personality determinants of the effects of participation*. Englewood Cliffs, NJ: Prentice-Hall.

Vroom, V. H. (1964). *Work and motivation*. New York: Wiley.

Vroom, V. H. (1980). Decision making and the leadership process. In P. Hersey & J. Stinson (Eds.), *Perspectives in leadership effectiveness* (pp. 63–78). Athens, OH: The Center for Leadership Studies.

Vroom, V. H., & Jago, A. G. (1974). Decision-making as a social process: Normative and descriptive models of leader behavior. *Decision Sciences*, *5*, 743–769.

Vroom, V. H., & Jago, A. G. (1978). On the validity of the Vroom–Yetton model. *Journal of Applied Psychology*, *63*, 151–162.

Vroom, V. H., & Jago, A. G. (1988). *The new leadership*. Englewood Cliffs, NJ: Prentice-Hall.

Vroom, V. H., & Yetton, P. W. (1973). *Leadership and decision-making*. Pittsburgh: University of Pittsburgh Press.

Wakabayashi, M., Graen, G., Graen, M., & Graen, M. (1988). Japanese management progress: Mobility into middle management. *Journal of Applied Psychology*, *73*, 217–227.

Walster, E., Berscheid, E., & Walster, G. W. (1976). New directions in equity research. In L. Berkowitz (Ed.), *Advances in experimental social psychology* (Vol. 9.). New York: Academic Press.

Watson, C. B., & Chemers, M. M. (1996, June). Leadership efficacy and collective efficacy. Presented to the meetings of the American Psychological Society, San Francisco.

Weber, M. (1947). *The theory of social and economic organization*. (A. M. Henderson & T. Parsons, Trans., T. Parsons, Ed.). New York: Free Press. (Original work published 1924)

Weick, K. (1969). *The social psychology of organizations*. Reading, MA: Addison-Wesley.

Weiner, B. (1979). A theory of motivation for some classroom experiences. *Journal of Educational Psychology*, *71*, 3–25.

Weiner, B., Frieze, I., Kukla, A., Reed, L., Rest, S., & Rosenbaum, R. M. (1972). Perceiving the causes of success and failure. In E. E. Jones, D. E. Kanouse, H. H. Kelley, R. E. Nisbett, S. Valins, & B. Weiner (Eds.), *Attribution: Perceiving the causes of behavior*. Morristown, NJ: General Learning Press.

Welsh, D. B., Luthans, F., & Sommer, S. M. (1993). Managing Russian factory workers: The impact of U.S.-based behavioral and participative techniques. *Academy of Management Journal*, *36*, 58–79.

Whitely, W., & England, G. W. (1980). Variability in common dimensions of managerial values due to value orientation and country differences. *Personnel Psychology*, *33*, 77–89.

Williams, M. L., & Podsakoff, P. M. (1988). A meta-analysis of attitudinal and behavioral correlates of leader reward and punishment behaviors. In D. F. Ray (Ed.), *Proceedings of the Southern Management Meetings* (pp. 161–163). Mississippi State University: Southern Management Association.

Wong, P. T. P., & Weiner, B. (1981). Memory discrimination for information typical or atypical of person schemata. *Social Cognition, 1,* 287–310.

Yammarino, F. J., & Bass, B. M. (1990). Long-term forecasting of transformational leadership and its effects among Naval officers: Some preliminary findings. In K. E. Clark & M. B. Clark (Eds.), *Measures of leadership.* Greensboro, NC: Center for Creative Leadership.

Yukl, G. A. (1971). Toward a behavioral theory of leadership. *Organizational Behavior and Human Performance, 6,* 414–440.

Yukl, G. A. (1989). *Leadership in organizations* (2nd ed.). Englewood Cliffs, NJ: Prentice-Hall.

Yukl, G. A., & Falbe, C. M. (1990). Influence tactics and objectives in upward, downward, and lateral influence attempts. *Journal of Applied Psychology, 75,* 132–140.

Yukl, G. A., & Tracey, J. B. (1992). Consequences of influence tactics used with subordinates, peers, and the boss. *Journal of Applied Psychology, 77,* 525–535.

Zajonc, R. B. (1965). Social facilitation. *Science, 149,* 269–274.

Zavalloni, M. (1980). Values. In H. C. Triandis & R. W. Brislin (Eds.), *Handbook of cross-cultural psychology: Social psychology* (pp. 73–120). Boston: Allyn & Bacon.

Znaniecki, F. (1918). Methodological note. In W. I. Thomas & F. Znaniecki (Eds.), *The Polish peasant in Europe and America.* Boston: Bodger.

Zullow, H. M., Oettingen, G., Peterson, C., & Seligman, M. E. P. (1988). Pessimistic explanatory style in the historical record. *American Psychologist, 43,* 673–682.

# Author Index

**193**

# Subject Index